Researching *and* Writing

A Portable Guide

Other *Portable* Volumes from Bedford/St. Martin's

RESEARCHING
and WRITING
A Portable Guide

MARCIA MUTH

Bedford/St. Martin's   BOSTON ◆ NEW YORK

For Bedford/St. Martin's

Developmental Editor: Karin Halbert
Production Editor: Kristen Merrill
Production Supervisors: Roger Naggar and Matthew Hayes
Marketing Manager: Karita dos Santos
Editorial Assistant: Christina Gerogiannis
Copyeditor: Jane Zanichkowsky
Text Design: Sandra Rigney
Cover Design: Donna Lee Dennison
Cover Art: Billy Boardman
Composition: Pine Tree Composition, Inc.
Printing and Binding: Haddon Craftsman, an R.R. Donnelley & Sons
   Company

President: Joan E. Feinberg
Editorial Director: Denise B. Wydra
Editor in Chief: Karen S. Henry
Director of Marketing: Karen Melton Soeltz
Director of Editing, Design, and Production: Marcia Cohen
Managing Editor: Elizabeth M. Schaaf

Library of Congress Control Number: 2005932490

Manufactured in the United States of America.

0   9   8   7   6
f   e   d   c   b   a

For information, write: Bedford/St. Martin's, 75 Arlington Street,
Boston, MA 02116 (617-399-4000)

ISBN: 0–312–44442–7
EAN: 978–0–312–44442–6

Acknowledgments

Page 25: Mark Krikorian, excerpt from "Re: Immigration: Ten Points for a
   Successful Presidential Candidate," from *National Review* (May 23, 2005): 33.
   Copyright © 2005 by National Review, Inc. Reprinted with the permission of
   National Review, 215 Lexington Avenue, New York, NY 10016.

*Acknowledgments and copyrights are continued at the back of the book
on pages 333–34, which constitute an extension of the copyright page.*

Preface for Instructors

This compact book is designed to guide students through the steps of investigating a research question and then writing a response to that question. These processes require that students investigate, evaluate, synthesize, and report information while honoring academic research conventions. Even students who are confident of their reading, writing, and thinking skills are likely to find research assignments complex and daunting. This book aims to advise students, bolstering their confidence as they strengthen the research and writing skills necessary for research projects in college and beyond.

The first two chapters help students begin on sound footing: first, by defining research goals and workable research questions, and second, by managing their projects with a realistic schedule, targeted sources, a working bibliography, a research archive, and useful records. Chapters 3, 4, and 5 explore searches in the library, on the Internet, and in the field. These three chapters supply practical advice about finding recommended sources, conducting productive searches, selecting relevant and reliable sources, consulting specialized resources, and gathering firsthand information.

The next four chapters guide students as they gather information from the sources that they have found. Chapter 6 emphasizes source evaluation. Chapter 7 outlines ethical academic practices for handling sources, while Chapter 8 thoroughly covers methods of capturing supporting evidence by using quotations, paraphrases, and summaries. Then Chapter 9 advises about how to pull together the research paper by focusing on the research question or the thesis that sums up its answer, organizing a sequence of ideas, adding supporting evidence, and integrating and citing source material.

The last four chapters, 10 through 13, review major documentation styles: MLA, APA, *Chicago*, and CSE (formerly CBE). The chapter for each style supplies a checklist for its recommended format and extensively illustrates its method of citing and listing sources. Each of these chapters also concludes with a sample student paper, annotated to highlight its conventional features. Additional student selections in the appendix illustrate ways of applying research conventions in common source-based assignments such as research outlines, annotated bibliographies, documented papers citing only a few sources, literary analyses, examinations, and reports on field research.

Throughout, this text offers practical help to students:

- abundant visual materials such as boxes, tables, charts, and graphics that help clarify research processes and decisions
- extensive tables—for example, "Finding Evidence and Opinions," "A Sampler of Sources Grouped by Discipline," and "Typical Features of Sources"—that help students think critically about source material
- unique Source Navigators (in chapters 2 and 10 through 13) illustrating how to locate identifying details in a variety of original sources from books to databases and how to transfer those details into source citations and lists
- practical emphasis on efficient searches for reliable and recommended sources
- consistent connections between strategies for selecting, evaluating, recording, and presenting information and its eventual use as supporting evidence
- frequent checklists for both research and writing to help students accomplish critical tasks and to gear advice to source-based papers
- discussion of plagiarism in the context of academic ethics and best practices for avoiding problems
- abundant illustration of conventions for citing and listing sources (Chapters 10 through 13), innovatively organized around two key questions: Who wrote it? What type of source is it?

Additional material on research and writing is available at Re: Writing (bedfordstmartins.com/rewriting), Bedford/St. Martin's extensive collection of free online student and instructor resources. For students, there are helpful research and reference aids, including tutorials, exercises, citation guides, model documents, and an annotated database of recommended research links. For instructors, Re: Writing offers such resources as *The Bedford Bibliography for Teachers of Writing, The Bedford/St. Martin's Workshop on Plagiarism,* and other free bibliographies, workshops, and online journals for professional development.

ACKNOWLEDGMENTS

Professors Donald Hoyt, California State Polytechnic University, Pomona; Pamela Laird and Donna Langston, both from University of Colorado at Denver and Health Sciences Center; and Dana Waters, Dodge City Community College, have generously recommended samples of student writing for this book. Mary Finley, University Library at California State University, Northridge, has provided timely advice about information competency and, as usual, recommended valuable sites. Special thanks go to all the student researchers and writers whose papers will enlighten and inspire others: Nick Broz, Alan Espenlaub, Brian Fenoglio, Sarah Goers, Stephanie Hawkins, Cindy Keeler, Whitney King, Jon Lindbloom, Angela Mendy, Susanna Olsen, Alex Poster, Ross Rocketto, Carrie Williamson, and Amanda Zeddy.

At Bedford/St. Martin's, I am grateful to many people. Joan Feinberg, Denise Wydra, Nancy Perry, and Karen Henry initially conceived of this project and supported its evolution to its present form. Because *Researching and Writing* is adapted from *The Bedford Guide for College Writers*, many hands have contributed to the parent book's research section and thus have strengthened the portable guide as well. Special thanks go to editors Michelle Clark and Genevieve Hamilton, who substantially refreshed the *Bedford Guide*'s research section, and Beth Castrodale, who encouraged its visual development and guided early steps in the development of this portable guide. Karin Halbert, my patient and insightful editor, nurtured the book to completion. Christina Gerogiannis assisted with manuscript preparation and efficiently attended to numerous details. Tammy Sugarman, Georgia State University, stalwartly supplied numerous documentation examples for this book, building on her earlier contributions to the *Bedford Guide*. Credit for a smooth production process goes to Elizabeth Schaaf and Kristen Merrill and to copyeditor Jane Zanichkowsky. Thanks also go to Sandra Rigney for the book's attractive design and to Sandy Schechter for clearing permissions.

My personal thanks go to the inspirational student researchers in my writing workshops, sponsored by the School of Education at the University of Colorado at Denver and Health Sciences Center. Anderson Muth and Elizabeth Muth also have enriched this book by recruiting contributions from fine student writers. Last, but never least, Rod Muth continues to share his expertise and to encourage the growth of mine.

Contents

ix

1

Defining Your Quest

Writing a research paper is a useful skill, essential not only in an academic community but also in the workplace. Although you'll draw on this skill for the rest of your life, learning to conduct research efficiently and effectively can be daunting. The Internet, television, books, newspapers, and magazines shower us with facts and figures, statements and reports, views and opinions—some half-baked, some revealing and trustworthy. College research requires you to sort through this massive burst of words, distinguishing fact from opinion, off-the-wall claims from expert interpretations.

As you investigate a topic and write a paper based on your findings, you will build valuable skills such as these:

- You'll learn how to find a topic and develop it into a focused and answerable research question.
- You'll draw from a wide range of sources—in the library, on the Internet, and in the field.
- You'll use library, Internet, and field research techniques to complement one another.
- You'll use your sources as evidence to support your own ideas, rather than simply repeating what they say.
- You'll do critical thinking—evaluating, analyzing, and synthesizing.
- You'll learn to cite and list your sources in a form that scholars and professionals follow in writing research reports and articles.

USING YOUR RESEARCH SKILLS

In College Courses

- Some courses require short papers using evidence from a few resources rather than a full research project, but instructors still expect you to find, evaluate, and document relevant sources.
- As you take advanced courses in your major, you may be expected to tackle an independent research project or conduct your own field study.
- Whenever you prepare a review of the literature or an annotated bibliography, you'll need to locate, evaluate, and summarize major sources on a topic or research question.

In the Workplace

- Employees at your company may routinely prepare research-based reports on regional markets, consumer preferences, market trends, or project feasibility.
- If you start your own business, you are likely to investigate print, electronic, and human resources on marketing, budgeting, and strategic planning.
- To advance in your career, you'll turn to publications whose editors, reporters, and columnists rely on the Internet, the library, and the results of subscriber surveys to stay current.

In the Community

- If you oppose plans for a new factory that might pollute a local river, your research on zoning laws and water quality will strengthen your appeal to the planning board.
- As a volunteer at the local women's shelter, you may want to persuade board members to open a second facility by reporting your findings about other community shelters.
- Research can be a great help when you or an organization intends to purchase something—be it a new kitchen for the community center or a new car for yourself.

CONTRIBUTING TO THE CONVERSATION

When you begin college, you may feel awkward, uncertain about what to say, and how to speak up. As you become a more experienced college student and writer, you will join the intellectual discussion around you by reading, thinking, and writing with sources. For many college papers, you will be expected to turn to articles, books, and Web sites for the evidence needed to support your main point or thesis and to develop your ideas about it. This expectation reflects the academic view that knowledge advances through exchange: Each writer reads and responds to the writing of others, building on earlier discussion while expanding the conversation.

JOINING THE ACADEMIC EXCHANGE

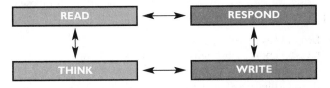

This research guide is designed to help you succeed in common research situations. Conducting any research requires time to explore, to think, and to respond. However, purposeful research can produce greater success in less time than random searching or optimistic browsing.

Purposeful research can help to build your confidence before you tackle an extensive research project. It can also increase your efficiency when you need good sources fast—perhaps because you've procrastinated, been overwhelmed by conflicting demands on your time, or feel uncertain about how to succeed as a college researcher.

To help you in all these cases, this research guide concentrates on five key steps: defining your quest and your question, searching for recommended sources, evaluating those you find, smoothly and gracefully adding evidence from them, and citing them correctly.

TURNING TO SOURCES FOR SUPPORTING EVIDENCE

The Assignment: Writing from Sources

Identify an idea, issue, situation, or problem that engages you. Develop a workable research question about it, one that is focused, intriguing, and provocative enough to allow for different perspectives. After conducting whatever research is necessary, synthesize the information you assemble to develop your own reasonable answer to the research question. Then write a paper, persuasively using a variety of source material to support and convey your conclusions.

Having a real audience can help you select what to include or exclude as you write your paper. If possible, try to use your paper to benefit your campus administration, your employer, or a particular cause or nonprofit group on campus or in your local community. Because your final paper answers your research question, that paper will be more than a list of facts. Reading and digesting the ideas of others is just the first step. During the process of writing, you'll also bring your own intelligence to bear on what you have discovered.

Other Assignments

Using library, Internet, and field sources, write a research paper on one of the following topics or another that your instructor approves. Follow the general directions supplied for the assignment just described.

1. Investigate workplace changes and trends in a particular industry or field. Include data from interviews conducted with people in the field.
2. Write a paper tracing efforts to control, reduce, or eliminate a particular health threat, including current data.
3. Discuss recent political, economic, or cultural changes in another country.
4. Compare student achievement in schools with different characteristics—for example, those with limited or extensive computer access or those with low and high numbers of students who move.
5. Study a change in home activities, such as adding home schooling or a homebased business, or in workplace activities, such as adding on-site child care or workout facilities.
6. Write a portrait of life in your town or neighborhood as it was in the past, using sources such as local library or newspaper archives, photographs or other visual evidence, and interviews with long-time residents or a local historian.

7. Write a short history of your immediate family, drawing on interviews, photographs, scrapbooks, old letters, unpublished records, and any other available sources.
8. Study the reasons students today give for going to college. Gather your information from pertinent sources as well as interviews or surveys of a variety of students at your college.
9. Investigate a current trend you have noticed on television, collecting evidence by observing news shows, other programs, or commercials.
10. Write a survey of recent films of a certain kind (such as horror movies, martial arts films, comedies, or love stories), supporting your generalizations with evidence from your film watching.

FINDING A REASON FOR RESEARCH

Does cell phone use cause brain tumors?

What steps can law enforcement take to help prevent domestic violence?

How do strict death penalty laws affect crime rates?

Is it true that about a million children in the U.S. are homeless?

Why is baseball exempt from antitrust laws?

You may have asked yourself questions like these. Perhaps you discussed them with friends, asked a teacher about the subject, or read an article about the issue. In doing so, you were conducting informal research to satisfy your curiosity.

In your day-to-day life, you also conduct practical research to help you solve problems and make decisions. For example, you may want to buy a digital camera, consider an innovative medical procedure, or plan a vacation. To become better informed, you may talk with friends, search the Internet, request product information from sales personnel, compare prices, read articles in magazines and newspapers, and listen to commercials. You pull together and weigh as much information as you can, preparing yourself to make a well-informed decision.

When one of your college professors assigns a research paper due in a month or two, you won't be expected to reveal the mysteries of the human brain or solve the problem of world hunger. On the other hand, you should expect to do far more than toss raw ingredients—facts, ideas, and information from others—on the table. Instead, the excitement lies in using research to cook up your own dish—taking your own perspective, drawing your own conclusions, and backing up your ideas with evidence from your sources.

The key is to start your investigation as professional researchers do—with a research question that you truly want to learn more about. Like a detective, you'll need to plan your work but remain flexible, ready to backtrack, jump ahead, slip by an obstacle, or set out in another direction altogether. Take some time to consider what goal or goals you'd like your research to accomplish—whether in your personal life, for a college class, or on the job.

Common Research Goals

Satisfy curiosity

Take a new perspective

Make a decision

Solve a problem

Analyze a situation

Substantiate a conclusion

Support a position

Advocate for change

Whatever your research goal, you're more likely to be successful if you also try to define the hunt in advance by considering questions such as these about your research situation and audience.

RESEARCH CHECKLIST

Refining Your Goals

☐ Does the assignment or class discussion suggest any specific research focus—certain kinds of supporting evidence, certain types of sources, or certain ways of presenting your material?

☐ Which of your ideas or opinions might you want to support with good evidence?

☐ Which of your ideas might you want to check, clarify, or change based on your research?

☐ Which ideas or opinions of others might you want to verify or counter?

☐ Do you want to analyze material yourself (for example, comparing articles or Web sites taking different approaches), or do you want to find someone else's analysis?

☐ What kinds of evidence do you want to use—for example, facts, statistics, or expert testimony? Do you also want to add your own firsthand observation of the situation or scene?

☐ Do you want to intrigue, inform, influence, or persuade your readers?

ASKING A RESEARCH QUESTION

What most effectively helps people in the military return to civilian life after a tour of duty?

How accurately do standardized tests measure achievement?

What can be done to assist families who lived in hurricane Katrina's path?

To define a narrow research question like the examples above, start with your own interests and research goals.

Log On

If you mentally "log on," paying attention to your own broad interests as well as the many ideas around you, you probably can identify a research topic that whets your curiosity. If you need ideas, listen to the academic exchanges around you. Perhaps the reading, writing, or discussion in a course intrigues you. For example, your sociology course might make you curious about family structures, or your geography course might alert you to the global threats to forests. To target your research from the beginning, try to narrow your interest from "family structures" to "blended families" or from "global threats to forests" to "farming practices that threaten rainforests." Although a limited research topic will help to focus your initial research, you also can continue to narrow your topic as you learn more about it.

Here are a few questions to help you find a research topic:

RESEARCH CHECKLIST

Discovering a Research Interest

☐ Which of your experiences have raised interesting questions or created unusual associations in your mind?

☐ What intriguing events or situations have you noticed while walking on campus, attending classes, working at your job, or watching television or sites with Web cams?

☐ What new perspectives on issues or events have friends, classmates, commentators, bloggers, or others offered?

☐ What problem would you like to solve?

☐ What decision might you need to make?

☐ What have you read about lately that you'd like to pursue further?

Scan Your Options

Before settling on a final research topic, take some time to find out more about it. Pay attention to a range of viewpoints; consider changes and trends that may affect the topic. Scanning your options can help you figure out exactly which narrow topic will best hold your interest and most effectively take shape in your paper.

Begin in the Library.   Suppose that you are looking for preliminary information on the sociology of the family or, more specifically, on "blended families." A good place to start is your college or local library. Most libraries subscribe to many specialized databases (like *Medline*, *PsycLIT*, and the *MLA Bibliography*). You will often be able to familiarize yourself with your topic and get a good feel for the range of sources available by scanning your options here.

Go Online.   You can also browse on the Internet, visiting Web sites and reading blogs or messages posted to newsgroups or Web discussion forums. Web search engines—such as Google and Yahoo!—can lead you to a wide range of Web pages (see p. 63 for URLs). Google (http://groups.google.com) also can help you locate newsgroups and mailing lists related to your topic. The number of sources you can locate on the Internet is vast—and growing daily—so you'll need to exercise discipline when you're online, especially in this early stage. (For more on Internet sources, see Ch. 4.)

Talk with Experts.   Consider discussing your topic with an expert in the field. If you're curious about America's fascination with the automobile, consider meeting with a professor, such as a sociologist or a journalist, who specializes in the area. Or talk with friends or acquaintances who are particularly passionate about their cars. Or spend time at an auto show, carefully observing and talking with the people who attend. (For more on interviewing, see pp. 71-72.)

Revisit Your Goals and Audience.   If necessary, refine the purpose of your research and your analysis of your audience in light of what you have discovered thus far. For example, perhaps your overview of campus programs has led you to a proposal by the International Students Office for matching first-year students with host families during holidays. You'd like to find out more about such programs—what they cost, how they work, what they offer foreign students, how they contribute to their college success, and how they benefit host families as well. At first, you thought that your purpose would be to persuade community members to participate. As you learn more, however, you decide that the real challenge is to persuade the Director of Student Activities to support the project.

Turn Your Topic into a Question

Once you have narrowed your interest and scanned your options, you can focus on drafting the question you want to answer.

TOPIC	Blended families
SPECIFIC QUESTION	How do blended families today differ from those a century ago?

TOPIC	Landscape architecture
SPECIFIC QUESTION	In what ways have the principles of landscape architecture shaped urban renewal in this city?

If no question springs to mind, you might try freewriting, mapping, or brainstorming about your topic, jotting down whatever questions come to mind. Then, select one that appears promising. Your instructor also may have some suggestions, but you will probably be more motivated investigating a question you design.

Test Your Question.   Ask these questions as you test for a workable research question:

- Is your question debatable? Does it allow for a range of opinions so that you can support your own view rather than explain something that's generally known and accepted?
- Is it interesting to you? Will your discoveries interest your readers?
- Is it narrow enough to allow for a productive investigation in the few weeks you have? Does it stick to a single focus?

BROAD QUESTION	How is the climate of the earth changing?
NARROWER QUESTION	How will El Niño affect global climate changes in the next decade?
BROAD QUESTION	Who are the world's best living storytellers?
NARROWER QUESTION	How is Irish step dancing a form of storytelling?
BROAD QUESTION	Why is there poverty?
NARROWER QUESTION	What notable welfare-to-work programs exist in the southeastern United States?

Although you should restrict your topic, a question can be too narrow or too insignificant. If so, it may be impossible to find relevant sources.

TOO NARROW	How did John F. Kennedy's maternal grandfather influence the decisions he made during his first month as president?

A question may also be so narrow that it's uninteresting. Avoid questions that can be answered with a simple yes or no or with a few statistics.

TOO NARROW	Are there more black students or white students in the entering class this year?
BETTER	How does the ratio of black students to white students affect campus relations at our school?

Instead, ask a question that will lead you into the heart of a lively controversy. The best research questions ask about issues that others take seriously and debate, issues likely to be of real interest to you and your readers.

Refine Your Question.   As you begin your research, you may find that your question seems rough or doesn't take you where you want to go.

Revise or replace a question that leads only to dull, predictable information or to irrelevant dead ends.

After drafting your question, use these questions to refine it.

RESEARCH CHECKLIST

Sharpening Your Question

☐ Is the scope of your question appropriate—not too immense and not too narrow?

☐ Will you be able to answer your question in the days and pages available for this project?

☐ Can you find enough current information about your question?

☐ Have you worded your question concretely and specifically so that it states exactly what you are considering?

☐ Does your question probe an issue that engages you personally?

Predict an Answer in a Working Thesis.   Some writers find a research project easier to tackle if they have not only a question but also an answer in mind. At this stage, however, you need to be flexible enough to change your answer, or even your question if your research turns up something unexpected.

You can state a proposed answer as a working thesis.

RESEARCH QUESTION   How does a school dress code benefit students?

WORKING THESIS   Instituting a school dress code decreases the incidence of school violence.

Remember that a working thesis is meant to guide your research, not hinder it. If you're only finding support for what you already thought was the case, then your working thesis may be too dominant, and you may no longer be conducting true research. Because of this possibility, some writers delay stating a working thesis until they've already done substantial research or even begun drafting. Your approach will probably depend on your research assignment, your instructor's expectations, and your own work style.

SETTING BOUNDARIES

Although answers to a research question can come from many sources—your experience, observation, imagination, or interaction with others—college instructors generally expect you to turn to the writings of others. In their books, articles, and reports, you can find pertinent examples, illustrations, details, and expert testimony—in short, reliable information that will show that your claims and statements are sound. That evidence should satisfy you as a writer and also meet the criteria of your college readers—your instructors and possibly your classmates.

Right now, you may not have a final research question in mind or feel confident that you know how to find the reliable sources that college readers will expect. Nevertheless, the expectations of college readers do set some boundaries for you. Keeping their preferences in mind can help you identify the relevant and reliable articles, reports, books, Web sites, and other resources that will add muscle to your paper. Such sources can supply facts, statistics, and expert testimony to answer your research question and to back up your points. (For more about finding reliable resources, see pp. 37–41.)

TWO VIEWS OF SUPPORTING EVIDENCE

COLLEGE WRITER	COLLEGE READER
• Does it answer my question?	• Is it relevant to the purpose and assignment?
• Does it seem accurate?	• Is it reliable, given academic standards?
• Have I found enough?	• Is it of sufficient quantity, variety, and strength?
• Is it recent enough?	• Is it current, given the standards of the field?
• Is it balanced enough?	• Is it typical, fair, and complex?
• Will it persuade my audience?	• Does the writer make a credible case?

Suppose, for example, that you want to propose solutions to your community's employment problem. You begin by turning that idea into a researchable question:

WORKING RESEARCH QUESTION

How can the residents of Aurora find educational opportunities to improve their job skills and career alternatives?

Because you already have several ideas based on your firsthand observations and the experiences of people you know, your initial research objectives are quite specific. First, you want to add accurate facts and figures that will show why you believe a compelling problem exists. Next, you want to visit the Web sites of local educational institutions and possibly locate someone to interview about existing career development programs. You expect that your instructor will agree that government statistics and academic Web sites are likely to be reliable sources of supporting evidence.

TABLE 1.1   Using Reliable Evidence to Answer Your Research Question

Types of Evidence	Definition	Example	Source
Facts	Information that could be confirmed or substantiated by an objective person	When employment opportunities drop, college enrollments tend to go up because people are motivated to increase their skills.	Colorado Commission on Higher Education, "Governor's Task Force to Strengthen and Improve the Community College System. Final Report, April 5, 2004," page 16, at <www.state.co.us/cche>
Statistics	Factual information presented in numerical form	According to the U.S. Census Bureau, 85% of Aurora residents over age 25 have graduated from high school, 4.6% more than the national average. However, only 24.6% of this group have graduated from college, only 0.2% better than the 24.4% national average.	"Profile of Selected Social Characteristics 2000" for Aurora, Colorado, and for United States, *U.S. Census Bureau Fact* at <http://factfinder.census.gov/home/saff/main.html?_lang=en>
Expert Testimony	Information from a knowledgeable person whose study, research, or experience is respected by others in the field	According to Daniela Higgins, director of the Center for Workforce Development, the Career Enrichment Program at Community College of Aurora wants to attract people looking for career advancement to improve their family resources.	"Program Provides Free College Education to People Who Need Improved Job Skills and Career Advancement," press release from Community College of Aurora at <www.ccaurora.edu/news/education.html>
Firsthand Observation	Your own unbiased, accurate eyewitness account	During my visit to Community College of Aurora to interview a workforce specialist, I observed campus publicity for programs in computer skills, paramedic and firefighter training, criminal justice, law enforcement, and early childhood education.	Your notes about your campus visit or your collection of campus materials

2

Managing Your Research Project

Once you've asked a research question that engages you, you've begun to define what you want to discover and what you'll eventually demonstrate in your research paper. This chapter will help you anticipate your research process, create a research schedule, survey your resources, establish a working bibliography, and build a research archive to organize information from all your sources—whether photocopies, printouts, or notes you've recorded.

PLANNING YOUR PROJECT

A research paper is often the most engaging and complex assignment in a course. Actively planning and managing your project will help you finish it successfully, right on time.

Anticipate the Research Process

The diagram of the research process (see p. 16) outlines the major stages most college researchers need to accomplish. Anticipating these stages—and planning the time to accomplish them—will help prepare you for even the most formidable research task.

THE RESEARCH PROCESS

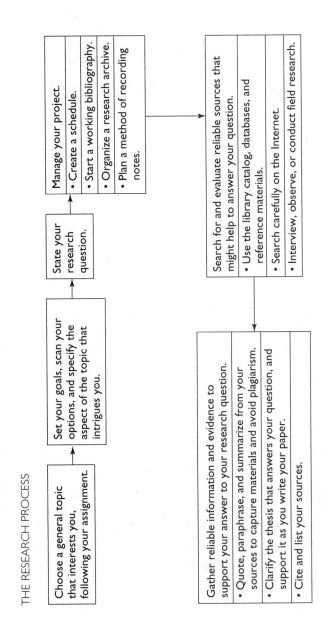

Choose a general topic that interests you, following your assignment.

Set your goals, scan your options, and specify the aspect of the topic that intrigues you.

State your research question.

Manage your project.
- Create a schedule.
- Start a working bibliography.
- Organize a research archive.
- Plan a method of recording notes.

Search for and evaluate reliable sources that might help to answer your question.
- Use the library catalog, databases, and reference materials.
- Search carefully on the Internet.
- Interview, observe, or conduct field research.

Gather reliable information and evidence to support your answer to your research question.
- Quote, paraphrase, and summarize from your sources to capture materials and avoid plagiarism.
- Clarify the thesis that answers your question, and support it as you write your paper.
- Cite and list your sources.

Create a Schedule

No matter what your question or where you plan to look for material, you will need a schedule to use your time efficiently. If your instructor doesn't give you a series of deadlines as part of your assignment, set

---

WORKING WITH A RESEARCH GROUP

Research groups, in class or at work, require cooperative effort but can reward all concerned with deeper and more creative outcomes than one individual could achieve. Your team might consolidate all its work or share the research but produce separate papers, presentation pages, or Web pages. With your instructor's approval, divide up the tasks so that all members are responsible for their own portions of the work. Then agree on your due dates and group meetings as the following schedule illustrates.

- *Week One:* Meet to get acquainted and to select someone to act as an organizer, e-mailing or calling to make sure things progress as planned; individually investigate interests and options for a project topic.
- *Week Two:* Meet again to select a topic, narrow it, and turn it into a research question that your instructor approves.
- *Week Three:* Individually survey available resources and contribute to a collaborative working bibliography. Meet to agree on assigned tasks, and then individually gather material for the group's research archive.
- *Weeks Four and Five:* Continue to find sources, read and evaluate them, and record notes.
- *Week Six:* Meet to evaluate the sources and information everyone has found and decide what is missing or weak. Draft a working thesis, and create a working outline for presenting what everyone has learned.
- *Week Seven:* Guided by the group's plan, individually draft assigned sections. Swap drafts, read them over, and respond with suggestions.
- *Week Eight:* Work together to consolidate the revised draft, read it carefully, and agree on final changes. Appoint one member to prepare a polished copy and one or two others to act as final editors and proofreaders.

some for yourself. You can be sure that a research paper will take longer than you expect. If you procrastinate and try to toss everything together in a desperate all-night siege, you probably will not be satisfied with the result. Instead, start with a clear-cut schedule that breaks your project into a series of small tasks.

SAMPLE SCHEDULE

- *Week One:* If you are not assigned a topic, start thinking about your interests. Using your library and the Internet, scan your options.
- *Week Two:* Begin narrowing your topic to a workable research question. Survey the available resources, and start your working bibliography and your research archive.
- *Week Three:* Begin your research in earnest. Locate and evaluate your most promising sources. Take notes and build your archive.
- *Week Four:* Continue narrowing your research, identifying promising sources, evaluating them as you go along, and taking efficient notes.
- *Week Five:* State your working thesis and begin planning or outlining your paper. Continue to update your bibliography and research archive, arranging your sources in the order in which you think you might use them.
- *Week Six:* Refine your thesis statement. Start your first draft, noting where your sources supply ideas and information as you write.
- *Week Seven:* Complete your first draft. Begin thinking about ways to revise and improve it. Seek feedback from a peer editor.
- *Week Eight:* Revise and edit your draft. Check that you have presented quotations properly. Carefully go over your documentation. Finally, proofread the entire paper, checking for any errors.

Each week you can make up a more detailed schedule, identifying tasks by the day or by the type to increase your efficiency while varying your activities.

DAILY SCHEDULE
Monday—finish library catalog search
Tuesday—start article indexes
Thursday—read printouts and add notes
Sunday night—organize files

ACTIVITY SCHEDULE
library search—EBSCOhost and InfoTrac
Web search—government sites
reading—new printouts

writing—revised research question—thesis?

SURVEYING YOUR RESOURCES

A short visit to the library or its Web site can help you set research priorities for answering your question. Your goal now is to determine whether you'll find enough ideas, opinions, facts, statistics, and expert testimony to address your question and to identify the most fruitful avenues for research.

If your preliminary search turns up a skimpy list of sources or, more likely, hundreds of sources, consider asking another question, especially a more specific one. Try to pick a question that is the focus of a dozen or twenty available sources. If you need help conducting a reliable search, ask a librarian for help.

Identify the Sources You Need

As you survey what's available, also decide which types of sources to concentrate on. Some research questions require a wide range of sources. Others are better suited to a narrower range, perhaps restricted by date or discipline. Target those most likely to yield the best information to answer your question. Understanding the types of information available in various print and electronic sources can help you plan your research. See Tables 2.1 on page 20 and Table 2.2 on page 21 and also Tables 6.1 and 6.2 on pages 90–93.

Use Keywords and Links

Keywords are terms or phrases that identify the topics discussed in a research source. As you look for information on the Internet or in databases, you will most likely perform keyword searches. When you enter the keywords into an electronic search engine (whether in a library catalog or on the Web), the engine will return to you a list of all the sources it can find with that keyword. Knowing how to use keywords to search is a skill useful not only in your research project but also throughout your college career and beyond.

Finding the best keywords for a particular topic and a particular search engine is essential. Start by using the main terms in your research question. As you survey your resources, jot down or print out the keywords you use, noting whether they produce too few or too many results. You are likely to find that some keywords work better than others and that certain combinations of keywords produce the best results. (For a list of search engines, see p. 63; for advanced search strategies, see pp. 64–68.)

As your keywords lead you to Web sites compiled by specialists or people interested in a particular area, you can browse through the

TABLE 2.1 Finding Evidence and Opinions in Print Sources

Type of Source	Facts and Statistics	Expert Testimony	Opinions
Scholarly Book	Extensive facts and data from reliable sources or original study	Written by expert scholars, researchers, or professionals	Author's thesis supported by own and other research
Popular Nonfiction Book	Facts and data included or not	Written by experts, practitioners, journalists, or others	Author's view or experience supported or not by research
Scholarly Journal	Facts and data from reliable sources or original study	Written by expert scholars, researchers, or professionals	Author's thesis supported by own and other research; readers' views expressed in letters or responses
News Magazine	Facts, data, and quotations from interviews, published reports, or unidentified sources	Written by freelance and staff journalists who may quote experts, participants, or observers	Magazine's focus reflected in articles; varied views in opinion columns, pro-con articles, and letters
Popular Magazine	Facts and data in popular form may not be attributed to original source	Written by staff and freelance writers who may quote others, including popular experts	Magazine's focus reflected in articles; varied views in columns and letters
Newspaper	Facts, data, and quotations from interviews, published reports, or unidentified sources	Written by local and wire-service journalists, columnists, and others who may quote participants, observers, or experts	Varied opinions in editorials (views of paper's editors), letters to the editor (views of readers), and columns (views of columnists)
Pamphlet or Booklet	Facts and data included or not	Written by experts, professionals, researchers, or others	Writer's or sponsor's opinion, view, or thesis presented
Reference Work	Extensive facts and explanations from reliable sources or experts	Written by scholars, specialists, and staff experts	One approach or several views explained

TABLE 2.2   Finding Evidence and Opinions in Electronic Sources

Type of Source	Facts and Statistics	Expert Testimony	Opinions
Online Reference Site	Topics or links with specialized facts or statistics	Expert academic sources	Varied academic links on research topics
Gateway Site for a Topic or Field	Pages with facts or links, such as <www.pollingreport.com>	Expert academic and field sources	Topic links and opinion sites, such as <www.publicagenda.com>
Online Document Collection	Documents on site with facts or statistics	Reliable authors and documents	Documents that present arguments or opinions
Professional Web Site	Resources, such as "Survey of the American Teacher" at <www.metlife.com> or InfoNation at <cyberschoolbus.un.org/index.asp>	Expert and professional views promoting sponsor's interests	Materials, advice, and sponsored reports that support group's views
Academic Web Site	Library links, such as "Community Information by Zip Code" at <http://library.csun.edu/Find_Resources/Government_Publications/zipstats.html>	Department or library links and lists of campus experts to interview	Links to campus or local newspaper with editorials and letters on current issues or to campus advocacy groups
Government Web Site	Agency reports, such as The World Factbook at <www.cia.gov>	Expert analysis of research studies, policy options, and consumer topics	Reports or pages that reflect mission of agency
Online Newspaper or News Service	Reports and boxes with news coverage or background	Quotations and background from participants, observers, and analysts	Editorials, letters to editor; featured columns, and polls of site visitors
Interest-Group or Personal Site	Facts and statistics that promote site's interests	Range from expert to partisan to oddball views	Advocacy and personal views that shape site content

21

information and resources gathered there. These sites often contain *links*—lists of related sites—also relevant to your research project. These links, in turn, often contain their own lists of related Web pages. By following these connections systematically, you can benefit from the work of others and rapidly expand your own knowledge. Be careful, however, not to look only for information that supports a preconceived notion. Research should be an opportunity to learn more about a topic, to answer an authentic question, not simply to collect evidence that supports what you already think.

KEYWORD SEARCHES

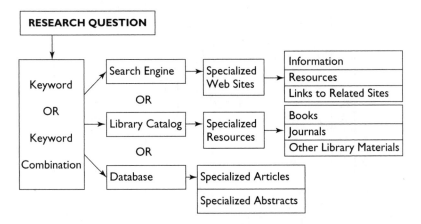

STARTING A WORKING BIBLIOGRAPHY

Your working bibliography will keep track of the resources—articles, books, Web sites, and other materials—that might help you answer your research question. Your working bibliography has two purposes:

> It guides your research by recording which sources you've examined and which you intend to examine.
>
> It helps you document or identify the sources you have used by recording detailed information about each of them.

Choose a Method for Compiling Your Working Bibliography.   Pick the method that suits you best, the one that you can use most easily and efficiently during the course of your research. Here are some options:

- Note cards, recording one source per card
- Small notebook

- Word-processing program
- Computer database
- Hand-held electronic storage tool

Keep Careful Records. Whatever your method, keeping accurate records from the beginning will simplify preparing the list of works cited or references that will eventually appear at the end of your paper. As you prepare that final paper, you'll be glad to have all the necessary titles, authors, dates, page numbers, and URLs (Internet addresses) neatly recorded—and you'll avoid a frantic, time-consuming trip back to the library. (For examples of correct documentation form, see Chs. 10–13.)

Start a bibliographic entry for each source you intend to consult. At this point, your information may be incomplete: "Dr. Edward Denu— cardiologist—interview about drug treatments." Later, once you locate a print or Internet source or conduct field research, you'll be able to fill in the complete bibliographical information. Eventually your records should include all the details needed to do two things:

- locate the source in the library or online
- list the source at the end of your paper with the others you've used

Though your assigned or chosen documentation style will determine the format for your final paper, the four styles illustrated in this book present much of the same information about each source. Learning to record this information when it's readily apparent (and to hunt for it when it's not) is a valuable skill that will save you time and improve the accuracy of your research writing.

Table 2.3 on page 33 summarizes what you'll need to record as you begin to gather sources, both the basics—the details nearly always required to identify each type of source—and the common additions or complications likely to crop up in varied sources. When in doubt, record more than you think you'll need so you don't have to return to the source later on. (See Chapters 10–13 for more about the specific conventions of the style you plan to use.)

The Source Navigators on pages 24–32 show how to find such information in several types of sources that you are likely to use as a college researcher. Each sample source is keyed to a menu, illustrating where to locate the details you'll need to record. Each sample source also is accompanied by a source note or card following Modern Language Association (MLA) style (see Ch. 10) with an entry ready to be copied directly from a working bibliography to a list of works cited for the final paper. See Chapters 10–13 for more Source Navigators and for specific formats for sources cited in your text and listed at the end of your paper.

SOURCE NAVIGATOR: Recording Source Notes on an Article from a Periodical

1 The complete name of the author
2 The title and any subtitle of the article (placed in quotation marks)
3 The title and any subtitle of the journal, magazine, or newspaper (underlined or italicized)
4 The full date of a magazine issue
5 The article's page numbers

Krikorian

①   ②
Krikorian, Mark. "Re: Immigration: Ten Points for a
                              ③
    Successful Presidential Candidate." National Review
    ④   ⑤
    23 May 2005: 33-35.

Outlines a plan to reduce illegal immigration through

stricter controls.

Figure 2.1 A source entry recorded in a computer file: an article in a monthly magazine, in MLA style

■ COVER ARTICLE

Re: Immigration

②

Ten points for a successful presidential candidate

① MARK KRIKORIAN

THE next presidential election may be years away, but potential candidates are already staking out positions on issues that should figure prominently. One of these is certain to be immigration, and one likely candidate for 2008 is already working to develop a tough, pro-enforcement image.

Unfortunately, that candidate is Hillary Clinton.

Her grade of F from Americans for Better Immigration, a group lobbying for stricter immigration rules, hasn't stopped her from dropping comments to reporters like "I am, you know, adamantly against illegal immigrants," and "People have to stop employing illegal immigrants." Of course, the only reason Hillary thinks she has a chance of outflanking the GOP on the right is that the president's immigration policies are terrible. It is therefore an opportune time to outline an immigration agenda for the 2008 presidential candidates. Here is a ten-point package, which includes both measures that a candidate should pledge to undertake on his own, and legislative changes that he should promote, as president.

1. *Unambiguous commitment to enforcement.* No candidate for chief executive can be taken seriously unless he enunciates a clear and unequivocal determination to execute the immigration law, whatever it happens to be. Presidential contenders don't come out and say they *oppose* enforcement, of course, but experience shows that's exactly what they mean when they offer the usual mealy-mouthed generalities.

It's not just a matter of pledging to pursue specific policies; rather, given the long history of government-ignored lawbreaking, the whole enforcement environment needs to change. A strong candidate will promise to end the climate of impunity for border-jumping, and illegal employment, and immigration fraud. In other words, apply to immigration the lessons of "broken windows" policing, learned from New York and elsewhere. (Under this policing, you crack down on all infractions, no

Mr. Krikorian is executive director of the Center for Immigration Studies.

matter how small, to reduce crime overall.) Equally important, the candidate should pledge that when the inevitable complaints come in from the many beneficiaries of illegal immigration, the White House will support those charged with enforcing the law, rather than hanging them out to dry, as has been the practice up to now.

2. *No Hobson's choice.* Comprehensive enforcement is a tactic; a candidate also needs to articulate a strategy for success. This entails rejecting the false choice between mass roundups and amnesty. Since everyone agrees that mass roundups like the ill-named Operation Wetback of the 1950s aren't going to occur, the anti-enforcement camp says that amnesty, and an unending stream of "temporary" workers, is the only alternative.

But a third way, and the only workable approach, is to use consistent, across-the-board enforcement as part of a strategy of attrition, causing fewer illegals to come and more of those already here to leave, so that the total illegal population declines from year to year, instead of continually rising. This is the same approach that worked so well with welfare reform, where the GOP rejected the Democratic vision of ever-growing welfare rolls, but didn't just throw all the recipients out on the street. A long-term, strictly enforced policy can stem the tide of immigration without resorting to mass roundups and without throwing in the towel with mass amnesty.

3. *Take amnesty off the table.* Amnesty should not even be a legitimate topic for discussion until *after* we regain control of the immigration system. Terms like "legalization," "normalization," and the ever-popular "phased-in access to earned regularization" are simply euphemisms for amnesty, i.e., giving legal status to illegal aliens. Having an amnesty at the front end of any immigration initiative guarantees failure. In 1986, nearly 3 million illegals were legalized, while promises of enforcement to prevent future illegal immigration were quickly abandoned. As a result, today's illegal population is twice as large as it was before the 1986 amnesty.

There is one kind of amnesty, however, that a presidential candidate could endorse—one modeled after parking-ticket or tax amnesties, giving illegal aliens 90 days to get right with the law by

③   ④

SOURCE NAVIGATOR: Recording Source Notes on an Article from a Database

1 The complete name of the author
2 The title and any subtitle of the article (placed in quotation marks)
3 The title and any subtitle of the journal (underlined or italicized)
4 The number of the journal volume
5 The year of the issue
6 The printed article's original page numbers
7 The name of the database, subscriber service, or library service (underlined or italicized)
8 The name and location (city and state, if needed) of the library you used
9 The access date when you used the source
10 The Internet address (URL or Uniform Resource Locator) or your search path

---

Reed

①   ②
Reed, Linda. "The Brown Decision: Its Long
                                          ③
    Anticipation and Lasting Influence." Journal of
        ④   ⑤   ⑥
    Southern History 70 (2004): 337-42. Expanded
    ⑦   ⑧
    Academic ASAP. InfoTrac. Boston Public Lib., MA.
        ⑨   ⑩
    28 July 2005 <http://infotrac.galegroup.com>.

Discusses the political, psychological, and cul-

tural effects of Brown v. Board of Education.

Figure 2.2   A source entry recorded in a computer file: an article in a scholarly journal available through a database, in MLA style

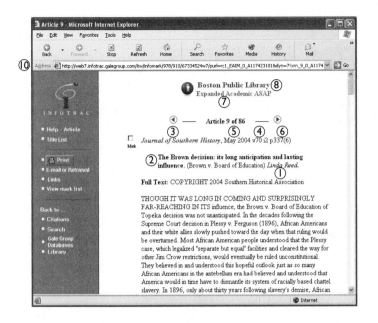

SOURCE NAVIGATOR: Recording Source Notes on a Book

1 The complete name of the author
2 The title and any subtitle of the book (underlined or italicized)
3 The place of publication, using the first city listed
4 The name of the publisher
5 The date of publication
6 The call number or library location

⑥   HF5387   Callahan

      C334

      2004

         ①   ②
Callahan, David. The Cheating Culture: Why More Americans Are Doing Wrong
                ③   ④   ⑤
        to Get Ahead. Orlando: Harcourt, 2004.

A look at how the competitiveness of American culture has led to an

epidemic of cheating in business, school, and sports.

Figure 2.3   A handwritten source card: a book with one author, in MLA style

①DAVID CALLAHAN

②the cheating culture

Why More Americans Are
Doing Wrong to Get Ahead

④
③   HARCOURT, INC.
ORLANDO   AUSTIN   NEW YORK   SAN DIEGO   TORONTO   LONDON

⑤

Copyright © 2004 by David Callahan

SOURCE NAVIGATOR: Recording Source Notes on a Page from a Web Site

1 The complete name of the author, if available
2 The title of the page (placed in quotation marks)
3 The name of the site (underlined or italicized)
4 The date of the last update
5 The name of any sponsoring organization
6 The access date when you used the source
7 The Internet address (URL or Uniform Resource Locator) or your search path

---

"AMA Calls on NCAA"

② ③ ④
"AMA Calls on NCAA to Ban Booze Ads." AMA. 28 Apr.
⑤ ⑥
2005. American Medical Association. 30 June
⑦
2005. <http://www.ama-assn.org/ama/
pub/category/15001.html>.

Brief article on the AMA's appeal to ban beer

commercials during college sporting and athletic

events.

Figure 2.4   A source entry recorded in a computer file: a page from a Web site, in MLA style

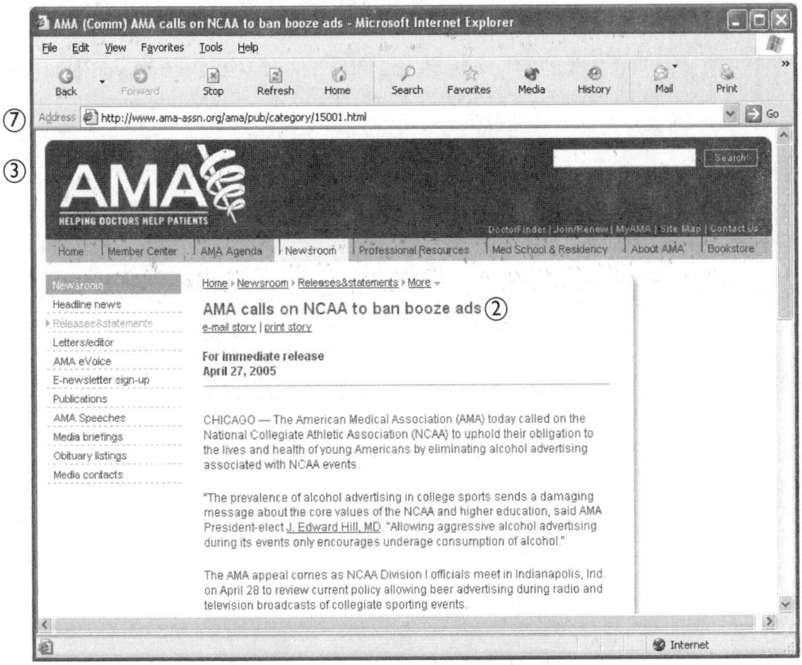
AMA (Comm) AMA calls on NCAA to ban booze ads - Microsoft Internet Explorer
⑦ Address http://www.ama-assn.org/ama/pub/category/15001.html
③ AMA
HELPING DOCTORS HELP PATIENTS
Home | Member Center | AMA Agenda | Newsroom | Professional Resources | Med School & Residency | About AMA | Bookstore
Home ▸ Newsroom ▸ Releases&statements ▸ More
AMA calls on NCAA to ban booze ads ②
e-mail story | print story
For immediate release
April 27, 2005
CHICAGO — The American Medical Association (AMA) today called on the National Collegiate Athletic Association (NCAA) to uphold their obligation to the lives and health of young Americans by eliminating alcohol advertising associated with NCAA events.
"The prevalence of alcohol advertising in college sports sends a damaging message about the core values of the NCAA and higher education, said AMA President-elect J. Edward Hill, MD. "Allowing aggressive alcohol advertising during its events only encourages underage consumption of alcohol."
The AMA appeal comes as NCAA Division I officials meet in Indianapolis, Ind. on April 28 to review current policy allowing beer advertising during radio and television broadcasts of collegiate sporting events.

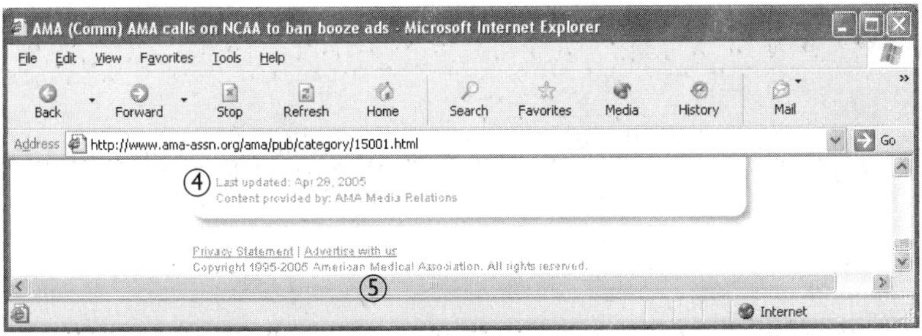
AMA (Comm) AMA calls on NCAA to ban booze ads - Microsoft Internet Explorer
Address http://www.ama-assn.org/ama/pub/category/15001.html
④
⑤

SOURCE NAVIGATOR: Recording Source Notes for a Field Source

1 The complete name of the person you interviewed or the setting you observed
2 A descriptive label, such as "Personal interview" or "E-mail interview"
3 The date you conducted the interview or observation

Cardone

① ② ③

Cardone, Amy. Personal interview. 20 Nov. 2005.

Anecdotal evidence. Describes sports injuries in children whom she's treated.

Figure 2.5   A source note recorded in a computer file: a personal interview, in MLA style

TABLE 2.3   Recording the Basics and Common Additions

Type of Information	The Basics	Common Additions
Author	Complete name of the author unless not identified	Names of co-authors, in the order listed in the source Name of any editor, compiler, translator, contributor, or editor of a special journal issue
Titles	Title and any subtitle of an article, Web page, or posting (placed in quotation marks) Title and any subtitle of a journal, magazine, newspaper, book, or Web site (underlined or italicized)	Title of a special issue of a journal Title of a series of books or pamphlets and item number
Publication Details for Periodicals	Volume number for a journal (or a magazine in APA or CSE) Section number for a newspaper	Issue number for a journal (and magazine in CSE), especially when page 1 begins each issue Any edition of a newspaper
Publication Details for Books	Place of publication, using the first city listed Name of the publisher	Edition number (4th) or description (revised) Volume number and total volumes, if more than one Names and locations of copublishers Publisher's imprint Total pages (CSE)
Publication Details for Electronic Sources	Name of the database, subscriber service, or library service (underlined or italicized) Name of any site sponsor	Details of any original or alternate print publication
Dates	Year of publication, full date (periodical), or date of creation or last update (electronic source) Your access date for an electronic source (printed or jotted on your hard copy)	Original date of publication for a literary work or classic
Location of Information	Article's opening and concluding page numbers	Paragraph, screen, or column numbers or section names
Location of Source	Call number or library area Name and location of the library where you used a database Internet address (URL or Uniform Resource Locator) or your search path	

STARTING A RESEARCH ARCHIVE

You can organize the information you accumulate from library, Internet, and field sources by creating a research archive. An *archive* is a place where information is systematically stored for later use. If you have ever found yourself staring at a pile of books, photocopies, and printouts, wondering which one contained the fact or quotation that you wanted to use, you know the importance of organizing. You can use several techniques to create a research archive.

File Paper Copies.   To use this method, try to get all important sources in a paper format: photocopy book passages and periodical articles, print out electronic sources, and keep questionnaires and other field material. Then put these pages in a separate file folder for each source, labeled with title or subject and author. Attach sticky notes next to key passages, or highlight them so you can locate them quickly. Make sure the source and page number are identified on your copy so that you can connect them to the corresponding source note in your working bibliography. If necessary, write that information on the photocopy.

Save Computer Files.   You can save Web pages, e-mail messages, posts to newsgroups and mailing lists, transcripts of chat sessions, and records from databases to a disk, a hard drive, or a network drive. Be certain that you carefully save or note URLs or search paths, your dates of access, and other similar details for these electronic sources. Give each file a descriptive name so that you'll be able to locate the information quickly later on. Clearly distinguish the sources you save from your own notes about sources. You can also organize the files in different electronic folders or directories, also named so you can easily tell what each contains.

Save Favorites and Bookmarks.   You can save the locations of sites on the Web within your browser so that you can easily locate them again. Microsoft Internet Explorer calls these saved locations *favorites,* while Netscape Navigator calls them *bookmarks.* You can also annotate these locations and organize them into folders, much as you organize files on a computer.

Save Search Results.   If a database or Internet search was very productive but you don't have time to locate each relevant source at that moment, note the keywords you used to search. Then return to the database or the search engine, and repeat the search at a later date. You can also print out the search results or save them to a computer file so you don't need to rerun the search.

RECORDING INFORMATION

No matter how you create your archive, remember two things: copy selectively and take notes. Selectively copying (either photocopying or saving to a computer file) will help you build your archive, but copying whatever you find will waste your money and time. Instead, try taking notes, annotating, highlighting, paraphrasing, and summarizing—all time-honored methods of absorbing, evaluating, and selecting information from a source. Such methods not only identify potentially useful material, they also prepare them for their smooth transfer and integration into a paper. (See Ch. 8 for more on quoting, paraphrasing, and summarizing and Ch. 7 on avoiding plagiarism.)

Capture the Essentials.   Make sure your notes are complete and accurate, ready to transfer information efficiently from your source to your draft. (For more on drawing information from sources, see Ch. 8.) If you want your paper to be a sound analysis or argument based on a variety of reliable sources, you'll need to separate the useful nuggets in each source from all the rest. Your research notes are the best place to do that. A good research note answers three essential questions:

- What's the source? Beginning with the author's last name and the page number (or other location) of the material you are recording will efficiently connect your research notes to the corresponding source note in your working bibliography.
- What's the topic? Adding a keyword at the top of each note will help you cluster related material and select its place in your paper.
- What's the information? Be selective, but carefully record every fact, statistic, authoritative view, quotation, or memorable phrase that you might eventually want to use.

Use a Sensible Format.   Many college researchers find that using note cards or word-processing files works better than taking notes on sheets of notebook paper. If you use note cards, aim to record only one note on each card. If you use a computer file, separate your entries clearly. When the time comes to organize your material, you can easily reshuffle cards or move around computerized notes to arrive at a logical order.

Take Accurate and Thorough Notes.   Read the entire article or section of a book before beginning to take notes. This method will help you decide what—and how much—to record without distorting the meaning. Put exact quotations in quotation marks, and take care not to quote something out of context or change the meaning. Double-check all statistics and lists. Make your notes and citations full enough that, once they're written, you are totally independent of the source from which they came.

Read as a Critic.   If you're tired or distracted, it's easy to stop thinking while you're recording notes. Instead, you need to read and write as a critic—approaching your sources skeptically and distinguishing what's significant for answering your research question and what's only slightly related. If you wish, add your own ratings (*, +, !! or −, ??) at the top or in the margin. When you feel that you're rereading what you have already learned from authoritative sources, you may be ready to stop reading, start shaping your paper, and perhaps begin identifing information gaps yet to fill.

Here are a few questions to help you set priorities for your research project.

RESEARCH CHECKLIST

Getting Organized

☐ Have you created a realistic research schedule based on your assigned deadlines? Have you reworked it to allow plenty of time for your research while meeting your other responsibilities?

☐ What has your quick survey of available library and online resources revealed? Do you expect to find enough—but not way too much—to answer your research question?

☐ Which types of sources might be best for beginning your research?

☐ Which method have you chosen for taking source notes for your working bibliography? Have you recorded a few entries to make sure your method will be easy and efficient to use?

☐ Which documentation style has been assigned for your project? If none has been assigned, have you asked your instructor which style is used most often in your field?

☐ Have you begun organizing your research archive—for example, by opening files and setting up folders on the computer or buying file folders for paper copies?

☐ Have you decided how you want to take research notes? Have you taken a few notes to test whether your method will be easy to keep up and will compile useful and accurate information?

3

Finding Sources
in the Library

By now you have narrowed your research question, started your working bibliography, and begun your research archive. Consult your schedule so that you stay on track, and revise it if necessary. This chapter will help you continue your research by using efficient strategies for searching the library for relevant and reliable sources.

SEARCHING FOR RELIABLE SOURCES

When you begin hunting for answers to your research question, you may be tempted to turn first to the Internet. However, even sites that supply useful material require you to do extra work—checking all the information presented as fact, looking for biases or financial motives, and searching for what's not stated rather than simply accepting what is. Such caution is required because anyone—expert or not—can build a Web site or post a message in a public forum. Information that appears on a Web site or circulates in e-mail messages may or may not be true; its repetition does not ensure its accuracy, reliability, or integrity because the Internet as a whole has no quality controls.

On the other hand, when your college library buys books, subscribes to scholarly journals, and acquires reference materials, whether print or electronic, these publications are expected to follow accepted editorial practices. Well-regarded publishers and professional groups turn to peer reviewers—experts in the field—to assess the strengths and weaknesses of an article or book before it is selected for publication. Guided by these reviewers and by professional editors, prospective authors revise for accuracy and edit for clarity. Their readers, in turn, count on these traditional quality controls to bring them material that meets academic or professional standards.

When you need to conduct an efficient search that meets academic expectations, take advantage of sources that already meet traditional quality standards. In addition, note sources recommended by your instructors, their academic departments, and the campus librarians—people trained to evaluate and manage information capably and to help others learn to do the same.

Seek Advice About Recommended Sources

Although popular search engines can turn up sources on nearly any topic, your challenge is not simply to find any sources but to find solid sources with the reliable evidence you need for a college paper. Very

---

RESEARCH CHECKLIST

Getting Source Recommendations

☐ Has your instructor suggested to the class where you might begin? Have you talked with your instructor after class or during office hours or e-mailed to ask for specific advice about resources for your topic? Have you checked the assignment sheet, syllabus, handouts, or class Web site?

☐ Does the department offering the course have a Web site with lists of resources available at the library or links to sites well regarded in that field?

☐ Does your textbook Web site provide links to additional resources or information?

☐ Have your classmates recommended useful academic databases, disciplinary Web sites, or similar resources?

☐ Which library databases does the librarian at the reference desk recommend for your course level and your topic?

☐ Which databases or links on your campus library's Web site lead to government (federal, state, or local) resources or to articles in journals and newspapers?

☐ Which resources are available on library terminals, in the new periodicals room, or in the reference area of your college library?

often your instructors will help to guide your search by specifying their requirements or general expectations. In addition, the short-cuts in the checklist on page 38 can help you find solid sources fast—ideally already screened, selected, and organized for you.

Start with Your Own Library

When you need reliable sources, your college library is usually the best place to begin your search. From its computer terminals, your home, or your dorm room, you can access many of its resources—catalogs, indexes, and databases, for example. Although much of the library's information is stored on printed pages, the way it has been for centuries, the tools for locating these pages and, increasingly, the information itself are taking electronic form. Today's researcher needs to navigate both the print and electronic worlds.

From your library's home page, you will find access to a wide variety of resources—the online catalog, periodical databases, online reference material, and guides to the Internet. Your library may also offer tours, online tutorials, or brochures explaining the library's organization and services. (See Figure 3.1 on page 40 for a sample library home page.)

RESEARCH CHECKLIST

Investigating Your Library

☐ Where can you find a Web site or pamphlet mapping locations of library holdings, describing library resources, and explaining services? How does your library use signs as guides?

☐ Where is the reference desk, and what hours is it open?

☐ How do you access the library's catalog? Can you search it or other library databases from your home computer or the campus network?

☐ Where are periodicals kept, and how are they arranged?

☐ What kinds of indexes or computerized databases are available, and how can you access them?

☐ Can you use interlibrary loan or a consolidated catalog to order material the library doesn't have?

☐ How long is the check-out period for books? How do you request items, renew them, or use other circulation services?

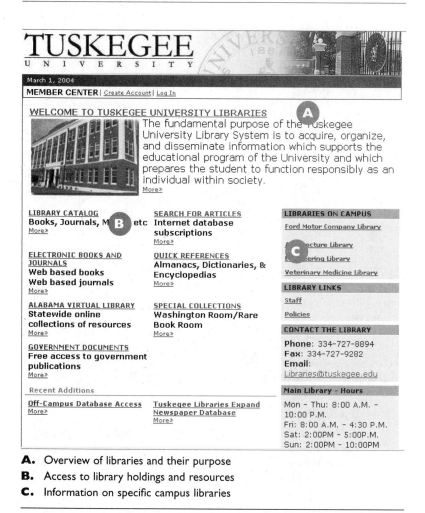

A. Overview of libraries and their purpose
B. Access to library holdings and resources
C. Information on specific campus libraries

Figure 3.1   Sample home page from the Tuskegee University Libraries

Reference librarians are available to help you answer questions, from specifics such as "What is the GNP of Brazil?" to general queries such as "Where can I find out about the Brazilian economy?" Before you look for sources for your paper, it pays to do a little research on the library itself, starting with the basic questions in the checklist on page 39.

Look for Resources Grouped by Discipline

Some researchers investigate current popular topics, such as social or environmental issues, and draw on expert resources to support their conclusions or recommendations. Others investigate questions of concern to a specific academic discipline. To help these researchers, many libraries supply electronic or printed lists of available resources that are well-regarded starting points for research within a field. These lists are valuable shortcuts for quickly finding a cluster of useful resources. Table 3.1 on pages 42–43 supplies only a small sampling of the specialized indexes, dictionaries, encyclopedias, handbooks, yearbooks, and other types of print and electronic resources you'll find on such lists. (For more extensive lists of specialized sources, visit <www.dianahacker.com/resdoc>. See also pp. 48–52 on databases and Ch. 4 on Internet research.)

USING THE ONLINE CATALOG

A library catalog provides information about the books, periodicals, videos, databases, and other materials available through the library. Typically, catalogs do not provide information about individual articles in periodicals. They do, however, provide you with the periodical's publication information (title, date, publisher, and so on), call number, location, and in some cases availability.

Become a Flexible Searcher.   When library catalogs were limited to printed file cards, they allowed searches only by author, title, or subject. Now, electronic catalogs may greatly expand these search options, as Table 3.2 on page 44 illustrates. Consult a librarian or follow the catalog prompts to find out which searches your library catalog allows. Try options that restrict a search by date, location, type of material, or other characteristics. Once you locate a relevant item, check its detailed record for alternative search terms that may help focus your search more productively. If your catalog adds online resources such as e-books or recommended Web sites to the items available at the library, use these selectively so that you are not distracted from your own research question.

Sort Your Search Results.   When your search produces a list of possible sources, click on the most promising individual items to learn more about them. See Figure 3.2 for a sample keyword search and Figure 3.3 for the sample online record for one source. In addition to the call number or shelf location, the record will identify the author, title, place of

TABLE 3.1 A Sampler of Sources Grouped by Field

Field	Specialized Indexes	Reference Works	Government Resources	Internet Resources
Humanities	Essay and General Literature Index	The Humanities: A Selective Guide to Information Sources	EDSITEment at <edsitement.neh.fed.us>	Voice of the Shuttle at <vos.ucsb.edu>
Art	BHA: Bibliography of the History of Art	Dictionary of Art (Grove)	National Gallery of Art at <www.nga.gov>	Art History Research Centre at <http://www.harmsen.net/ahrc/>
Film and Theater	Film Literature Index	McGraw-Hill Encyclopedia of World Drama	Smithsonian: Film, Theater and TV at <www.si.edu/art_and_design/film_theater_and_tv/>	Theatre History Sites on the WWW at <www.win.net/~kudzu/history.html>
History	Historical Abstracts	Dictionary of Concepts in History	The Library of Congress: American Memory at <memory.loc.gov/ammem>	Gateway to World History at <www.history.ccsu.edu/History_Web_links.htm>
Literature	MLA International Bibliography	Encyclopedia of the Novel	National Endowment for the Humanities at <www.neh.gov>	American Studies Web at <www.georgetown.edu/crossroads/asw/>
Philosophy	Philosopher's Index	Routledge Encyclopedia of Philosophy	The Library of Congress: Electronic Resources at <www.loc.gov/rr/ElectronicResources>	Philosophy Resources on the Internet: <www.EpistemeLinks.com>
Social Sciences	Social Sciences Citation Index	International Encyclopedia of the Social and Behavioral Sciences	Fedstats: One Stop Shopping for Federal Statistics at <www.fedstats.gov>	SOSIG: Social Science Information Gateway at <sosig.esrc.bris.ac.uk>
Business	Business Index	International Encyclopedia of Economics	SEC EDGAR Database at <www.sec.gov/edgar.shtml>	Hoover's Online: The Business Network at <www.hoovers.com>
Communications	Communication Abstracts	Communication Yearbook	Plain Language.gov at <plainlanguage.gov>	Online Communication Studies at <www.lib.uiowa.edu/gw/comm>
Criminal Justice	Current Law Index	Encyclopedia of Crime and Justice	U.S. Department of Justice at <www.usdoj.gov>	Internet Legal Resource Guide at <www.ilrg.com>
Education	Education Index	International Encyclopedia of Education	National Center for Education Statistics at <nces.ed.gov>	ERIC: Education Resources Information Center at <eric.ed.gov>

Ethnic Studies	Chicano Index	Asian-American Almanac	African American History at <memoryloc.gov/ammem/>	NativeWeb at <www.nativeweb.org>
Political Science	ABC Pol Sci: A Bibliography of Current Contents: Political Science and Government	State Legislative Sourcebook: A Resource Guide to Legislative Information in the 50 States	Fedworld at <www.fedworld.gov/>	Political Resources on the Web at <www.politicalresources.net> National Security Archive at <www.gwu.edu/~nsarchiv>
Psychology and Sociology Women's Studies	Psychological Abstracts Women's Studies Abstracts	International Encyclopedia of Sociology Women in World History: A Biographical Encyclopedia	National Institutes of Health at <www.nih.gov> U.S. Department of Labor: Women's Bureau at <www.dol.gov/wb/welcome.html>	Social Psychology Network at <www.socialpsychology.org> Institute for Women's Policy Research at <www.iwpr.org>
Science and Technology	General Science Index	McGraw-Hill Encyclopedia of Science and Technology	National Science Foundation at <www.nsf.gov>	EurekAlert! Your Global Gateway to Science, Medicine, and Technology News at <www.eurekalert.org>
Chemistry	Chemical Abstracts	Kirk-Othmer Encyclopedia of Chemical Technology	EnergyFiles: Chemistry at <www.osti.gov/energyfiles/>	CHEMINFO at <www.indiana.edu/~cheminfo/cisindex.html>
Earth Sciences	Bibliography and Index of Geology	Facts on File Dictionary of Earth Science	USGS (United States Geological Survey): Science for a Changing World at <www.usgs.gov>	CIESIN: Information for a Changing World at <www.ciesin.org>
Engineering	Applied Science and Technology Index	Van Nostrand's Scientific Encyclopedia	Scientific and Technical Information at <www.osti.gov>	EEVL: The Internet Guide to Engineering, Mathematics and Computing at <www.eevl.ac.uk/index.htm>
Environmental Studies Life Sciences	Environmental Abstracts Biological Abstracts	Encyclopedia of Environmental Science Encyclopedia of Human Biology	EPA: U.S. Environmental Protection Agency at <www.epa.gov> National Agricultural Library at <www.nal.usda.gov>	EnviroLink at <envirolink.org> Health Web at <healthweb.org>
Mathematics	Mathematical Reviews	Encyclopedic Dictionary of Mathematics	The NASA Homepage at <www.nasa.gov>	Math Archives Undergrads' Page at <archives.math.utk.edu/undergraduates.html>
Physics and Astronomy	Physics Abstracts	Handbook of Physics	U.S. Department of Energy: Office of Science at <www.erdoe.gov>	Astronomy Resources from STScI at <www.stsci.edu/resources>

TABLE 3.2 Searching an Electronic Catalog

Type of Search	Explanation	Examples	Search Tips
Keyword	Terms that identify topics discussed in the source, including works by or about an author, and may generate long lists of relevant and irrelevant sources	• workplace mental health • geriatric home health care • Creole cookbook • Jane Austen novels	Use a cluster of keywords to avoid broad terms (whale, nursing) or to reduce irrelevant topics using same terms (people of color; color graphics)
Subject	Terms that are assigned by library catalogers, often following the *Library of Congress Subject Headings* (LCSH)	• motion pictures (not films) • developing countries (not third world) • cookery (not cookbooks)	Consult the *LCSH*, a set of large red books often shelved near the catalog terminals, to find the exact phrasing used
Author	Name of individual, organization, or group that leads to list of printed (and possibly online) works by author	• Hawthorne, Nathaniel • Colorado School of Mines • North Atlantic Treaty Organization	Begin, as directed, with an individual's last name or first; for a group, first use a keyword search to identify its exact name
Title	Name of book, pamphlet, journal, magazine, newspaper, video, CD, or other material	• *Peace and Conflict Studies* • *Los Angeles Times* • *Nursing Outlook*	Look for a separate search option for titles of periodicals (journals, newspapers, magazines)
Identification Numbers	Library or consortium call numbers, publisher or government publication numbers	• MJ BASI, local call number for Count Basie recordings • DS272.G27 2004, for book *The Persians*	Use the call number of a useful source to find related items shelved nearby
Dates	Publication or other dates used to search (or limit searches) for current or historical materials	• Elizabeth I558 (when she became queen of England) • science teaching 2005	Add dates to keyword or other searches to limit the topics or time of publication

publication, and date. Often it will describe what the book contains, how long it is, and which subject headings define its scope. Though each library presents information slightly differently, the elements generally are the same. Use these clues to help you select and evaluate your options wisely. (For more on evaluating sources, see Ch. 6.)

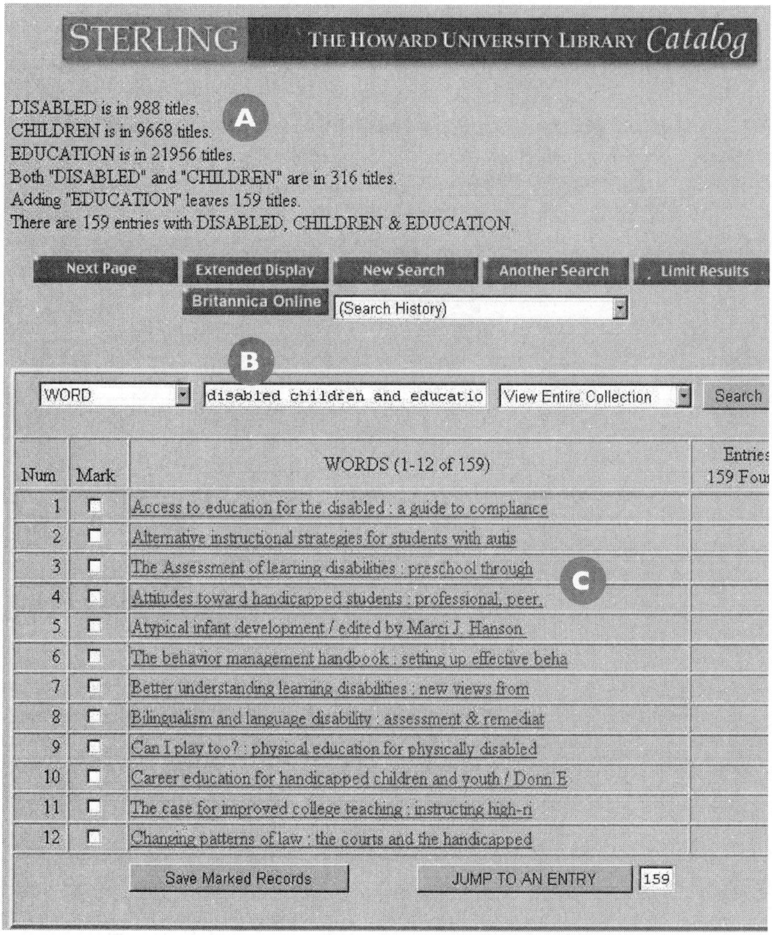

A. Number of results for individual and combined search terms
B. Keyword search window
C. Results screen (linked to full entries)

Figure 3.2 General results of a keyword search on "disabled children and education" using an online library catalog

STERLING   The Howard University Library *Catalog*

| Previous Record | Next Record | Back to Browse | Another Search | New Search |

| MARC Display | Export | Britannica Online | (Search History) |

WORD ▾ disabled children and educatio View Entire Collection ▾ Searcl

Title   **A** **B**etter understanding learning disabilities : new views from research and the
                 implications for education and public policy / edited by G. Reid Lyon ... [et a
Imprint   Baltimore, Md. : Paul H. Brookes Pub. Co., c1993.

LOCATION **B**	CALL #	STATUS
Founders Library	LC4705 .B48 1993	CHECK SHELF

Descript   **C** xxi, 362 p. : ill. ; 24 cm.
Bibliog.   Includes bibliogaphical references and index.
Local note **D** 35969020152588
Subject   **E** Learning disabilities -- United States -- Congresses.
                   Learning disabled children -- Education -- United States -- Congresses.
Alt author   Lyon, G. Reid, 1949- **F**
ISBN   **G** 1557661162

A. Book title, author, and publication information
B. Location and library call number
C. Number of pages, illustrations, height of book
D. Description of bibliography
E. Alternate subject headings (often hyperlinked)
F. Other works by the same author (often hyperlinked)
G. International Standard Book Number (ISBN)

Figure 3.3   Specific record selected from keyword search results

Browse for Items on the Shelves.   A book's call number, like a building's address, tells where the book "resides." This number is carefully chosen so that books on the same subject end up as neighbors on the shelves. College libraries generally use the classification system devised by the Library of Congress. Its call letters and numbers guide you to items grouped by subject. (See Figure 3.4.) Other libraries use the older and more familiar Dewey decimal system, which uses numbers to assign items to broad categories. In either case, reserve some of your research time for browsing because you will almost certainly find interesting materials on the shelf next to the ones you found through the catalog. The two common classification systems are outlined here. Both have added

LIBRARY OF CONGRESS CLASSIFICATION SYSTEM

A	General Works	L	Education
B	Philosophy, Psychology, Religion	M	Music and Books on Music
C	Auxiliary Sciences of History	N	Fine Arts
D	History: General and Old World	P	Language and Literature
E	History: America	Q	Science
F	History: America	R	Medicine
G	Geography, Anthropology, Recreation	S	Agriculture
H	Social Sciences	T	Technology
J	Political Science	U	Military Science
K	Law	V	Naval Science
		Z	Library Science

DEWEY DECIMAL CLASSIFICATION SYSTEM

000–009	General Works	500–599	Natural Sciences
100–199	Philosophy	600–699	Applied Sciences
200–299	Religion	700–799	Fine and Decorative Arts
300–399	Social Sciences, Government, Customs	800–899	Literature
400–499	Language	900–999	History, Travel, Biography

Library of Congress classification number ——— **Human ecology** *(May Subd Geog)*
[GF1-GF900]
Here are entered works on the relationship of humans to the natural environment. Works on the relationship of humans to their sociocultural environment are entered under Social ecology. Works on the composite of physical, biological, and social sciences concerned with the conditions of the environment and their effects are entered under Environmental sciences. Works on the interrelationships of organisms and their environments, including other organisms, are entered under Ecology.

Used for ——— UF   Ecology—Social aspects
Environment, Human
Human environment

Broader topics ——— BT   Ecology
Related topics ——— RT   Ecological engineering
Human beings—Effect of environment on
Human geography
Nature—Effect of human beings on

Narrower topics ——— NT   Community life
Ecofeminism
Hazardous geographic environments
Human settlements
Landscape assessment
Population
Quality of life
Social psychology
Survival skills

Figure 3.4   *Entries from the* Library of Congress Subject Headings

newer fields, such as computer science, mass communications, and environmental studies, to related areas.

Consult Catalogs at Other Libraries.   Most college and university library catalogs are available over the Internet or through regional, state, or other consolidated catalogs. Use these catalogs to find books or other materials that you can borrow through interlibrary loan or by visiting a nearby library. If you're not sure how to access such catalogs ask a librarian. You may be able to connect directly to them via the Internet or through your own library's catalog.

SEARCHING DATABASES: PERIODICAL INDEXES AND BIBLIOGRAPHIES

Information on current topics often appears first in periodicals rather than books. Periodicals are journals, magazines, newspapers, and other publications issued at regular intervals. Many indexes—guides to material published within other works—exist to help you locate articles in periodicals. Bibliographies—lists of sources on a particular topic—also can lead you to relevant materials, often those you would never think to trace in a catalog. (For more on timeliness and other characteristics of sources, see the charts on pp. 58 and 60.)

If you have questions about which database to use or how to access it, ask a reference or subject-area librarian. Many library indexes and databases are not available free to the general public; your library selects these resources and subscribes to them so that you—and other campus researchers—can find the most current and reliable sources as quickly and easily as possible. Academic librarians, often expert research advisors, are specially trained to help you search efficiently in the most appropriate databases. They are available in person, generally at the reference desk, and often by e-mail, telephone, appointment, or live chat online. (See also pp. 66–68 on keyword searches and pp. 64–68 on advanced electronic searches.)

Check the Periodical Indexes.   In a periodical index, you'll find every article—listed by author, title, and subject—for the periodicals and time period covered by the index. The index also includes the source information you'll need to find each article in the library, usually the periodical title, date, volume or issue number, and page numbers.

Electronic indexes—often called periodical databases—are organized as a series of records or entries on a particular item, such as a newspaper or journal article. You can easily search for these records using author, title, subject, or keyword. Electronic indexes may include more information on each article than traditional print indexes do, such as a short summary or abstract or even the full text of the article, which you can print or download for later use. Electronic indexes may complement, replace, or duplicate print indexes; for instance, *MLA Online*, *ERIC*, and *PsychLIT* are available in both forms.

Each periodical index includes entries only for its specific collection of periodicals, so finding the right article is largely a matter of finding the right index. Before you use a periodical index, ask these questions.

RESEARCH CHECKLIST

Finding the Right Index

☐ Is your subject covered in this index? Does the index cover a broad field or a very specific subject in depth?

☐ Does the index cover the period you're interested in? If the index is electronic, how far back does it go? How often is it updated?

☐ Does the index cover scholarly journals written for an expert audience or popular magazines for a more general audience?

☐ Does the index simply identify an article, add a summary or abstract, or supply a link to its full text?

☐ Is the index an online subscription service available to students on a library terminal, campus network, or home computer? Is it a public index available on the Web and conveniently linked from the library's Web site?

☐ Are older print or CD-ROM indexes, sometimes needed for historical research, available in the reference area or elsewhere in the library?

Consider General Indexes. Several indexes can help you if you're looking for magazine or newspaper articles addressed to the general population.

The *Readers' Guide to Periodical Literature* started publication in 1900, so you can use the current or retrospective indexes to locate popular press coverage of events at any time in the twentieth century—for example, articles published days after the bombing of Pearl Harbor in December 1941. (See Figure 3.5 for sample entries.)

The *New York Times Index,* dating back to 1851, can help you track down that newspaper's current or historical coverage of events.

EBSCOhost and *InfoTrac* include the full text of many articles written for a fairly general audience. (See Figure 3.6 for a sample entry.)

NewsBank, with daily updates, indexes nearly five hundred local U.S. papers.

Lexis-Nexis carries mainly full-text articles from newspapers, wire services, and other general-interest publications.

Try Specialized Indexes.   Discipline-specific indexes are more likely to analyze scholarly journals with peer-reviewed articles that have been critiqued by other experts before being accepted for publication. Such articles are aimed at a more specialized audience and provide more analysis than articles in popular magazines. If you are looking for literary criticism, research on social issues, or scientific or medical research only summarized or reported in the popular press, turn to indexes such as these:

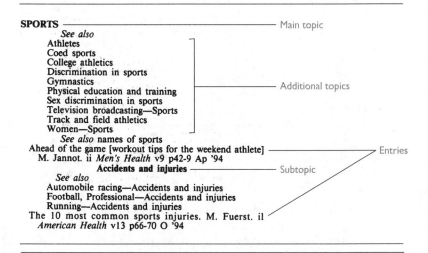

Figure 3.5   *Entries from the* Readers' Guide to Periodical Literature

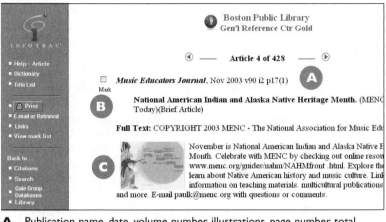

A. Publication name, date, volume number, illustrations, page number, total pages in article

B. Article title and author

C. Text of short article

Figure 3.6 Search result from InfoTrac index

Humanities Index or *Humanities Abstracts*

Social Sciences Index or *Social Sciences Abstracts*

Business Periodicals Index

PAIS International (an index focusing on public affairs)

For more examples of specialized indexes, see the sampler on pages 42–43, or visit <www.dianahacker.com/resdoc>.

Although indexes are wonderful aids, their very richness can bog down or distract a researcher. Ask yourself questions like those in the checklist on page 52 to help you select the most promising articles and stay focused on your search.

RESEARCH CHECKLIST

Selecting Sources from a Periodical Index

☐ Does the title or description of the article suggest that it will answer your research question? Or does the entry sound intriguing but irrelevant?

☐ What does the title of the periodical suggest about its audience, interest area, and popular or scholarly orientation? How likely are the articles in that periodical to supply what you need to find?

☐ Does the date of the article fit your need for current, contemporary, eyewitness, or classic material?

☐ Does the length of the article suggest that it's a short review, a concise overview of a topic, or an exhaustive discussion? How much detail will you need about its topic?

☐ Is the periodical containing the article likely to be available on your library's shelves, in its microform files, or among its online resources?

Look for Bibliographies. When you use a bibliography—a list of sources on a specific subject—you take advantage of the research others have already done. Every time you find a good book or article, look at the sources the author draws on; some of these may be useful to you, too. Look for a section at the back of a book labeled "Bibliography" or perhaps "For Further Reading." If the author has quoted or referred to other works, look for a list called "References" or "Works Cited" at the end of the work. If the book or article uses footnotes or endnotes, check those, too, for possible leads.

Sometimes you may locate a book-length bibliography on your subject, compiled by a researcher and published so that other researchers (including you) won't have to duplicate the work. Bibliographies cite a wide variety of materials—books and articles but also films, manuscripts, letters, government documents, and pamphlets—and they can lead you to sources that you wouldn't otherwise find.

For example, *Essential Shakespeare* lists the best books and articles published on each of Shakespeare's works, a wonderful shortcut when you're looking for worthwhile criticism. If you're lucky, adding the word *bibliography* to a subject or keyword search will turn up a list of sources with annotations that describe and evaluate each one.

CONSULTING REFERENCE MATERIALS

Many other library resources are available to you beyond what you can access from your library's home page. One of the most overlooked resources in the library is its staff. Besides knowing the library better than anyone else, librarians are constantly working with its catalog, databases, and additions to the collections. If you need help locating or using the library's amazing array of reference material, consult a librarian.

Spending research time in the library can save you a lot of time and effort in the long run. Remember, the library and all of its resources—whether electronic or print—are specifically designed to help researchers like you to find information quickly and efficiently. Here you can familiarize yourself with a topic or fine-tune your research by filling in detailed definitions, dates, statistics, or facts.

Reference Guides.   Use resources such as the *Guide to Reference Books*, a directory of sources arranged by discipline, to find reference sources related to your topic.

General Encyclopedias.   These multivolume references, such as the *New Encyclopaedia Britannica* and *Encyclopedia Americana*, may be especially valuable when you first scan or survey a topic. Although they can supply a missing fact here or there, they'll serve you best by preparing you to move on to more specialized resources.

Specialized Encyclopedias.   These references cover a field in much greater depth than general encyclopedias do. The following titles illustrate their variety:

> *Dictionary of American History*
>
> *Encyclopedia of the American Constitution*
>
> *Encyclopedia of World Cultures*
>
> *The Gale Encyclopedia of Science*
>
> *New Grove Dictionary of Music and Musicians*

Dictionaries.   Large and specialized dictionaries cover foreign languages, abbreviations, and slang as well as the terminology in a field. Examples include *Black's Law Dictionary, Stedman's Medical Dictionary,* or the *Oxford Dictionary of Natural History.* In unabridged dictionaries, often available on dictionary stands, you can learn what the most obscure words mean as well as how to pronounce them.

Handbooks and Companions. These concise surveys of terms and topics relating to a specific subject feature articles that are generally longer than dictionary entries but more concise than those in encyclopedias. Check with a reference librarian to see if specialized handbooks, such as the following, are available for your topic.

> *Blackwell Encyclopaedia of Political Thought*
>
> *Bloomsbury Guide to Women's Literature*
>
> *Dictionary of the Vietnam War*
>
> *Oxford Companion to English Literature*

Statistical Sources. If numbers are a key type of evidence for your research, you can find sources for statistics in the library and on the Web.

- The *Statistical Abstract of the United States.* Perhaps the most useful single compilation of statistics, this resource contains hundreds of tables relating to population, social issues, economics, and so on.
- *Gallup Poll.* Good resources for public-opinion statistics, the surveys conducted by the Gallup organization are published in annual volumes, in a monthly magazine, and on the Web.
- *<www.census.gov>.* The federal government collects an extraordinary amount of statistical data and releases much of it on the Web. Check also <www.fedworld.gov> and <www.fedstats.gov> for lists of other government statistics available on the Web.

Atlases. If your research has a geographical angle, maps and atlases may be useful. Besides atlases of countries, regions, and the world, others cover history, natural resources, ethnic groups, and many other special topics.

Biographical Sources. Useful directories list basic information—degrees, work history, honors, addresses—for prominent people. You can use tools such as *Biography Index* and the *Biography and Genealogy Master Index* to locate biographical resources, which include the following:

> *American Men and Women of Science*
>
> *The Dictionary of American Biography*
>
> *The Dictionary of National Biography*
>
> *Who's Who in Politics*
>
> *Who's Who in the United States*

LOCATING SPECIAL MATERIALS

Your library is likely to have other collections of materials, especially on regional or specialized topics, but you may need to ask what's available.

Periodicals on Microform.   This technology puts a large amount of printed material—for example, two weeks' worth of the *New York Times*—on a durable roll of film (microfilm) that fits into a small box or on a set of plastic sheets the size of index cards (microfiche). The machines used to read microforms often print out full-sized copies of pages.

Primary Materials on Microform.   Many libraries also have primary, or firsthand, material in microform. For example, the *American Culture Series* reproduces books and pamphlets (1493 to 1875) along with a good subject index, making it possible to view colonial religious tracts or nineteenth-century abolitionist pamphlets without traveling to a museum or rare books collection. The *American Women's Diaries* collection provides firsthand glimpses of the past through the words of New England and Southern women who traveled west as pioneers.

Primary Materials in Digitized Format.   Firsthand materials such as diaries, letters, speeches, and interviews are increasingly available to libraries in digitized databases that can be searched using keywords, authors, titles, or other means. Examples include *Black Thought and Culture, Oral History Online,* and *North American Immigrant Letters, Diaries, and Oral Histories* (1840 on).

Resources from Organizations.   Your library may collect pamphlets and reports distributed by companies, trade groups, or professional organizations. The *Encyclopedia of Associations,* organized by subject or group name, or the *United States Government Manual,* listing government agencies, can lead you to useful materials and contacts, especially for field research.

Government Documents.   The federal government of the United States is the most prolific publisher in the world and, in an effort to make information accessible to citizens all over the country, makes an increasing number of documents available on the Web along with indexes like these:

- *Monthly Catalog of United States Government Publications,* which is the most complete index to federal documents available

- *CIS Index*, which specializes in congressional documents and includes a handy legislative history index
- *Congressional Record Index*, which indexes reports on what happens in Congress each day

Besides congressional hearings, presidential papers, and reports from federal agencies, the government has published something on practically any topic you can think of, as the following sampling suggests:

Ozone Depletion, the Greenhouse Effect, and Climate Change

Placement of School Children with Acquired Immune Deficiency Syndrome

Small Business and the International Economy

Violence on Television

If you plan to use government documents, reports, or statistics in your research, don't be shy about asking a librarian for help. The documents can be difficult to locate both on the shelves and on the Web.

SELECTING RELEVANT AND RELIABLE SOURCES

Many college researchers view library research, whether online or in the dusty stacks of bound periodicals, as an exercise in optimistic accumulation. They gather as large an archive of sources as possible, all the while fervently hoping that those materials will somehow congeal in an answer to their research question. As your working bibliography and archive grow, pause occasionally to convert your optimism to selectivity. Return to your research question to help you select relevant sources—sources that are likely to help you develop and support a compelling answer to your specific research question. In addition, consider the reliability of your sources—the extent to which you and your academic readers will have confidence in their assertions and evidence.

If you planned to survey common Internet hoaxes for a paper about online practices, you might deliberately turn to sources that are, by definition, unreliable. However, investigating such sources is very different from accepting and repeating their phony claims as if they were accurate supporting evidence. Instead, you usually want to turn right away to sources that are reliable. The charts on pages 58 and 60 explain how to recognize different types of sources, gauge their currency, and select those appropriate for your research question.

Each type of source analyzed in these charts might be credible and useful for a paper. For certain research questions, you might want to use sources as varied as reports from journalists, advice from practitioners in the field, accounts of historical eyewitnesses, or opinions on civic policy. However, college instructors often expect you to turn not to popular sources but to scholarly ones—also identified as peer-reviewed or refereed sources—with characteristics such as these:

- in-depth investigation or interpretation of an academic topic or research problem
- discussion of previous studies, which are cited in the text and listed at the end for easy reference by readers
- use of research methods accepted across several fields or within a discipline
- publication by a reputable company or sponsoring organization
- acceptance for publication based on reviews by experts (peer reviewers) who assess the quality of the study
- preparation for publication supervised by academic or expert editors or by authors and professional staff

Your instructors may be more confident of the standards and quality controls of established publications, appearing in print or in simultaneous print and online versions, than of the procedures of newer or unfamiliar electronic sources. Your campus librarian can help you limit your searches to peer-reviewed journals or check the scholarly reputation of sources that you find. You also can look for a periodical's editorial policies or advice to contributors to find out more about its procedures and standards. (Also see Ch. 6 for more on evaluating sources.)

Besides assessing the reliability of a source, you need to consider its relevance to your research question. Because you may not be certain where your answers to that question will go, you also may not be certain which sources will be useful. Look for sources that challenge your existing point of view as well as those that support it. Favor sources that deepen your reasoning and enrich your store of evidence. Try to select those that might be meaty contributions to your understanding, not light filler.

Before turning to the wealth of Web resources available, take a moment to assess where you are in your research project. If you have a

TABLE 3.3 Understanding Print Sources and Their Applications

Type of Source	Likely Appearance	Typical Publication Time Frame	Examples	Best For
Scholarly Book	In-depth discussion for an academic audience, often a plain-cover hardbound with research findings, references, and few, if any, illustrations	Months or years, probably following months or years of research and writing	*The Information Society: A Skeptical View, The Psychology of Aggression, Theodore Roosevelt and His Times*	In-depth analysis and research into established academic topics
Popular Nonfiction Book	Trendy or topical hardbound or paperback, often with an eye-catching cover and information, advice, or instructions for general readers	Months or years, possibly following months or years of writing	*Dude, Where's My Country?, Ten Minutes from Normal, General Ike, A Short History of Nearly Everything*	Overview of current issue, advice, personal experience, or life story
Scholarly Journal	Quarterly or monthly text-heavy publication for specialists, often with a scholarly sponsor and prominent table of contents listing long articles	Months (or longer), probably following months or years of research and writing	*American Economic Review, PMLA* (Publications of the Modern Language Association), *Science and Technology Review*	In-depth, up-to-date research on discipline-specific topics
News Magazine	Weekly or monthly publication with color cover, photographs; and short articles on events and societal trends	Days or weeks, following current or long-term investigation	*Time, Newsweek, U.S. News & World Report*	The latest news on regional, national, or international topics
Popular Magazine	Colorful weekly, biweekly, or monthly publication with attention-grabbing cover, sidebars, photographs, and special-interest articles	Days, weeks, or months, following immediate or long-term development	Range from *Atlantic Monthly, National Geographic,* and *Smithsonian* to *People* and *US* (serious topics to hobbies or celebrities)	Current information on popular issues, trends, and subjects that interest readers
Newspaper	Daily, weekly, or monthly publication with oversized pages, headlines, columns, photographs, graphics, and stories on events and trends	Days or weeks, following current or long-term investigation	*New York Times, Wall Street Journal, Chronicle of Higher Education,* your local or regional newspaper	The latest news and opinions on local, regional, state, national, or international topics
Pamphlet or Booklet	Brief paperbound publications, appearing irregularly, individually, or serially, often sponsored by a scholarly, civic, business, government, or other group	Days or months, following development of material	*GE Annual Report, The Unicorn Tapestries, Children of John and Sophia Walz, Healthy Moves*	In-depth coverage of specific topics; viewpoints, or recollections
Reference Work	Book or multivolume encyclopedia, handbook, fact book, or other guide, usually in library's reference area	Months or years, probably following months or years of research and writing	*Encyclopedia of the Harlem Renaissance, Oxford Dictionary of Literary Quotations, Facts on File, Atlas of World Cultures*	Concise background, definitions, facts, statistics, biographies, and other specifics

clear idea of what's left to accomplish, you will find it easier to stick to your research schedule and, in the final stage, to write your paper. Ask yourself the questions in the following checklist, and then catch up or reorganize as needed.

RESEARCH CHECKLIST

Managing Your Project

☐ Are you on schedule? Do you need to adjust your timetable to give yourself more or less time for any of the stages?

☐ Are you keeping your materials up-to-date — listing new sources in your working bibliography and labeling and storing new material in your archives?

☐ Are you using your research question to stay on track and avoid digressions?

☐ Are you selecting materials instead of simply accumulating them? Are you considering both relevance to your question and reliability?

☐ Do you have a clear idea of where you are in the research process?

TABLE 3.4 Understanding Electronic Sources and Their Applications

Type of Source	Likely Appearance	Typical Publication Time Frame	Examples	Best For
Online Reference Site	Prominent search box, search options for fields or topics, links to gateways or resources	Immediate, daily or regular updates	<http://infomine.ucr.edu>, <www.ipl.org>, <http://lii.org>, <www.teoma.com> (see p. 63)	Quick access to pre-screened resources and links for researchers
Gateway Site for a Topic or Field	Prominent focus on discipline or topic with search or category options	Regular or irregular updates, depending on sponsor or Web master	*The American Civil War Homepage at* <http://sunsite.utk.edu/civil-war>	Quick access to pre-screened resources and links on specific subjects
Online Document Collection	List of available documents, groups of documents, or search options such as author or title	Regular or irregular updates, depending on materials or Web master	<http://bartleby.com>, <http://gutenberg.org>, <http://memory.loc.gov>	Easy access to large collections of texts
Professional Web Site	Conspicuous promotion of sponsor: scholarly or field group, nonprofit agency, corporation, or foundation (.org, .net, or .com)	Regular or irregular updates, depending on sponsor	American Educational Research Association at <www.aera.net>, Better Business Bureau at <http://bbb.org>	Resources or specialized materials related to sponsor's interests
Academic Web Site	Attractive presentation of institution (.edu) and its campus units	Regular or irregular updates, depending on unit maintaining page	College Web sites such as your library, department, or course home page	Disciplinary and cross-disciplinary campus resources
Government Web Site	Prominent focus on federal, state, local, or other agencies (.gov), often with links and a search box	Regular or irregular updates, depending on agency	Gateways such as <www.firstgov.gov>, agencies such as <http://factfinder.census.gov> or <www.epa.gov>	Statistics, reports, legislation and policies, consumer publications
Online Newspaper or News Service	Banner headline of organization with breaking news, section options, and archives	Immediate updates as events occur and archives of past coverage	Online *New York Times, Wall Street Journal,* or local newspapers	The latest national or international news and views
Interest-Group or Personal Web Site	Logo for partisan, special-interest, or discussion group or individual page or blog (Web log)	Regular or irregular updates, depending on individual or group	<www.blogforamerica.com>, <www.tyr.org>, <www.artsjournal.com>	Views, resources, and opinions requiring evaluation of bias

4

Finding Sources
on the Internet

Conducting academic research on the Internet—including the vast, disorganized arena called the World Wide Web—can challenge even an experienced researcher. Because the Internet's resources are so numerous, you can easily be swamped by too many options. In addition, these resources vary greatly in purpose and quality. They may reflect the quirks of an individual, the collective intuition of a group of like-minded people, the marketing savvy of a profit-driven business, the beliefs of an advocate who acknowledges only part of a story—or the substantial work of another inquisitive researcher. (See, for example, the range of electronic sources and their applications on p. 60.) Refining your search skills can help you locate the sources that you need.

USING THE INTERNET FOR RESEARCH

A quick search for information about Yellowstone National Park turns up nearly anything you might want to find: contacts for making cabin reservations, photographs of family trips to Yellowstone, the Greater Yellowstone Coalition's spirited defense of the park's ecosystem, scientific studies of regrowth following the 1988 fire, teaching modules on fire management, the Old Faithful Webcam, and technical reports such as the official Yellowstone Wildland Fire Management Plan. Unfortunately, because of the sheer bulk of information, searching for relevant materials can be both too easy and too difficult. Many of the strategies you have used to tap the resources of your library will also help you to access the nearly limitless—and ever-growing—resources of the Internet. (See pp. 42–43 on sources and p. 44 on strategies for using the online catalog.) In addition, understanding a few basic principles can help a great deal.

Select Your Search Engines

Unlike a library, the Internet has no handy, systematic catalog. Instead, researchers must rely on search engines to identify its vast resources. However, search engines are not unbiased, objective searchers. Each has its own system of locating material, categorizing it, and establishing the sequence for reporting results. The best search site is the one you learn to use well. In addition to following general search strategies, you should note each site's "search tips" and "help" instructions.

One search site, patterned on a library catalog or index, might be selective, designed to advance the investigations of students, faculty, and professionals. Another might carry extensive advertising but separate it from search results, while a third organizes search results so that the sites that pay advertising fees ("sponsors") pop up first in the list, even though sites listed on later pages might better match the searcher's needs. Take a close look at the practices of your favorite search engine (which may be described on an "About" page), and consider trying some others to find those that most efficiently supply the reliable sources you need. (For a list of leading search sites, see p. 63.)

If you are uncertain about your topic, try a directory site like *Digital Librarian* or Google Directory that begins searches with categories. Next, think of searching like a zoom lens. If you zoom into "no results" or "no pages found," then you can step back and add more information until you start to focus on sites you want to explore. By tinkering with your words, you can improve your searches and locate Web pages with titles and ideas closer to your research goals. This process is much easier than starting with a general prompt and finding thousands of potential sites.

Look for Recommended Internet Resources

Instead of beginning your Web research with a few keywords and your favorite search engine, go first to online resources recommended by your instructor, department, campus library, or other reliable source. What are the advantages of well-chosen site recommendations? They save the time required to search and screen randomly chosen sites. (For more on evaluating sources, see Ch. 6.) More important, they can take you directly to respected resources that have been prepared by experts (scholars or librarians), directed to academic researchers (like you), and

LEADING INTERNET SEARCH SITES

Subject Catalogs, Directories, and Guides

Ask Jeeves <www.ask.com>
Digital Librarian (Margaret Vail Anderson)
Encyclopaedia Britannica Online
Google Directory (Open Directory Project)
 <http://directory.google.com/>
Infomine: Scholarly Internet Resource Collections
 <http://infomine.ucr.edu>
Librarians' Internet Index <http://lii.org/>
Michigan eLibrary <http://mel.org/>
University of California Berkeley: Find Electronic Resources
 <www.lib.berkeley.edu/find/types/electronic_resources.html>
Yahoo!

Indexes with Content Gathered by Computer "Spiders" or "Robots"

AlltheWeb <www.alltheweb.com>
Alta Vista
Google
Google Scholar <http://scholar.google.com>

Sites That Search Multiple Indexes at One Time

Dogpile
InfoSpace
Ixquick
Metacrawler
MetaEureka
Search.com
SurfWax

used successfully by others on campus. Of course, no recommendation can replace your careful consideration of the appropriateness of a resource for your research question.

How can you locate recommended sources? Browse to find collections of links to resources such as these on your library or other campus Web site:

- Self-help guides or Internet databases organized by area (social sciences or business), topic (literary analysis), or type of information, such as the *Auraria Library Statistics Guide* at <http://library.auraria.edu/findit/subj_guides/statistics/statistics.html>.

- Research Web sites sponsored by another library, academic institution, or consortium such as the Internet Public Library at <www.ipl.org>.

- Other research centers or major libraries with their own collections of links, such as the Library of Congress page "Newspaper & Current Periodical Reading Room" at <www.loc.gov/rr/news/lists.html>.

- Specialty search engines for government materials—<www.fedworld.gov>, <www.firstgov.gov>, or <www.google.com/unclesam>—along with advice about using them such as that on the California State University Northridge Web site at <http://library.csun.edu/Find_Resources/Government_Publications/index.html>.

- Specialty search engines for specific materials such as images at <www.ditto.com>.

- Collections of e-books, including reference books and literary texts now out of copyright, such as *Bartleby.com* at <www.bartleby.com/> and *Project Gutenberg* at <www.gutenberg.org/>.

- Web databases with "unrestricted access" (not online subscription services restricted to campus users) as varied as the country-by-country data of *InfoNation* at <cyberschoolbus.un.org/infonation3/menu/advanced.asp> and the health resources of *MedlinePlus (Pub Med)* at <www.nlm.nih.gov/medlineplus/sitemap.html>.

- Community resources or organizations, often useful for local research and service learning reports, such as the information on Austin, Texas, at <www.lib.utexas.edu/refsites/austin.html>.

CONDUCTING ADVANCED ELECTRONIC SEARCHES

Search engines contain millions of records on Web sites, much as a database or library catalog contains records on books, periodicals, or other materials found in a library. Generally, search engines can be searched by broad categories such as *education* or *health* or by more specific keywords. (For more on keywords see pp. 66–68.)

When you limit your search simply to keywords and broad categories, however, you may be overwhelmed with information not directly related to your research question. For example, Figure 4.1 illustrates a keyword search for sources on *foster care* on Google that produced more

A. Search terms
B. Total number of entries located
C. Highlighted search terms found in entries

Figure 4.1 Results of a keyword search for *foster care* using Google, reporting more than 4 million entries

than 4 million entries. A keyword search may be ideal if you search for a highly specialized term or topic, such as a "marathon training diet" for long distance runners. For a more general topic—such as *foster care*—you may turn up seemingly endless lists of results.

Several techniques are available for more sophisticated searches of the Web, databases, and library catalogs. Some of these techniques can expand your search, but most researchers want to limit the scope of their searches in order to find more results relevant to their research interests. As Figure 4.2 shows, an advanced search produced fewer sources on one aspect of foster care—placing older children in foster care.

Use Wildcards.   Wildcards are symbols that tell the search engine to look for all possible endings to a word. For instance, if you search for the keyword *runner*, you'll get every entry containing that word but not entries containing only *run*, *runs*, or *running*. Using a wildcard symbol such as run*, you can search for all words that begin with *run*, thus increasing the range of your results. The most common wildcard symbols are an asterisk (*) for multiple letters, numbers, or symbols and a question mark (?) for single characters. Check your search engine's symbols by clicking on search tips.

Combine Terms in Boolean Searches.   A Boolean search, named after the nineteenth-century mathematician George Boole, lets you specify the relationships between your keywords and phrases. Common Boolean search terms include *AND* (all terms must appear in a result), *OR* (one or more of the terms must appear), and *NOT* (one or more terms can appear, but another must not).

Search for: history AND California
Result: all entries containing both *history* and *California*
Search for: history OR California
Result: all entries containing *history* or *California* or both
Search for: history NOT California
Result: all entries containing *history* but not containing *California*
Search for: history AND California NOT Los Angeles
Result: all entries containing *history* and *California* but not those containing *Los Angeles*

Select Limitations for Advanced Searches.   Many search engines will automatically combine terms for Boolean searches when you select the advanced search option. Google and Metacrawler, for example, allow

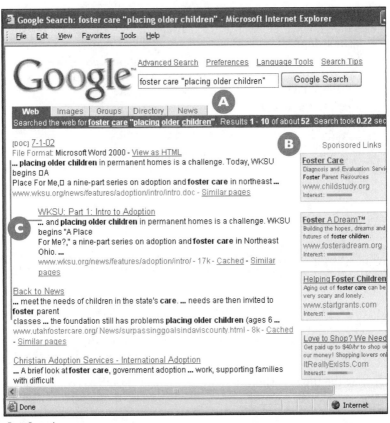

A. Search terms
B. Total number of entries located
C. Highlighted search terms found in entries

Figure 4.2   Advanced search results on *foster care + placing older children* using Google, reporting 52 entries

you to limit searches to all, exactly, any, or none of the words you enter. Look for directions for limitations such as these:

- A phrase such as *elementary school safety,* requested as a unit (exactly these words) or enclosed in quotation marks to mark it as a unit
- A specific language (human or computer) such as English or Spanish

- A specific format or type of software such as a .pdf file
- A date range (before, after, or between dates for creation, revision, or indexing)
- A domain such as .edu (educational institution), .gov (government), .org (organization), or .com (commercial site or company), which indicates the type of group sponsoring the site
- A part of the world, such as North America or Africa
- The location (such as the title, the URL, or the text) of the search term
- The audio or visual media enhancements
- The file size

FINDING SPECIALIZED ONLINE MATERIALS

You will find that you can locate a variety of material online, ranging from e-zines (electronic magazines) to conversations among people interested in your topic.

Look for Electronic Publications.   Wide public access to the Internet has given individuals and small interest groups an economical publication option. Although such texts must be used cautiously, you can locate a wide range through the Etext Archives at <www.etext.org/index.shtml>.

Browse the Blogs.   Globe of Blogs at <www.globeofblogs.com> indexes many blogs (short for Web logs), providing access to the personal, political, and topical observations and commentaries of individuals around the globe. Given the rapid growth of blogs, you may want to use RSS (often expanded as "Real Simple Syndication") software to alert you to breaking news or to sample wide-ranging commentary on a current topic of interest to you. Introductory versions of these feeds are available free at sites such as <newsgator.com> or <bloglines.com> (sponsored by AskJeeves).

Keep Up with the News.   Try sites such as <http://news.google.com> for easy access to current national or international coverage of major stories by thousands of newspapers or news services. Click on "About Google News" if you want to rearrange the page to suit your interests, track a topic during the preceding month, or focus on a specific country or news source. RSS feeds are available for news as well as specialized topics, such as historical events on the current date from *Encyclopaedia Britannica Online,* as illustrated on the "On This Day" page at <http://newsletters.britannica.com/onthisday/otd_sample.html>.

Search Newsgroups and Mailing Lists. Newsgroups and mailing lists, among the oldest forms of Internet communication, generate an enormous amount of text each day. Both types of exchange support the discussion of topics such as adult education or immigration among people with a shared interest. If you're working on a current issue, consider consulting the archives of such groups. You will need to read cautiously but may find detailed analyses by interested members of the public or acknowledged experts. Google (at <groups.google.com>) allows you to search for mailing lists and newsgroups.

Find Chat Transcripts. Major news organizations, such as ABC News, use chat to interview public figures or industry leaders in advertised sessions attended by hundreds or even thousands of participants. You can view transcripts of these sessions by visiting <http://abcnews.go.com> and searching under "chat." Similarly, major search sites, such as Yahoo!, host regular chat sessions on topics including entertainment and finance. Yahoo! also provides transcripts of past sessions. (See also pp. 76–77.)

Ask yourself these questions to improve the quality and appropriateness of the Internet materials that you find and select.

RESEARCH CHECKLIST

Conducting Productive Web Searches

☐ Which recommended sites have you used to locate links related to your research question?

☐ Does your search engine organize results so that sponsored sites, popular sites, or selected sites that match the query come first?

☐ How does your search engine recommend identifying wildcards and combining terms?

☐ Which limitations (such as phrasing, dates, or domain) have produced the most relevant results for your advanced searches?

☐ Do the first ten or twenty results of your searches have titles or descriptions that suggest that they'll help answer your research question? If not, how might you change your search terms?

☐ Which productive search terms have you reused with another search engine? How did the various search results compare?

5

Finding Sources in the Field

The goal of field research is the same as that of library and Internet research — to gather the information you need to answer your research question and then to marshal persuasive evidence to support your conclusions in your research paper. The only difference is where you conduct the research. Many rich, unprinted sources lie beyond the library and the Internet, providing opportunities to explore matters that few researchers have investigated.

GATHERING INFORMATION IN THE FIELD

When you interview, observe, or ask questions of people, you generate your own firsthand (or primary) evidence. You may find a special satisfaction in looking for local responses to vexing questions or in probing significant issues differently or more deeply than others have. In addition, after you consolidate or tabulate your findings, you also may enjoy sharing them with others, using your own data to substantiate or expand your answer to your research question.

Almost any paper will be enriched by authentic and persuasive field sources. And you'll almost certainly learn more about your topic by going into the field and developing firsthand knowledge of it. This section introduces research techniques that have proven useful for college students who want to turn to sources in the field. Before you begin, however, be sure to find out from your instructor whether you need institutional approval for research involving other people ("human sub-jects approval").

Interview the Ordinary or the Expert

The interview—whether for a news broadcast, a celebrity magazine ar-ticle, or a research project—is a familiar type of field research. The suc-cess of the interview conversation may depend on both parties, but your careful preparation as an interviewer will enhance the likelihood that you'll discover what you want to learn. Carefully select the person or people you want to interview. If you want to hear the perspective of an expert in the field, identify someone with the appropriate credentials or experience. If you want to investigate the views of a group, look for someone typical or representative, or select several individuals who might hold complementary views.

Arrange your interview ahead of time. Contact the person initially to request an interview, to gain permission to quote his or her comments in your written paper, and to agree on a date and time when you can meet for about an hour. If a face-to-face interview isn't possible, set a time when you can call for a telephone interview or, if necessary, ask the individual to respond to questions that you e-mail (see pp. 75–76 on cor-responding with others). Before the interview itself, consider your re-search question, pinpoint what you want to learn from your interview, and write out an appropriate series of questions. If you need advice about these, talk with your instructor, or test the questions in a mock in-terview with someone from your class. A mock interview might also help you sharpen your interviewing skills—talking comfortably, listening carefully, following up on an intriguing point or skipping past an un-productive question, and tactfully drawing the conversation back to your questions.

Tips for Interviewing

- Go to the location set for the interview or place your call on time, showing that you respect your interviewee's busy schedule.
- Bring your questions with you, written out clearly so that you can easily refer to them yet flexibly rearrange them as the interview progresses.
- Be prepared to tape record the interview if you have familiar equip-ment available and if your interviewee gives permission to do so. Always come prepared to write down notes to supplement or re-place recording, as needed. (For a telephone interview, federal law requires that you announce in advance that you are recording the

conversation; of course, common courtesy requires that you record it only with the consent of your interviewee.)

- During the interview, focus on the person you are interviewing, not on yourself (even if you feel nervous), so that you hear what is actually said.

- As the interview concludes, thank your interviewee, and arrange for an opportunity to follow up in case you need to check the accuracy of any direct quotations or to clarify any comments.

- When you have left the interview location, stop to record any additional notes while they are fresh in your mind, including any pertinent details of the setting, the interviewee's appearance or mannerisms, or the tone of the exchange.

Observe an Environment

An observation may provide essential information about a setting such as a business or a school. If so, you will need to make an appointment and, as soon as you arrive, identify yourself and your purpose. Some receptionists will insist on identification. You might ask your instructor for a statement on college letterhead declaring that you are a bona fide student doing field research. Follow-up field trips may be necessary if you find gaps in your research or if you need to test new ideas by further observation.

Tips for Observing

- Establish a clear purpose—exactly what you want to observe and why.

- Take notes so that you don't forget important details when you review your findings and incorporate them into your paper.

- Record facts, telling details, and sensory impressions. Notice the features of the place, the actions or relationships of the people who are there, or whatever relates to the purpose of your observation.

- Consider using a still or video camera if you have equipment available and can operate it without being distracted from the scene you are observing. Photographs can illustrate your paper and help you interpret your observations or remember details while you write. If you are filming or taking photographs in a private place, be sure to get written permission from the owner (or other authority) and from any people you film or photograph.

- Pause, look around the setting, and check over your notes before you leave the observation site. Fill in any missing details, and confirm that your notes accurately record what you have actually observed—even if it surprised you—rather than what you'd hoped or expected to see.

- Thank the person who has arranged or approved your observation so that you will be welcome again if you need to gather additional information.

Distribute a Questionnaire

Questionnaires are widely used to gather the responses of a number of people to a fixed set of questions. For example, a marketing department might want to find out how readers react to a magazine's new features, partisans of a ballot issue might wonder how women are likely to vote, and workplace experts might wish to learn how many applicants for jobs in a particular sector are likely to hold a college degree. To answer such questions, professional researchers may carefully design their questions and randomly select representative people to respond to them in order to reach reliable answers.

Because your survey will not be as extensive as a professional one, you should avoid generalizing about your findings as if they were proven facts. It's one thing to say that "many of the students" who filled out a questionnaire on reading habits hadn't read a newspaper in the past month; it's another to claim that this is true of 72 percent of the students at your school—especially when you gave questionnaires only to those who ate in the dining hall the day you were there and many of those students just tossed their forms into the trash.

A far more reliable way for you to use questionnaires is to treat them as group interviews: assume that the information you collect represents typical views, use it to build your overall knowledge of the subject, and cull the responses for interesting or persuasive details or quotations. Use a questionnaire when you want to concentrate on what a group thinks as a whole rather than on what a particular individual has to say or when you find an interview that would cover all your questions impractical. (See Figure 5.1 for an example of a student questionnaire.)

Tips for Using a Questionnaire

- Ask yourself what you want to discover with your questionnaire. Then thoughtfully invent questions to fulfill that purpose.
- State your questions clearly, and supply simple directions for easy responses. Test your questionnaire on classmates or friends before you distribute it to the group you want to study.

QUESTIONNAIRE

Thank you for completing this questionnaire. All information you supply will be kept strictly confidential.

1. What is your age? _____
2. What is your class?
   _____ First year   _____ Junior
   _____ Sophomore   _____ Senior
3. How old were you when you first began using the Internet? _____
4. How do you currently access the Internet? Indicate which of the following statements is true for you.
   _____ With my own computer   _____ With computers at the library or campus lab
   _____ Someone I live with has a computer   _____ I never use a computer
   with Internet access
   _____ Other (please specify): _____
5. Approximately how many hours a week do you use the Internet? _____
6. What is your primary reason for using the Internet?
   _____ Personal   _____ School-related   _____ Work-related
7. Check all of the ways in which you use the Internet.
   _____ E-mailing
   _____ Recreational Web surfing
   _____ Conducting optional research for a class
   _____ Conducting mandatory research for a class
   _____ Conducting personal research (such as planning travel, evaluating
   products, or searching for a job)
   _____ Managing your financial accounts
   _____ Visiting chat rooms
   _____ Shopping online
   _____ Posting résumés or job applications
   _____ Designing or posting Web sites
   Other: _____
8. For which of the activities above do you use the Internet most? _____
   _____
9. On a scale of 1 to 5, rate how comfortable you are using the Internet.
   (not very comfortable)   1   2   3   4   5   (very comfortable)
10. Do you feel that you could benefit from further instruction in using the Internet?
    _____ Yes   _____ No   _____ Maybe

Figure 5.1   A questionnaire asking college students about Internet use

- Ask questions that call for checking alternative answers, marking yes or no, circling a number on a five-point scale, or writing a few words so that responses are easy to tally. Try to ask for just one piece of information per question.

- If you wish to consider differences based on age, gender, or other variables, include some demographic questions.

- Write unbiased questions that will solicit factual responses. Do not ask, "How religious are you?" Instead ask, "What is your religious affiliation?" and "How often do you attend religious services?" Based on responses to the last two questions, you could report actual numbers and draw logical inferences about the respondents.

- When appropriate, ask open-ended questions that call for short written responses. Although these will be difficult to tally and fewer people are likely to respond, the answers may supply worthwhile quotations or suggest important issues or factors when you mull over the findings.

- If possible, distribute your questionnaires at a set location or particular event, and collect them as soon as they are completed. If necessary, ask respondents to return them to your campus mailbox or some other secure location. The more immediate and convenient the return location, the higher your return rate is likely to be.

- Use a blank questionnaire or make an answer grid so that you can quickly and accurately tally the responses from the completed forms. Mark and then add up the answers selected for each question. Total the responses as well if you want to be able to say that a certain portion or percentage of the respondents selected a specific answer.

- For fill-in or short answers, an easy procedure is to type each respondent's answer into a computer file. (Identify each questionnaire with a code number, and note it along with the answer if you might want to return to the individual questionnaire.) You can rearrange the answers in the file, looking for logical groups, categories, or patterns that accurately reflect the responses and enrich your analysis.

CORRESPONDING WITH OTHERS

Although some believe that letter writing is a dying art, sending a traditional business letter or a formal e-mail request is another way to gather field material. You might use this method to contact an individual who cannot be available for an in-person interview or a telephone call. In addition, you can check your library or the Internet for directories of professional organizations, businesses, government agencies, or special-interest groups whose members or representatives might supply expert information about your research question. If you visit an organization's Web site, look for an e-mail option for sending your request, a correspondence address, a FAQ page (that answers frequently asked questions), or downloadable PDF files of brochures or other materials.

Tips for Corresponding

- Plan ahead, and allow plenty of time for responses to your requests.
- Make your letter or e-mail message short and polite. Identify yourself, explain what you want to find out, and request what you need. Thank your correspondent for helping you.
- If you want specific information from an individual, send your questionnaire or a short list of pointed questions. If you e-mail your message, insert the questions from your questionnaire into the message.
- Enclose a stamped, self-addressed envelope for a reply by mail. If you are sending an e-mail message, include your e-mail address in the message.

ATTENDING PUBLIC AND ONLINE EVENTS

College organizations frequently bring interesting speakers to campus. Check the schedules of events on bulletin boards and in your campus newspaper. In addition, professionals and special-interest groups sometimes convene for a regional or national conference. These meetings can be fertile sources of fresh ideas for your research. Attending a lecture or conference can be an excellent way to begin to learn the language of a discipline.

Tips for Attending Events

- Take notes on the lectures, which are usually given by experts in the field and supply firsthand opinions or research findings.
- Ask questions from the audience or corner a speaker or two later for an informal talk.

- Record who attended the event, how the audience reacted, or other background details that could prove useful in writing your paper.
- Depending on the nature of the gathering, a speaker might distribute copies of the paper presented or be willing to send a copy to you. Conferences often publish their proceedings—usually a set of all the lectures delivered—but publication generally takes months or even years after the conference. Try the library for proceedings of past conferences.

Be on the lookout, as well, for blog (Web log) or online discussions—such as the chat sessions sponsored by search engines like Yahoo! or sites like CNN Online—that are relevant to your research topic. (For more on using online discussions, see pp. 68–69.) You can participate as an observer or perhaps even ask a question. Remember to use your chat program to record the discussion for later review. You can learn how to record a transcript by consulting the program's online help.

6

Evaluating Sources

As you work on a research paper, from start to finish you need to evaluate—in other words, judge—your sources. Evaluating sources means exploring the ideas, opinions, facts, and beliefs they express and assessing the utility of that information as you strive to answer your research question.

EVALUATING POSSIBLE SOURCES

You may dream that your research will instantly turn up the perfect source. Like the perfect wave, the perfect snowy slope, or the perfect day, such a source is likely to be hard to come by. After all, by what standards will you judge perfection? And what are the odds that you will find such perfection ever, much less during your limited research schedule? Instead of looking for perfect sources, most college researchers evaluate sources on the basis of their own practical needs, the standards of their readers, and the shared concern of writers and readers for reliable, relevant evidence.

Evaluate Sources as a Practical Researcher

Your situation as a writer may determine how long or how widely you can search for what you need or how deeply you can delve into the sources you find. For example, if you are worried about finishing your paper on time or about juggling several assignments at once, you will need to search efficiently, evaluating sources first in terms of your own practical criteria.

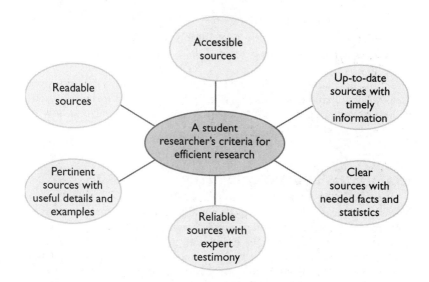

Evaluate Sources as Your Readers Would

You will want to consider what your readers expect of the sources you select and the way that you use them. If you are uncertain about college requirements, start with recommended sources that are easily accessible, readable, and up-to-date—and chock full of the reliable facts, statistics, research findings, case studies, observations, examples, illustrations, and expert testimony that will persuade your readers.

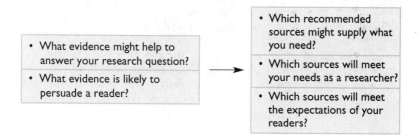

Evaluate Sources for Potential Evidence

When you select sources and eventually select evidence from sources to support the points that you make in a research paper, you are likely to ask three basic questions:

- Which of your sources are reliable?
- Which of these sources are relevant to your research question?
- What evidence from these sources is most useful for your paper?

After all, how could an unreliable source successfully support your ideas? And what could unsuitable or mismatched information contribute to your paper? The difficult task, of course, is learning how to judge what is reliable, relevant, and useful.

EVALUATING LIBRARY AND INTERNET SOURCES

Not every source you locate will be equally reliable or equally useful to you. You will need to examine sources from the Web with special care. Like other firsthand materials, individual postings, Web logs ("blogs"), and Web sites will reflect the biases, interests, or information gaps of their writers or sponsors. Commercial and organizational sites may supply very useful material, but they'll provide only what supports their objectives—selling their products, serving their clients, enlisting new members, or persuading others to support their activities or views. Sites recommended by your library will have been screened by professionals, but each will have its own point of view or approach, often a necessary bias to restrict its focus.

Even so, your selection of sources can itself simplify evaluation. For example, when you draw information from an article in a print or online peer-reviewed journal, the process of evaluation for that article actually began when the editors of the journal first read the article and then asked expert reviewers to evaluate whether it merited publication. Similarly, a serious book from a major publishing company or university press probably has been submitted to knowledgeable reviewers. Such reviewers may be asked to assess whether the article or book is well reasoned, logically presented, and competently researched. However, such reviewers can't decide if the work is pertinent to your research question or if it contains evidence useful for your paper. For this reason, a key part of the job of conducting research is thinking critically about sources so that you can select the best evidence for your purposes. (For more about the characteristics of various types of sources, see the charts on pp. 58 and 60 and 90–93.) Figure 6.1 illustrates a sample evaluation of the componenets of a Web site that provides both informative and persuasive materials about its topic.

How do you know what evidence is best? Do what experienced researchers do—ask a series of key questions in order to evaluate your

A. Identifies group as organization (.org), not school (.edu) or company (.com)
B. Uses engaging animal graphics
C. Appeals for support
D. Explains purpose of group and provides link to contact information
E. Provides special features slanted toward animal lovers and ASPCA activities
F. Offers free newsletter to involve readers
G. Links to information about controversies and recommends action

Figure 6.1   Evaluating the purpose, audience, and bias of a Web site offering informative and persuasive materials

sources. The basic questions remain the same whether your source is print or electronic. (For additional advice on evaluating field sources, see p. 88.) The following checklist suggests how you can use the time-tested journalist's questions—who, what, when, where, why, and how—to evaluate each print or electronic source that you consider using.

RESEARCH CHECKLIST

Evaluating Sources

Who?

- ☐ Who is the author of the source? What are the author's credentials and profession? What might be the author's point of view?
- ☐ Who is the intended audience of the source? Experts in the field? Professionals? General readers? People with a special interest? In what ways does the source's tone or evidence appeal to this audience?
- ☐ Who is the publisher of the source or the sponsor of the site? Is it a corporation, a scholarly organization, a professional association, a government agency, or an issue-oriented group? Have you heard of this publisher or sponsor before? Is it well regarded? Does it seem reputable and responsible? Is it considered academic or popular?
- ☐ Who has reviewed the source prior to publication? Only the author? Peer reviewers who are experts in the area? An editorial staff?

What?

- ☐ What is the purpose of the publication or Web site? Is it to sell a product or service? To entertain? To supply information? To publish new research? To shape opinion about an issue or cause?
- ☐ What bias or point of view might affect the reliability of the source?
- ☐ What kind of information does the source supply? Is it a primary source (a firsthand account) or a secondary source (an analysis of primary material)? If it is a secondary source, does it rely on sound evidence from primary sources?
- ☐ What evidence does the source present? Does it seem trustworthy, sufficient, and relevant given what you know about the subject? Does its argument or analysis seem logical and complete,

or does it leave many questions unanswered? Does it identify and list its sources? If it is electronic, does it supply appropriate, active links?

When?

☐ When was the source published or created? Is its information current?

☐ When was it last revised or updated? Is its information up-to-date?

Where?

☐ Where have you found the source? Is it a pre-screened source available through your campus library? Is it a Web site that popped up during a general search?

☐ Where has the source been recommended? On an instructor's syllabus or Web page? On a library list? In another reliable source? During a conference with an instructor or librarian?

Why?

☐ Why should you use this source rather than others?

☐ Why is its information directly relevant to your research question?

How?

☐ How does the selection of evidence in the source reflect the interests and expertise of its author, publisher or sponsor, and intended audience? How might you need to qualify its use in your paper?

☐ How would its information add to your paper? How would it help answer your research question and provide compelling evidence to persuade your readers?

Who Is the Author?

Make every effort to learn about each author's credentials, affiliations with institutions or organizations, and reputation among peers. Try to make sure that any author who shapes or supports your ideas is reliable and trustworthy.

Print Credentials.   Check an article or a book for the author's background or biography, especially in any preface, introduction, or concluding note. National newsmagazines (for example, *Newsweek, Time,* and *U.S. News & World Report*) usually identify any expert authors before or next to their contributions. However, most of their articles are written by reporters who try to substantiate the facts and cover multiple points of view, perhaps compiling regional contributions. On the other hand, some other magazines select facts that mirror the opinions of their editors.

Internet Credentials.   If your source is a Web site, look for a link on its home page to information about the author and an e-mail address that you could use to contact the author about his or her background. If your source is a posting to a newsgroup or a mailing list, deduce what you can from the writer's e-mail address and any signature file. Try a Web search for the person's name, looking for associated sites or links to or from the author's site. If you can't find out anything about the author, it is best not to use the information in your paper, though it might provide useful background.

Field Credentials.   When you conduct field research, you may be able to select your sources. If you are investigating safety standards for infant car seats, for example, a personal interview with a local pediatrician will probably produce different information than an interview with the manufacturer's sales representative. You can also affect the results of your research by distributing a questionnaire to a certain group of people or by observing a particular setting. Delve deeply, widely, and fairly.

Reputation.   The best measure of someone's expertise is the regard of other experts. Do others cite the work of your source's author? Does your instructor or someone else on campus who knows the field recognize or recommend the author? Is the author listed in a biographical database?

Material with No Author Identified.   If no author is given, try to identify the sponsoring organization or publisher. On a Web site, check the home page or search for a disclaimer, contact information, or an "About This Site" page. If a print source doesn't list an author, consider the nature of the publication: Is the article published in a nationally respected newspaper like the *Wall Street Journal* or in a supermarket tabloid? Is the brochure published by a leading organization in its field?

Who Is the Intended Audience?

A source written for authorities in a field is likely to assume that readers already have plenty of background knowledge. For this reason, such sources typically skip general overviews and tailor their detailed discussions to experts. In contrast, sources written for general audiences usually define terms and supply background. For example, for your paper on current treatments for HIV, you locate an article in a well-known medical journal that discusses the most favorable chemical composition for an effective protease inhibitor drug. Instead of beginning with this article, written by a physician for other physicians, you might turn first to a source that defines *protease inhibitor* and discusses how it helps HIV patients. Considering the intended audience can help you identify sources appropriate for your project.

Who Is the Publisher or Sponsor?

Experienced researchers know that the person, organization, government agency, or corporation that prints or electronically distributes a source also may shape its content. Like authors, publishers often hold a point of view. Businesses are likely to present their own products and services more favorably than those of competitors. Political sponsors, such as the Democratic Party or the National Rifle Association, are likely to publish materials supporting policies they favor. To learn about a Web site sponsor, look for a disclaimer, a mission statement, or an "About" description (as shown in Figure 6.1).

As you evaluate a source, ask critical questions about what might motivate its publisher. Is a Web site created for commercial (.com) purposes, such as selling a product or service? Is it sponsored by an organization (.org, as in Figure 6.1) or a government agency (.gov)? Is it devoted to a specific cause? Is it the work of an individual with strong opinions but little expertise? Is a newsgroup or mailing list limited to a particular interest? Is a publisher noted for its works in a specific field or with a specific political agenda? Does a periodical have a predictable point of view? For example, a faith-based publication will take a different view than a news magazine, just as a conservative publication will differ from a liberal one. Because these questions can be difficult, even for experienced researchers, consult with a librarian if you need help finding answers.

Who Has Reviewed the Source Before Publication?

Consider whether a publisher has an editorial staff, an expert editor, or an advisory board of experts. Does it rely on peer reviewers to critique articles or books under consideration? Does it expect research to meet professional standards? Does it outline such standards in its advice for prospective authors or its description of its purpose or mission? Does any sponsor have a solid reputation as a professional organization?

What Is the Purpose?

Understanding the purpose or intention of a source will help you decide whether it is likely to supply solid evidence for your project. A reference book in a library serves a different purpose than a newspaper editorial, a magazine advertisement, or a Web site that promotes a product or service. Asking critical questions is crucial: Is the purpose of this source to explain or inform? To report new research? To persuade? To offer another viewpoint? To sell a product? Does the source acknowledge its purpose in its preface, mission statement, or "About Us" or FAQ (Frequently Asked Questions) page?

What Might Be the Bias of the Source?

A *bias* is a preference for a particular side of an issue. Because most authors and most publishers have opinions on their topics, there's little point in asking whether they are biased. Instead, ask how that viewpoint affects the presentation of information and opinion. What are the author's or sponsor's allegiances? Does the source treat one side of an issue more favorably than another? Is that bias hidden or stated? Having a strong bias does not invalidate a source. However, if you recognize such bias early on, you may want to look for other viewpoints that will help you avoid lopsided analyses or arguments.

What Kind of Information — Primary or Secondary — Does the Source Offer?

A *primary source* is a firsthand account written by an eyewitness or a participant. It contains raw data and immediate impressions. A *secondary source* is an analysis of the information contained in one or more primary sources. For example, primary sources for investigating the Korean War might include diaries or letters written by military personnel, accounts of civilian witnesses, articles by journalists who were on the scene, and official military reports. If a military historian used those accounts as background or evidence in a study of military strategy or if a peace activist used them in a book on consequences of warfare for civilians, these resulting works would be secondary sources.

Most research papers benefit from both primary and secondary sources. If you repeatedly cite a fact or an authority quoted in someone else's analysis, try to go to the primary source itself. For example, statistics can be used by those on both sides of an issue; often only the interpretation differs. After all, a bombing raid that spared 70 percent of a village also leveled 30 percent of it. Going to the original research or statistics (published as a primary source) can help you to learn where the facts end and the interpretation begins.

When Was the Source Published?

In general, you should try to rely on current sources. In most fields, new information and discoveries appear every year, so the evidence in a source needs to be up-to-date or at least still timely. New information may appear first in Web postings, media broadcasts, and periodicals such as newspapers and eventually magazines, though such sources may not allow the time needed to consider information thoughtfully. Later, as material is more fully developed or examined, it may be treated in scholarly journal articles and books. In contrast, older materials can supply a historical, theoretical, or analytical focus. (See pp. 58 and 60 for more about the timeliness of various publications.)

Where Did You Find the Source?

Is it recommended by your instructor? Is it located on the library's Web page or in its book collection? When instructors or academic units direct you to sources, you benefit from their experience teaching students as well as their subject-matter expertise. On the other hand, when you find a Web source while randomly browsing or pick up a magazine at the dentist's office, you'll need to do all the source evaluation yourself.

Why Would You Use This Source?

Why use one source rather than another? Is the information it contains useful for your purposes? Does it provide strong quotations or hard facts that would be effective in your paper? Does it tackle the topic in a relevant way? For one paper, you might appropriately rely on an article from a popular magazine; for another, you might need the findings published in the scholarly article on which the magazine article was based. As you look for the best possible sources for your purpose, always ask yourself not only "Will this do?" but also "Would something else be better?"

How Would This Source Contribute to Your Paper?

The evidence in a source—its ideas, information, facts, and expert or other opinions—can tell you a great deal about its reliability and usefulness for your research project. Is its evidence complete, up-to-date, and carefully assembled? Is its argument or analysis convincingly supported by the evidence? Is there enough evidence to support the claims being made? Does visual material enhance the source rather than distract from its argument or information? Does the source formally identify its own sources in citations and a bibliography? If the source leaves important questions unanswered, you might want to look elsewhere for your own evidence. Even if the source seems highly reliable, it needs to be relevant to your research question and your ideas about how to answer that question. An interesting fact or opinion could be just that—interesting. Instead, you need facts, expert opinions, information, and quotations that relate directly to the purpose and audience of your research paper.

EVALUATING FIELD SOURCES

Although the general criteria for evaluating print and electronic sources may also apply to field resources, you might want to ask these questions as well.

RESEARCH CHECKLIST

Evaluating Field Sources

☐ Does your source seem biased or prejudiced? If so, is this viewpoint so strong that you have to disregard some of the source's information?

☐ Does your source provide evidence to support or corroborate claims? How does it compare to the evidence of others?

☐ Does your source report the thoughts of someone else or recount actions that he or she hasn't witnessed? Can you cross-check this information by turning to another source or a different type of evidence?

☐ Does your source seem to respond consistently, seriously, and honestly? If a respondent has told you about past events, to what extent might time have eroded memory?

Each type of field research can also raise particular questions. For example, if you are observing a particular event or setting, are people aware that they are being observed? Often, knowing that they are being observed can change people's behavior. If you have tried to question a random sampling of people, do you feel that they are truly representative? Or, if you have tried to question everyone in a group, have you been thorough enough? It is important for you to think critically about field sources as well as those from the library and the Web.

RECONSIDERING YOUR PURPOSE AND YOUR RESEARCH QUESTION

As you evaluate your sources, you will critically examine each individual source, assessing its specific strengths, shortcomings, and possible contributions to your paper. Once you have gathered and evaluated a reasonable collection of sources, it's time to step back and consider them as a group—lifting your eyes from the maples, red oaks, and elms to the forest as a whole.

- Have you found enough relevant and credible sources to satisfy the requirements of your assignment? Have you found enough to suggest sound answers to your research question?
- Are your sources thought-provoking? Can you tell which information is generally accepted, which is controversial, and which may be unreliable? Have your sources engaged and enlightened you while substantiating, refining, or changing your original ideas?
- Are your sources varied? Have they helped you achieve a reasonably complete view of your topic? Have they suggested other perspectives, approaches, alternatives, or interpretations that you will want to acknowledge? Have they deepened your understanding and helped you reach well-reasoned, balanced conclusions?
- Are your sources appropriate? Do they answer your question with the kind of evidence that your readers will find persuasive? Do they have the range and depth necessary to achieve your purpose and satisfy your readers?

Use these questions to check in with yourself. Make sure that you have a clear direction for your research—whether it's the same direction you started with or a completely new one. Perhaps you are ready to answer your research question, refine your thesis, and begin to draft a paper that pulls together your own ideas and those of your sources. On the other hand, you may want to find additional sources that support or challenge your assumptions about the topic. Maybe you need to hunt for specific counterevidence that responds to strong evidence against your position—or change your working thesis to account for that evidence. On the other hand, you might want to pursue a new direction that seems more tantalizing than your original one.

The following charts, mentioned earlier in this chapter, will help you choose solid sources regardless of where you are in your research process.

TABLE 6.1   Typical Features of Print Sources

Type of Source	Location Information	Typical Audience	Authors or Expert Contributors	Quality Controls
Scholarly Book	Library online catalog or database	Specialists, researchers, students, professionals	Scholars, researchers, specialists, professionals	Peer reviews, editorial standards
Popular Nonfiction Book	Library online catalog, public library, or bookstore	General readers interested in book's topic	Informed writers, journalists, specialists, professionals	Reviews for publisher, editorial standards
Scholarly Journal	Library periodical index (print or online) or periodicals area	Specialists, researchers, students, professionals	Scholars, researchers, specialists, professionals	Peer reviews, editorial standards
News Magazine	Library periodical index (print or online), periodicals area, or newsstand	General readers interested in current events	Freelance and staff journalists, editorial staff	Editorial and journalistic standards
Popular Magazine	Library periodical index (print or online), periodicals area, or newsstand	General readers interested in magazine's focus	Freelance and staff writers, editorial staff, guest contributors	Editorial standards
Newspaper	Library periodical index (print or online), periodicals area, or newsstand	General or local readers	Freelance and staff journalists, editorial staff, columnists	Editorial and journalistic standards
Pamphlet or Booklet	Library collection (such as government, business, historical, or civic material)	Specialists, professionals, students, general or local readers	Range from specialists and researchers to sponsoring groups or individuals	Editorial standards and expertise of sponsor
Reference Work	Library online catalog, database, or reference area	Specialists, researchers, students, professionals	Scholars, specialists, and staff experts	Selection of contributors, editorial standards

Sponsor or Publisher	Possible Purposes of Publication	Content for Researchers	Use of Source Citations
Major, specialty, or university publisher such as University of Chicago Press	Explore issues or topics in the field, advance knowledge, sell books	In-depth library or field research that meets academic standards	Yes—supplies in-text citations, notes, or bibliography
Major or specialty publisher such as Simon & Schuster	Present popular issues, explore trends, provide advice, sell books	Substantial research, investigative journalism, experience, or opinion	Maybe—might identify sources in chapters, notes, or bibliography
Scholarly or professional organization such as Modern Language Association	Explore topics of concern to journal readers and specialists in the field	In-depth library or field research or professional critique that meets field's standards	Yes—supplies in-text citations, notes, and references following field's format
Commercial or specialty publisher such as Time Warner	Cover news, promote magazine's viewpoint, sell advertising and magazine	News reports supported by facts, observation, interviews, and investigation	Maybe—might mention or quote popular or expert sources but does not list references
Commercial or specialty publisher such as Rodale or National Geographic	Cover popular topics and readers' interests, sell advertising and magazines	Current advice, expert views reduced to popular applications	Maybe—might mention or quote sources but does not list references
Newspaper publisher or media group	Cover news, events, and issues; sell advertising and newspapers	News reports supported by facts, observation, interviews, and investigation	Maybe—might mention or quote popular or expert sources but does not list references
Government, civic, business, health, or other group; family or individual	Supply information in short form, promote sponsor or writer's specialty	Concise advice, information, opinion, or research findings	Maybe—might supply full, some, or no source citations, depending on purpose and sponsor
Major or specialty publisher	Present accurate information on topic, sell books	Concise and accurate facts, definitions, and background	Maybe—may or may not list or recommend sources

TABLE 6.2   Typical Features of Electronic Sources

Type of Source	Recommended Sites and Examples	Typical Audience	Authors or Expert Contributors	Quality Controls
Online Reference Site	<http://mel.org>, <http://sunsite.berkeley.edu>, and <http://hw.ac.uk/libWWW/irn/pinakes/pinakes.html>	Researchers, scholars, professionals, students	Librarians, information specialists	Site selection criteria and standards
Gateway Site for a Topic or Field	Voice of the Shuttle at <vos.ucsb.edu> or *Social Science Information Gateway* at <www.sosig.ac.uk>	Researchers, scholars, professionals, students	Librarians, information specialists in field	Site selection criteria and standards
Online Document Collection	<http://etext.lib.virginia.edu> or Historical Documents at <http://thomas.loc.gov>	Researchers, scholars, professionals, students, general readers	Librarians, information specialists, topic specialists	Site selection criteria
Professional Web Site	Links to corporations, nonprofits, and foundations at *Fortune* <www.fortune.com> or the Foundation Center <http://fdncenter.org>	Professionals, business people, consumers, students, interested readers	Professionals, scholars, business people, organization staff	Site objectives; public or customer service standards
Academic Web Site	Lists of Web pages such as at <www.utexas.edu/world/univ>	Students, graduates, faculty, staff, parents, visitors	Campus units, groups, and Web staff	Campus criteria for inclusion
Government Web Site	Federal index at <www.firstgov.gov> or Google's search engine at <www.google.com/unclesam>	Public visitors, other agencies, researchers, specialists, companies	Agency information specialists, staff, and consultants	Agency mission, research and editorial standards
Online Newspaper or News Service	*News & Periodical Resources on the Web* at <http://lcweb.loc.gov/rr/news/lists.html>, *Arts & Letters Daily* at <www.aldaily.com>	General or local readers, researchers, professionals, students	Journalists, editorial staff, columnists	Journalistic and editorial standards
Interest Group or Personal Web Site	American Academy of Pediatrics at <www.aap.org/advocacy.html>, Global Advocacy Sites at <http://danenet.wicip.org/bcp/global_advocacy.html>, <www.salon.com/blogs>	Issue-oriented visitors, students, researchers	Activists, concerned citizens, individuals	Individual or group objectives and standards

Sponsor or Publisher	Possible Purposes of Publication	Content for Researchers	Use of Source Citations
Library or information organization	Assist scholars, researchers, and students	In-depth sources for academic, professional, or personal research	Yes — lists Web links, often grouped and annotated
Library, information, or professional organization	Assist and engage scholars, researchers, and students in specialty	In-depth sources for research in discipline	Yes — lists Web links, often grouped and annotated
Library or special-interest sponsor	Assist scholars, researchers, and students to access documents	Easy access to selected texts	Yes — supplies links to documents and maybe background for texts
Professional group, nonprofit agency, corporation, or foundation	Promote interests of organization; attract and assist members, clients, or site visitors	Promotion of organization and its research, civic, economic, or other interests	Maybe — may present information, with or without sources, or supply links
College or university	Assist campus community, attract students, promote family and public support	Promotion of campus programs and activities, including research	Maybe — may supply campus information, academic texts, or resource lists or links
Federal, state, local, or foreign government agency	Fulfill agency objectives by providing public information and assistance	Authoritative information for citizens, policy makers, and agencies	Maybe — may present reports with sources or popular information without sources
Newspaper or media group	Cover news, current events, and timely issues	Accurate news reports supported by facts, observation, interviews, visuals, and investigation	Maybe — might mention or quote popular or expert sources
Partisan or special-interest group or individual	Promote special interests of group or individual	Range from academic to partisan to individual interests	Maybe — may or may not identify sources or use reliable sources

7

Using Sources
Ethically

Once you have selected and evaluated sources likely to help you answer your research question, you're ready to record all the valuable evidence and persuasive reasoning that can support your paper's conclusions. Even though your desk is stacked with books and your research archive overflows with printouts and photocopies, keep a sharp eye on your schedule. Almost every college paper requires more time than expected for drafting, revising, and editing.

In addition, a research paper is likely to require extra time for weaving in source materials and crediting them according to the system required by your instructor or expected in your field. This chapter and the next two will help you learn to recognize general conventions — widely shared expectations — for recording, identifying, and integrating material from sources. These chapters will alert you to common problems and suggest useful solutions that can help strengthen your final paper. You'll also want to refer to one of the four documentation chapters, Chapters 10 to 13, to find specific advice about identifying and listing sources in the documentation style you are expected to use in your paper.

SHOWING RESPECT IN ACADEMIC WRITING

Although research can be a complex, lively process, enriched by the exchange of ideas and findings, discussions of research ethics sometimes reduce that topic to one issue: plagiarism. Plagiarists intentionally present someone else's work as their own — whether they dishonestly submit as their own a paper purchased from the Web, pretend that passages copied from an article are their own writing, appropriate the ideas or theories of others without identifying their sources, or paste in someone else's graphics without acknowledgment or permission.

Plagiarism is viewed especially seriously in college because it shows a deep disrespect for the intellectual work of the academic world — analyzing, interpreting, creating, investigating, and assessing ideas. Depending on institutional policies and honor codes, plagiarism may have serious consequences — failing a paper, failing a course, or being dismissed from the institution. Behind these tough policies lies the critical issue of respect. Educating yourself about the standards of your

TABLE 7.1   Avoiding Plagiarism

Plagiarism Problem	Remedy
You have dawdled instead of starting your paper. Someone gives you the addresses for two Web sites, one selling papers for $29.95 and the other for $49.95. The visuals on the sites show smiling students, but you aren't smiling because you know that this choice is wrong. In addition, the sample paper topics don't sound quite like your assignment, your instructor expects to receive both your annotated bibliography and your draft (not just a final paper), and you wonder whether the college uses a plagiarism-detection system that would easily catch you.	Don't buy a paper, but go immediately to throw yourself on the mercy of your instructor. Explain that you have fallen behind; ask for help and a time extension, even if it carries a penalty. Cancel all your social plans for the next week or so, and follow the advice in this book about finding recommended sources. Consider this one of your most valuable college experiences: You have saved the cost of a phony paper; you have not jeopardized your very expensive education; you won't need to explain to your family why you have failed a course or been suspended; and you have shown intellectual integrity and personal maturity.
You're investigating a serious research question about a problem that affects a family member. You started your research right away, taking lots of notes from sources. Now, however, your note file is getting long, and you're mixing up which ideas you quoted from sources, which you summed up, and which you thought up yourself. You're beginning to worry that your disorganization will lead to plagiarism because you won't be able to credit your sources accurately.	Stop where you are and get organized. Set up a linking system so that you can tell what comes from where. Record the author's last name or a brief source title and page number when you begin taking any notes from a source, add divider lines between notes from different sources, or move your existing notes to separate files, each clearly labeled as the only file for that source. Reread pp. 22–33 on keeping a working bibliography; turn to Chapter 8 on recording source notes. Use any unidentified leftover notes as background, but don't add them to your paper if you can't credit your source.

(continued)

TABLE 7.1   Avoiding Plagiarism (continued)

Plagiarism Problem	Remedy
You had an hour between classes and found a new book on reserve in the library. You had to write quickly to avoid being late to class. Here's part of what you found in your research notebook later that day: InDfCult, HUP, Cambridge, Carol Padden, Tom Humphries, 5 122 For Df voice/technol = issue Relates to cult def	Go back to the library. This time, record clear information (without potentially confusing abbreviations) about *Inside Deaf Culture*, written by Carol Padden and Tom Humphries and published in Cambridge, MA, by Harvard University Press in 2005. Then turn back to p. 122. Decide what you want to do: Quote these authors or sum up their view. Use quotation marks to identify their exact words. Otherwise, rewrite their ideas in your own words and sentences so that you don't plagiarize by "parroting" your source (see Ch. 8).
You have worked hard to find reliable sources, but you're having trouble beginning your paper. You e-mail your friends and eat all the leftover pizza. The afternoon is nearly gone by the time you finally figure out how to get started. Soon you're busily writing a few sentences, then cutting and pasting in quotations and notes, then writing again. You suddenly wonder how you'll be able to figure out where it all came from when you have to add your source citations. What if your instructor thinks that you are plagiarizing if you don't identify a few sources or add the page numbers for quotations?	Backtrack as fast as you can. For each chunk you've pasted in, add obvious notes to yourself (using color, brackets, or your software's comment feature) so that you will know exactly where to add a formal source citation later. For yourself, note at least the basics — the author's name and the page number in the original. Put quotation marks around any words directly from the source — using color for them in your draft if you need a temporary reminder about the need to present these words accurately. See pp. 107–13 on weaving source material into your paper.

institution, your instructor, and your profession (once you've successfully moved from college to the workplace) can protect you from making ethical errors that may carry heavy consequences. Table 7.1 also illustrates how to avoid or remedy common situations that can generate ethical problems.

LEARNING TO BECOME A CREDIBLE RESEARCHER

Careful researchers acknowledge their intellectual obligations and their respect for the researchers, scholars, and writers who came before them. Careful researchers respect readers who are likely to be curious about the discoveries, reasons, and evidence marshaled by others. Finally, careful researchers respect themselves. Instead of trying to evade the intellectual responsibilities and benefits of a college education, they try to figure out the practices that will give their writing credibility with academic readers. In short, they learn how to write solid research papers from the best teacher of all — experience.

Look for the Details

Although the details about where to place a punctuation mark or how to identify the exact words of a source may seem finicky when you write your first research papers, many of these conventions are widely accepted academic practices. On the other hand, some details reflect the needs or traditions of a specific field or discipline. After all, it's not surprising that astrophysicists and physical therapists and philosophers might favor different ways of crediting sources and reporting their own research findings. This book, for example, explains four styles commonly required in college papers — but many other styles exist, each serving the needs of the particular journal, professional group, or discipline that uses it.

Learning the conventions of the style (or styles) you'll be expected to use during college is primarily a matter of learning what to watch for. The four popular citation styles in this book are MLA style (Ch. 10), APA style (Ch. 11), *Chicago* style (Ch. 12), and CSE style (Ch. 13). Each style is explained and extensively illustrated, including a sample student paper, in its own chapter. Try to refer to that chapter all along the way, from beginning your working bibliography to handing in your final paper. Once you select or are assigned a style, you should stick to its guidelines consistently for the project involved. If you need more detail than this book provides, the chapter about each style will identify the full book that explains it so that you can get a copy at your bookstore or library.

Your instructor may assign the specific style for a paper or expect you simply to use the most common style in your major area or that of the course. Sometimes an instructor will ask you to use the style required in a particular professional journal. Then, of course, you'll follow the journal's directions for its authors and use its articles as models, but you're likely to find that its style is derived from or similar to one of the four presented here.

The entries for the four styles may look quite different, as the box on page 98 shows. Those examples show how the same book and the same article would be listed in the final list of works cited, reference list, or bibliography in four different papers, each following one of the styles.

FOUR STYLES FOR LISTING SOURCES: THE POWER OF CONVENTION

MLA (Modern Language Association) Style

Bolman, Lee G., and Terrence E. Deal. Escape from Cluelessness: A Guide for the Organizationally Challenged. New York: AMACOM, 2000.

Ravitch, Diane. "Education after the Culture Wars." Daedalus 131.3 (2002): 5–21.

APA (American Psychological Association) Style

Bolman, L. G., & Deal, T. E. (2000). *Escape from cluelessness: A guide for the organizationally challenged.* New York: AMACOM.

Ravitch, D. (2002). Education after the culture wars. *Daedalus, 131*(3), 5–21.

(Chicago *Manual of Style*)

Bolman, Lee G., and Terrence E. Deal. *Escape from Cluelessness: A Guide for the Organizationally Challenged.* New York: AMACOM, 2000.

Ravitch, Diane. "Education after the Culture Wars." *Daedalus* 131, no. 3 (2002): 5–21.

CSE (Council of Science Editors) Reference-Number Style

1. Bolman LG, Deal TE. Escape from cluelessness: a guide for the organizationally challenged. New York: AMACOM; 2000. 244 p.

2. Ravitch D. Education after the culture wars. Daedalus 2002; 131(3): 5–21.

Once you begin to look carefully at these examples, you'll spot many differences: punctuation, capitalization, abbreviations, use of italics or underlining, spacing, sequence of information, and even the presentation of an author's first name or initials.

At first glance, you may wonder how you'll ever remember all these details, even for the one style you are likely to use most often. The good news is that you don't have to remember the details. In fact, all you have to do is look up what you need to know and then make sure that your final paper follows what's expected. And there's more good news — the more often you use a style, the easier it becomes. In fact, some researchers become so accustomed to their usual style that they begin to believe it's the only correct style. They may even argue about how something must be done without realizing that their view is true only within the limits of their one style.

Keep Sight of the Goals

No matter which style you use for your current paper and no matter how strange its details may seem to you, all four major styles expect you to achieve these common objectives:

- Supply an immediate, brief reference in the text itself at the very moment you refer to a source. This brief reference — your in-text citation — instantly acknowledges and could be a name in your sentence, a note placed in parentheses, or a note number keyed to a later list, depending on the style.

- Provide the essentials in this brief reference — the name, date, or number necessary for a reader to locate full identification of the source later in the paper.

- Add, if needed, the page number or other location information a reader would require to locate the exact material used, particularly a direct quotation or specific paraphrase in your own words.

- Consolidate a full but efficient list that supplies all the publication details about each source at the end of the paper, thus avoiding tedious repetition throughout the paper.

- Follow consistent patterns for citing and listing sources so that readers who are used to the style know exactly what to expect and where to find the details needed to find the source itself.

- Credit first the author (or authors) — those to whom you and other researchers are intellectually indebted. Then vary entry forms by type of source — the kinds or genres that may alert other researchers to the source's likely depth, currency, or detail. To help you get used to these patterns, Chapters 10 to 13 organize sample entries around these two key questions: Who wrote it? What type of source is it?

As you learn to recognize such conventions and apply them in your own papers, you, too, will begin to take them for granted. The more you take such conventions for granted, the further you'll have grown toward mastering the assumptions common in your field. In addition, from a practical perspective, learning these practices is also your best protection against making mistakes that might look to others like intentional plagiarism.

USING TIME EFFECTIVELY

If you're attending classes, probably working part-time, possibly raising children, and likely worrying about student loans or credit card payments or health insurance, you're no doubt short of time. And using time well is one of the most effective ways to avoid questionable research practices. If your time is short, however, don't take shortcuts. (After all, your instructors have the same electronic resources that you do, and many campuses subscribe to antiplagiarism software.) Instead, continue to use your energy and your valuable time productively as you gather and incorporate information from your sources.

Remember that the value of every source remains potential until you successfully capture its facts, statistics, expert testimony, examples, or other information in a form that you can incorporate into your paper (see Ch. 8). In addition, you must accurately credit, both in the text of your paper and in a final list of sources, each source whose words or ideas you use. To increase your confidence and your efficiency, try the time-tested methods illustrated in this book as you record, integrate, and credit your sources appropriately (see pp. 127–29).

Though these traditional methods can't be fully implemented instantaneously, their steady use can save you from a deadline crisis — and from the temptation to make a poor ethical decision that might jeopardize your goals for the future. When you use your time efficiently, add source information skillfully, and credit each source conscientiously, your research probably will accomplish its purpose: answering your research question so that your paper satisfies you and meets your readers' standards.

FOLLOWING ACCEPTED PRACTICES

No matter how you record your notes, they should achieve two crucial purposes: conservation and transfer. First, your notes conserve pertinent source material so that you can find it when you need it. Second, because your notes consolidate and miniaturize dense books, articles, and other documents, they help you transfer and credit what's relevant to your own paper.

As you begin to mine your sources for information, be sure that you understand exactly how your instructor expects you to credit sources. Turn to the appropriate style chapter in this book for specific examples of its methods of citing and listing sources. Even if you do not intend to plagiarize — to use another writer's words or ideas without appropriately crediting them — a paper full of sloppy or careless short-cuts can look just like a paper deliberately copied from unacknowledged sources.

Specify the source of a detail, an idea, a summary, a paraphrase, or a quotation as you record it in your notes. Transfer that acknowledgment into your first draft and every version that follows. You generally do not need to identify a source if you use what is called "common knowledge" — quotations, expressions, or information widely known and widely accepted. If you are uncertain about whether you need to cite a source, ask your instructor, or simply provide the citation.

Table 7.2 on pages 102–03 reviews accepted methods of adding source material and identifies good research practices. Using these practices will help prevent common errors that may call into question your integrity or your attentiveness as a research writer. In addition, see Chapters 8 and 9 for more about conserving and transferring materials from sources.

Ask yourself the following questions as you consider how to meet college and professional research standards.

RESEARCH CHECKLIST

Learning How to Conduct Research Ethically

☐ Have you reviewed your campus standards for ethical academic conduct? Have you checked your syllabus or course handouts for any explanation about how those standards apply in your course?

☐ Are you accurately and regularly recording entries in your working bibliography?

☐ Are you carefully distinguishing your own ideas from those of your sources when you record notes or gather material for your research archive?

☐ Are you sticking to your research schedule so that you can avoid a deadline crisis?

(continued)

TABLE 7.2 Using Accepted Methods to Add and Credit Source Material

Method	Objectives of Method	Good Practices to Avoid Errors
Quotation	Select and identify the exact words of a source in order to capture its vitality, authority, or incisiveness for your paper.	• Supply complete identification of the source. • Provide the page number or other location of the quotation in the source. • Use both opening and closing quotation marks. • Repeat the exact words of the source or properly indicate changes.
Paraphrase	Reword the detailed ideas of a source in your own words and sentences, with credit to the original, in order to capture the content of a passage.	• Read carefully so that you can paraphrase accurately without distorting the source. • Supply complete identification of the source. • Provide the page number or other location of the original passage in the source. • Rephrase or add quotation marks to identify words or phrases from the source that creep into your paraphrase. • Apart from brief quotations, use your own words and sentences to avoid following the pattern, sequence, or wording of the original. • Clearly distinguish between the paraphrase and your own ideas to avoid confusing switches.
Summary	Very briefly express the main point or key ideas of a source or passage in your own words, with credit to the original source, in order to capture its essential ideas or conclusion in your paper.	• Read carefully so that you can summarize accurately without distorting the source. • Supply complete identification of the source. • Rephrase or add quotation marks to identify words or phrases from the source that creep into your summary. • Give specific credit to the source for ideas that you include in your discussion. • Clearly distinguish between the summary and your own ideas to avoid confusing switches.

In-Text Citation	Credit each quotation, paraphrase, summary, or other reference to a source in short form by giving the author's last name in the text of the paper; in parentheses, or in a note — adding the page number; date, or other details required by your citation style.	• Supply consistent citations without forgetting or carelessly omitting sources. • Spell names of authors and titles correctly. • Provide accurate page or other location references, especially for direct quotations, paraphrases, or other specific information. • Add any other information such as dates or note numbers required by your citation style (see Chs. 10–13).
Concluding List of Works Cited or References	Credit each source cited in the text with a corresponding full entry in a list of sources at the end of the paper.	• Provide consistent entries without forgetting or carelessly omitting sources. • Match each source citation in the text with an entry in the final list. • Supply every detail expected in an entry, even if you must return to the library or go back online to complete your source notes. • Follow the exact sequence, capitalization, punctuation, indentation pattern, and other details required by the style you are using (see Chs. 10–13). • Check that each entry in your final list appears in the expected alphabetical or numerical order.

☐ Have you analyzed your typical paper-writing habits to identify any, such as procrastination, that might create ethical problems for you? How do you plan to change such habits to avoid problems?

☐ Have you become aware of any research skills (such as quoting, paraphrasing, or summarizing) that you need to master or polish? If so, have you used this book's index or table of contents to identify which chapters explain those skills?

☐ Have you found the chapter in this book that explains the documentation style you'll use in your paper? Have you familiarized yourself with the chapter's features, such as its opening directory of examples, its checklists, and its sample paper?

☐ Have you identified and followed campus procedures for conducting field research involving other people?

☐ Have you recorded contact information so that you can request permission to include any visual materials from sources in your paper?

☐ If your research is part of a group project, have you honored your agreements with your instructor and your peers, meeting your obligations in a timely manner?

☐ If you feel ill-prepared for your research assignment, have you sought help from your instructor or staff at the library, writing center, computer lab, or other campus facility?

☐ Have you asked your instructor's advice about any other ethical issues that have arisen during your research project?

8

Drawing Information from Sources

Sources alone do not make for an effective research paper. Instead, the ideas, explanations, examples, and details from your sources need to be integrated—combined and mixed—with your own thoughts and conclusions about the question you have investigated. Together they eventually form a unified whole that conveys your perspective to your audience, along with the reasons and evidence that logically support it.

Ideally, your final paper will demonstrate the level of authority that you have achieved during your research process. Often, however, novice researchers find their confidence a bit shaky, especially because research papers are complex assignments. To make sure that your voice isn't drowned out by your sources, keep your research question and your working thesis—maybe still evolving—in front of you as you record information.

On the other hand, to make sure that you identify and credit your sources appropriately, work carefully, treating your sources with the respect they deserve. Keep in mind your goals and your audience as you read, quote, paraphrase, summarize, and otherwise record potentially useful materials from your sources.

READING FOR INFORMATION
AND SUPPORTING EVIDENCE

Before you spend time taking notes on outside material, read critically to decide what the source offers to you. If you cannot understand a source that requires specialized background, don't take notes or use it in your paper. If its ideas, facts, claims, or viewpoint seem unusual, incorporate

105

only what you can substantiate in other unrelated sources. On the other hand, if its evidence seems accurate, logical, and relevant, consider exactly how you might want to record it and eventually add it to your paper.

Pick a Comfortable System.   Once you have decided that you should record the information you're reading, the method that you use is up to you. You might want to stick to the same system you selected for your working bibliography (see p. 22) or switch to one that will help you draft your paper easily. For instance, if you find that note cards are easy to drop into your backpack and simple to reorganize, you might prefer this traditional note-taking method. On the other hand, if you'd rather move material in and out of an electronic draft, you might prefer to open a new file for each source or for each subtopic.

Identify What's from Where.   Whatever your system, be certain that you clearly note the author of the source, a brief title if needed, and the page number (or other location) where a reader could find the information. To cite and list each source correctly, you will need to connect each content note to your corresponding bibliography note.

Besides linking your notes with your sources, you also need a reliable system for identifying which ideas are yours and which are your source's. For example, you might mark your source notes with these labels:

". . .": quotation marks to set off all the exact words of the source

para: your paraphrase, translating a passage from the source into your own words

sum: your overall summary of the source's main point

paste: your cut-and-paste, quoting an entire passage pulled from an electronic document

JN (your initials) or [ ]: your own ideas, connections, reactions, or conclusions

Not only will a system like this help you avoid accidental plagiarism — for instance, confusing your paraphrase or cut-and-paste with your own ideas — it will also help you to highlight and develop your original thinking as your paper evolves.

Meet Your Needs.   In addition, if you know or can predict what you're likely to need from a certain source, you might limit your notes to a certain type, quantity, or emphasis, as these examples illustrate:

- facts and statistics that substantiate a situation
- examples that illustrate comparable or possible situations

- examples that you observed or identified through your field work
- analytical systems that may help you classify or organize
- similar or contrasting viewpoints or research findings
- historical events that provide background or suggest trends
- expert opinions, including reasons, for predicting certain outcomes
- unexpected views that may make you reconsider your assumptions
- novel solutions that may stimulate your creativity

Read Actively.   Many readers simply record whatever they read, hoping that their notes will include buried treasure. However, reading actively can help you search more deeply for the reasons and evidence necessary to develop a compelling answer to your question or challenge you to think more deeply and more creatively about just which answers are possible. Record your own comments in a special research notebook, or try active reading techniques such as these:

- Jot your own notes relating one reading to others or combining ideas from several sources.
- Look for strengths and weaknesses, especially if they challenge your own preconceptions.
- Try to figure out what a persuasive writer takes for granted or what a dull one doesn't express effectively; then reassess the merits of each view.
- Write out your own views, passionately or calmly.
- Sum up the changes in your own thinking as you have tried to answer your research question: Where did you begin? Where are you now? How and why have you changed your views?

BUILDING TRADITIONAL SKILLS: QUOTING, PARAPHRASING, AND SUMMARIZING

Three time-tested methods of experienced researchers can help you take notes efficiently, carefully, and ethically:

- Quoting: transcribing a writer's exact words directly from the source
- Paraphrasing: rewording or translating what the writer says into your own words
- Summarizing: reducing the writer's main point to its essentials

See the box on page 108 for examples of these methods.

SAMPLE PARAPHRASE, QUOTATIONS, AND SUMMARY

Passage from Original Source

Obesity is a major issue because (1) vast numbers of people are affected; (2) the prevalence is growing; (3) rates are increasing in children; (4) the medical, psychological, and social effects are severe; (5) the behaviors that cause it (poor diet and inactivity) are themselves major contributors to ill health; and (6) treatment is expensive, rarely effective, and impractical to use on a large scale.

Sample Paraphrase

The current concern with increasing American weight has developed for half a dozen reasons, according to Brownell and Horgen. They attribute the shift in awareness to the number of obese people and the increase in this number, especially among youngsters. In addition, excess weight carries harsh consequences for individual physical and mental health and for society's welfare. Lack of exercise and unhealthy food choices increase the health consequences, especially because there's no cheap and easy cure for the consequences of eating too much and exercising too little (51).

Passage from Original Source

Biology and environment conspire to promote obesity. Biology is an enabling factor, but the obesity epidemic, and the consequent human tragedy, is a function of the worsening food and physical activity environment. Governments and societies have come to this conclusion very late. There is much catching up to do.

Sample Quotations

Although human biology has contributed to the pudgy American society, everyone now faces the powerful challenge of a "worsening food and physical activity environment" (Brownell and Horgen 51).

As Brownell and Horgen conclude, "There is much catching up to do" (51).

Sample Summary

After outlining six reasons why obesity is a critical issue, Brownell and Horgen urge Americans to eat less and become more active (51).

Works Cited Entry (MLA Style)

Brownell, Kelly D., and Katherine Battle Horgen. <u>Food Fight: The Inside Story of the Food Industry, America's Obesity Crisis, and What We Can Do about It</u>. Chicago: Contemporary-McGraw, 2004.

Because you have to decide which method to use, these three methods can generate carefully selected, even polished, notes. Such notes can easily slip right into the draft of your paper, including the appropriate source citation, of course. On the other hand, you can't always predict what you'll need and thus may spend time refining notes that you'll never use at all.

In addition, research writers tend to use different methods to start their drafts. Some writers simply dive into the pool—writing easily from their own outlines or lists, embedding source information and notes as they swim along. Other writers prefer to begin by identifying and arranging a series of quotations or other notes in a logical order. After they've constructed this diving platform, they're ready to take the plunge—surrounding their quotations and source notes with their own observations and interpretations. Despite such variations in research and writing methods, you would be wise to master these traditional skills, building your strengths and your deep reserves so that you are ready for whatever challenges the future may hold.

Quote Accurately

Effective quotation depends on careful selection. Record only a quotation that promises to lend its vitality, originality, or authority to your discussion. Use a quotation to support your point, not to pad your paper. Instead of copying a long passage, choose the words that most clearly relate to your discussion while respecting the meaning of the original. If your source describes a military clash as "an appalling outcome of weak policy and failed negotiation," don't convert this to the "outcome of . . . policy and . . . negotiation."

Children and sports   Leonard 140
"... [in organized sports] children may be subject to intense emotional
stress caused by fear and anxiety, concern about physical safety, and
doubts about performance and outcomes. This anxiety may emerge if
children are ignored, chastised, or made to feel that they are no good.
Scanlan and Passer's study of preadolescent male soccer players showed
that losing players evidenced more postgame anxiety than winning players.
Children who experience anxiety in sport competition may try to avoid failure
by shying away from active participation, by developing excuses, or by
refusing to try new things." [Good quote!]

Figure 8.1   A sample note card directly quoting a source (paraphrased in
Figure 8.2)

Quoting directly means repeating a writer's precise wording, set off
by quotation marks. Record the quotation accurately, including punctuation and capitalization. Use an ellipsis mark—three dots (. . .)
mid-sentence or four dots (. . . .) counting the period concluding a sentence—to show where you leave out any original wording. (See
pp. 126–29.) See Figure 8.1 for an example of a note card quoting a
source.

RESEARCH CHECKLIST

Quoting from a Source

☐ Have you limited your quotations to impressive, persuasive passages that might strengthen your paper?

☐ Have you checked your quotation against the original to be sure
that it repeats your source word for word?

☐ Have you marked the beginning and the ending of the quotation
with quotation marks?

☐ Have you used ellipses (. . .) to mark any spot where you have
left out words in the original?

☐ Have you identified the source of the quotation in a launch
statement (see p. 124) or in parentheses (or another format)?

☐ Have you specified the page number where the quotation appears in the source?

Paraphrase Carefully

Paraphrasing means rewording to translate a passage from a writer's words into your own language. A paraphrase is generally about half the length of the original; it expresses the ideas and emphasis of the original using your words and sentences. Besides avoiding plagiarism, a creative paraphrase expresses ideas in your own style without awkwardly jumping between it and your source's style.

An effective paraphrase conveys the ideas of the original in fresh language; it avoids following the original too closely by shadowing its sentence patterns or echoing its wording. If the original asserts that "The play wittily rewards virtue, punishes vice, and validates societal norms," your paraphrase should go beyond rearranging the sentence or altering a few words (as in "The play punishes vice, rewards virtue, and validates its society's norms"). Instead, try to translate the original into your own language and credit its source: "According to Smith, this comedy reinforces social codes by honoring good conduct and chastising bad" (47). Should you need to include exact wording from the source, set it off with quotation marks, blending direct quotation with paraphrase. See Figure 8.2 for an example of a note card paraphrasing a source. See Figure 8.3 for an example of a note card summarizing a source.

RESEARCH CHECKLIST

Paraphrasing from a Source

☐ Have you read the passage critically to be sure that you fully understand it?

☐ Have you paraphrased accurately, reflecting both the main points and the supporting details in the original?

☐ Does your paraphrase use your own words without repeating or echoing the words or the sentence structure of the original?

☐ Does your paraphrase stick to the ideas of the original without tucking in your own thoughts?

☐ Have you reread and revised your paraphrase so that it reads smoothly and clearly?

☐ Have you identified the source of the paraphrase in a launch statement (see p. 124) or in parentheses (or another format)?

☐ Have you specified the page number where the passage appears in the source?

Summarize Fairly

Summarizing is a useful way of incorporating the general point of a whole paragraph or section of a work. You briefly state the main sense of the original in your own words and tell where you got the idea. A summary is generally much shorter than the original; it expresses only the most important ideas — the essence — of the original.

RESEARCH CHECKLIST

Summarizing a Source

☐ Have you fairly stated the author's thesis, or main point, in your own words in a sentence or two?

☐ Have you briefly stated any supporting ideas that you wish to summarize?

☐ Have you stuck to the overall point without getting bogged down in details or examples?

☐ Has your summary remained respectful of the ideas and opinions of others, even if you disagree with them?

☐ Have you revised your summary so that it reads smoothly and clearly?

☐ Have you identified the source of the summary in a launch statement (see p. 124) or in parentheses (or another format)?

☐ Have you specified the page number where any specific passage appears in the source?

Children and sports Leonard 140	Paraphrase about half the length of original passage
Stress and anxiety on the playing field can result in children backing away from participating in sports because they fear rejection if they perform poorly. This anxiety and stress is a result of the child's fears of being hurt or not being good enough. A study by Scanlan and Passer confirms these findings, showing that boys who lose in soccer have more anxiety after losing a game than boys who win.	Emphasis of original maintained with word choice and order reworked to avoid plagiarism

No interpretation or evaluation of original passage included |

Figure 8.2   A sample note card paraphrasing a source (quoted in Figure 8.1)

Reasons for moving to Las Animas	Aaron Sanchez Interview, 3-11-04

In 1964, my father Octavio and his family (father, mother, four brothers, three sisters) moved to Las Animas because they couldn't make enough money where they were living in New Mexico. The inheritance from his mother's father went to her brothers, and she got nothing. They moved to the Las Animas region, settling in a <u>colonia</u> (labor camp).

Subject heading

Label identifies person interviewed and date

Main points clearly broken out

Terse, even fragmentary, notes convey gist of key point in the interview

Figure 8.3   A sample note card summarizing a source

Using Other Note-Taking Systems. As you develop your own comfortable system for recording notes and as you practice traditional note-taking skills, you should find that your notes are increasingly pertinent to your project and increasingly likely to be useful as you draft your paper. Other more contemporary ways to integrate useful notes with your research archive include techniques such as these:

- Jot a summary on the first page of a printout or photocopy.
- Add a paraphrase in the margin next to a key section of a printout.
- Identify a lively or concrete quotation with a highlighter.
- Record key quotations (including sources and page numbers) in a computer file so that you can easily reorganize them to find an effective sequence.
- Record summaries of sources on sticky notes so that you can quickly rearrange them in various orders.
- Use a graphics program or a big sheet of poster board to sketch out a "storyboard" for the main "events" that you want to cover in your paper.

Learning to select appropriate quotations and to write useful paraphrases and summaries takes time and practice. As you combine these traditional skills with other notes, use the following questions to help you continue to improve your research skills.

RESEARCH CHECKLIST

Taking Notes

☐ For each research note, have you identified the source (by the author's last name or a key word from the title) and the exact page? Have you added a subject heading to each note?

☐ Have you made a companion bibliography card or note for each new source you discovered during your reading?

☐ Have you remained true to the meaning of the original source?

☐ Have you quoted sparingly—selecting striking, short passages?

☐ Have you quoted sources exactly? Do you use quotation marks to identify significant words, phrases, and passages from the original sources? Do you use ellipsis marks as needed to show where any words are omitted?

☐ Are most notes in your own words—paraphrasing or summarizing?

☐ Have you avoided paraphrasing that parrots the source too closely?

☐ Have you carefully distinguished the exact words of a source, your account of its ideas, and your own reactions or interpretations so that you can accurately credit both words and ideas?

9

Pulling Together Your Research Paper

Like a wide horizon with a vast sky, college research is open territory as you tackle any of an array of questions. For this reason, you may see no end to your research process—finding, evaluating, and recording information from sources—even though you need to move toward a finished paper. You may, in fact, be worried about when to stop digging and start drafting. However, you've probably already begun writing your paper.

Stating a research question, and possibly a working thesis, automatically begins the planning for your paper. It establishes the limits, direction, and purpose for your paper. Every source you select for your working bibliography can strengthen your source citations and source list. And every content note you record may become a critical chunk of text—whether that note is a traditional quotation, paraphrase, or summary or your own comparison, interpretation, or conclusion.

CONVERTING YOUR NOTES TO A DRAFT

Turning your notes into text generally requires positioning them in a sequence, fitting them in place, and reworking them so that they advance your case. Your source notes need your interpretation to transform them into effective evidence. As a researcher and writer, you have to think critically about each fact. What does it mean in the context of your paper? Is it strong enough to support the weight of the claim you're going to base on it? Do you need supplemental evidence to shore up an interesting but possibly ambiguous fact?

You'll also need to synthesize your sources and evidence, to weave them into a unified whole. If you have a sure sense of your paper's direction, you may find this synthesis fairly easy. On the other hand, if your research question or working thesis has changed, perhaps because you have unearthed persuasive information at odds with your original direction, consider these questions:

• Taken as a whole, what does all this information mean?
• What does it actually tell you about the answer to your research question?
• What's the most important thing you've learned?
• What's the most important thing you can tell your readers?

You may have your own tried-and-true system of moving from research notes to a rough draft. If so, feel free to stick to your own system. On the other hand, you may be worried about how to pull together your paper—perhaps the longest and most complex one you've ever written. In this case, try some of the suggestions in the following sections to help you accomplish these key steps:

• Refocus on your research question.
• Organize the sequence of your paper.
• Synthesize your points and your support: launch, capture, and cite your source material.

RETURNING TO YOUR RESEARCH QUESTION

Refocusing on your research question can help you get back to the essentials—why you began your investigation and what you had hoped to learn. Concentrating for the moment on these big issues may help you clarify what you'll want to emphasize in your paper. Sometimes this process is easy: You know what the question is; you know what the general answer is; you just need to let the pieces fall into place.

At other times, you may want to try some of the following "starter" activities to help you specify and state your focus. When you try one of these, just write without reviewing your notes or sorting through your research archive. Later on you can refine, reorient, or qualify your statement, as needed.

Write Out Your Question and Your Answer.   Write down your research question in its original form or as you have reshaped or refined it during your research process. Then, in a few sentences, simply write out your most direct answer to your question.

Address Your Reader. Writing directly to a friendly and interested reader, explain your most important conclusions about your question. Imagine that you're sending the reader an e-mail, a postcard, or a short note addressed "Dear Reader."

Make a Personal Statement. Write an informal, personal account of where you began and where you ended up. For example, "I wondered why . . . , and I found out . . ."

List Your Key Points. If you find it difficult to sum up your conclusions, make a list of your strongest or most important points instead. Later on, you can convert your list to sentences, perhaps using them to introduce the sections of your paper.

Write Out Your Current Thesis Statement. A thesis is a clear, concise statement of the main point you want to make in your paper. Once you've written it out in a sentence or so, your thesis can help you decide what to say and how to say it. It can also alert readers in advance to the scope and message of your paper. Make your thesis precise and concrete, and don't claim more than you can demonstrate in your paper. If your paper is argumentative—that is, if you take a stand, propose a solution, or evaluate something—then you should make your stand, solution, or appraisal clear.

TOPIC	Americans' attitudes toward sports
RESEARCH QUESTION	Is America obsessed with sports?
THESIS	The national obsession with sports must end.

WRITING CHECKLIST

Stating Your Thesis

- ☐ Does your thesis identify your topic and your approach to it?
- ☐ Does your thesis sum up your overall answer to your research question, specifying your main point or conclusion?
- ☐ Can your thesis help you decide which supporting points to discuss, which evidence to emphasize, and which sequence to follow as you arrange the sections of your paper?
- ☐ Will your thesis help prepare a reader for the rest of your paper?
- ☐ Can you refine the wording of your thesis to make it clearer, more direct, or more compelling?

ORGANIZING A SEQUENCE OF IDEAS

In writing your paper, it isn't enough to describe the steps you took in answering your research question or to string data together in chronological order. You aren't writing a memoir; you're reporting the significance of what you found out. Your goal is to arrive at an organization that fulfills your purpose.

Test a Possible Order. If you began with a clear research question, you may not have much difficulty selecting and organizing your evidence to answer it. But research questions often change. Don't be afraid to ditch an original question that no longer works and to reorganize around a newly formed question. Conduct some experiments, organizing your paper or electronic notes first in one order, then in another, until they begin to pull together. As an overall direction for your paper emerges, turn it into a working plan that can guide your writing even if you still feel uncertain about exactly where every point belongs.

Try an Outline. Whether you work on paper or on the computer, preparing an informal or formal outline may help you define a sequence for your draft (see pp. 115–16). Word processors often offer an outline tool in the View menu. As you think critically about your organization, you can assign outline levels to your headings or to individual paragraphs, letting the word processor automatically fashion your sequence in outline form. After you have outlined your text, you can display headings by hiding text or manipulate text while you reorganize your thinking.

You can also use the computer to develop a personalized system of coding using bold, italics, underlining, color, or other highlighting. Some writers like to organize their ideas around italicized questions, while others prefer bold headings. Some use a color scheme to show pro and con thinking; others highlight their main pro and con points. Think about the software features that can make your ideas more visual and easier to organize.

In whatever way you prepare your outline, remember that it is only a skeleton until you flesh it out with details. Use your outline as a working plan, but change the subdivisions or the order of the parts if you discover a better way as you draft. If you don't want to start at the beginning, start wherever you feel most comfortable. You can draft sections in any order; later on, you can add clear connections between parts of your paper.

Consider Beginning with the Findings of Others. A common way to begin a research report is to identify the research question your paper will explore and to explain why you find the question intriguing or significant. Such an opening often logically leads into a brief review of other studies of the same perplexing question or of a related topic. After all, if those other studies had fully and indisputably answered the question, there'd be no need for your investigation. Thus, reviewing this research background or history justifies your fresh look at the issue.

In addition, your review of past studies or major points of view can also enhance your credibility as a thorough researcher. Be careful, however, to avoid tediously listing study after study. Instead of discussing a source simply because you found and read it, include it only if it is genuinely relevant to your answer to your research question. In addition, try to group studies thematically or chronologically. As you summarize, synthesize, and interpret them, a reader can immediately see how they relate to each other as well as to your approach and your research question. (For more on adding evidence from sources, see pp. 120–24.)

Experiment with Your Finish.   Depending on the kind of paper you are writing, you might prefer to start out slowly with a clear account of an event to draw your readers into the paper. You could then build up to

---

WRITING CHECKLIST

Developing Your Ideas

- ☐ Are your ideas presented and developed in an order that will seem easy to follow and logical to readers?
- ☐ Are your points explained thoroughly enough to be clear to readers without becoming tedious or drifting off the topic?
- ☐ Do your reasons, your evidence, and your references to sources all seem relevant to the purpose and position of your paper?
- ☐ Do you use different strategies in your paper when they seem appropriate? For example, do you compare or contrast past studies or alternative solutions? Do you analyze possible causes or effects? Do you substantiate pertinent trends or propose solutions?
- ☐ Do you state clearly the reasons for your conclusion—your answer to your research question? Do you support these reasons with appropriate, varied, and persuasive evidence?
- ☐ Do you consider the expectations of your readers, such as the approaches or methods they favor, the types of sources or quantity of evidence that they'll find compelling, or the extent to which they value the synthesis of ideas?

a robust finish, saving your strongest argument until the end—after you have had the chance to present all the evidence to support your thesis. For example, if your paper argues that American children are being harmed by the national obsession with sports, you might organize your paper something like this:

- Begin with a factual account of a real event, putting you and your reader on the same footing.
- Explore that event's implications to prepare your reader for your view.
- State your thesis (main idea): for example, "The national obsession with sports must end."
- Support your thesis with persuasive reasons supported by evidence from well-chosen sources, moving to your strongest argument.
- Then end with a rousing call to action:

> For the sake of our children and the future of our country, isn't it time that we put the brakes on America's sports mania? The youth of America have been sold a false and harmful bill of goods. Let's stop such madness and step off the carousel now. We owe that to the children of America and to ourselves.

DECIDING WHERE YOU NEED SUPPORTING EVIDENCE

Sometimes you will know exactly what your paper needs from your sources. In fact, as you plan and organize, you may tuck in notes to yourself—add Bryant here, cover Texas and Oregon studies there, find some more statistics. Other times, you may sense that your paper isn't as strong as you want it to be, but you may not know exactly what to add or where to add it.

Support Your Statements.   One way to determine where you need to supply supporting evidence is to examine your plan or even your draft, point by point.

- What does each of your points claim or promise to a reader?
- Where do you provide supporting evidence from sources to demonstrate the claim or fulfill the promise?

The answers to these questions—your statements and your supporting evidence—often fall into a common alternating pattern:

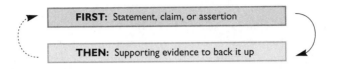

FIRST: Statement, claim, or assertion

THEN: Supporting evidence to back it up

When you spot a string of assertions without much support, you have found a place where you might need more evidence from your sources. Select your evidence carefully so that it substantiates the exact claim, statement, or assertion that precedes it. Likewise, if you spot a string of quotations or source materials, introduce or conclude each of them with an interpretive statement that explains the point each substantiates.

When Carrie Williamson introduced the topic of her paper, "Rainforest Destruction," she made a general statement and then supported it by quoting facts from a source. Then she repeated this statement-support pattern, backing up her next statement in turn.

The tropical rainforests are among the most biologi-
cally diverse communities in the world. According to the — *Statement*
Web site <u>World Rainforest Information Portal</u>, "more than
50 percent of all species live in tropical rainforests," and
"a typical four-square-mile patch of rainforest contains up — *Evidence: Statistics*
to 1,500 species of flowering plants, as many as 750 tree   *about species*
species, 125 mammal species, 400 bird species, 100 rep-
tile species, 60 amphibian species, and 150 butterfly
species" ("Biodiversity"). These amazing communities
that depend on each part being intact in order to function properly and successfully are being destroyed at an — *Statement*
alarming rate. Each year "an area larger than Italy"
(Soltani) is destroyed. Many rainforest conservationists   *Evidence: Facts*
debate what the leading cause of deforestation is.   *about destruction*
Regardless of which one is the major cause, the fact re-   *Statement identify-*
mains that both logging and slash-and-burn farming are   *ing cause-and-effect*
    debate
destroying more and more acres of rainforests each year.   *Statement preview-*
    ing points to come

Build Your Own Credibility.   By using this statement-support pattern from the very beginning, Carrie did more than support her opening statements; she also reassured her readers that she was a trustworthy writer who would try to supply convincing evidence throughout the rest of her paper. She further strengthened this impression of her reliability by conscientiously following the conventions of MLA style (see Ch. 10). Both of her sources—an article from a library database and a Web page—were electronic, and neither provided the page numbers that customarily appear with quotations. As a result, Carrie couldn't supply page numbers with her quotations. In addition, the Web site had a well-known sponsor but didn't identify the writer of the passage she quoted. Despite these complications, the nature of each source was clear when Carrie added entries for both sources to her list of works cited:

"Biodiversity." World Rainforest Information Portal. 2001. Rainforest
    Action Network. 4 Feb. 2003. <http://www.rainforestweb.org/
    Rainforest_Information/Biodiversity/>.

Soltani, Atossa. "Every Tree Killed Equals Another Life Lost." Wood and
    Wood Products 100.3 (1995): 86-. Expanded Academic ASAP. InfoTrac.
    Dodge City Community College Lib., Dodge City, KS. 31 Jan. 2003.
    <http://web1.infotrac.galegroup.com>.

TABLE 9.1   Using the Statement-Support Pattern

Statement, Claim, or Assertion	Possible Supporting Evidence
Introduces a topic	Facts or statistics to justify the importance or significance of the topic
Describes a situation	Factual examples or illustrations to convey the reality or urgency of the situation
Introduces an event	Accurate firsthand observations to describe an event that you have witnessed
Presents a problem	Expert testimony or firsthand observation to establish the necessity or urgency of a solution
Explains an issue	Facts and details to clarify the significance of the issue
States your point	Facts, statistics, or examples to support your viewpoint or position
Interprets and prepares readers for evidence that follows	Facts, examples, observations, or research findings to define and develop your case
Concludes with your recommendation or evaluation	Facts, examples, or expert testimony to persuade readers to accept your conclusion

Develop Your Evidence with the Statement-Support Pattern.
Consider your paper's overall purpose, organization, and line of reasoning. For example, evidence from sources may help you to define key terms, justify the significance of a problem or controversy, analyze causes or effects, compare similar problems or situations, back up your stand on an issue, support your solution to a problem, or interpret a literary work effectively.

Table 9.1 on page 122 shows some of the many ways the statement-support pattern can be used to strengthen your paper. In addition, you can use the following checklist to help you decide whether—and where—you might need supporting evidence from sources.

WRITING CHECKLIST

Adding Supporting Evidence

☐ What does each statement promise that you'll deliver? What evidence would ensure that you have effectively kept this promise?

☐ Are your claims, statements, and assertions backed up with supporting evidence? If not, what evidence might you add?

☐ What evidence would most effectively persuade your readers? How much evidence would they expect?

☐ What criteria for useful evidence are most important to your readers? What evidence would best meet these criteria?

☐ When you read through your draft, which parts sound weak or incomplete to you?

☐ What facts or statistics would clarify or substantiate your answer to your research question?

☐ What examples or illustrations would make the background or the current circumstances clearer and more compelling for readers?

☐ What comments by a reliable expert would enlighten your readers about your research question or the situation that it involves?

☐ What firsthand observation would add authenticity?

☐ Where have peer readers or your instructor suggested adding more evidence or stronger evidence?

LAUNCHING, CAPTURING, AND CITING SOURCE MATERIAL AS YOU DRAFT

You need to follow each detail and each idea—whether a quotation, summary, or paraphrase—drawn from your reading or field research with a source identification. Noting your sources as you draft is easy and efficient, saving time later while avoiding omissions or errors that might look like plagiarism. (See Chs. 10–13 for citation examples.) Once you have decided where you want to add supporting information from a source, avoid dropping those ideas into your paper as if they had just arrived by flying saucer. Instead, weave them in so that they effectively support the point you want to make. As you integrate each idea from a source, take three steps.

Launch Your Source Material

Launch each quotation, paraphrase, summary, or other reference to a source with an introduction that tells readers who wrote it or why it's in your paper. College instructors are likely to favor launch statements that comment on the source, connect it to the paper's research question or thesis, or relate it to other sources. For this reason, you want to use your launch statements to show not only that you have located and read your sources but that you have absorbed and applied what they say about your own research question.

In your first draft, when you're struggling to get everything added in a logical sequence, your launch statements may be rough. However, as you revise and edit your paper (see pp. 129–32), you can continue to specify the connections you want to make, especially watching for the spots where you assume that readers will automatically see what you expect them to see. The following strategies suggest ways of strengthening your launch statements. These examples follow MLA style, but the chapter about the style you are using will show how to cite sources correctly in that style.

- Identify the name of the author in the sentence that introduces the source:

  As Wood explains, the goal of American education continues to fluctuate between gaining knowledge and applying it (58).

- Add the author's name in the middle of the source material:
  In *Romeo and Juliet*, "That which we call a rose," Shakespeare claims, "By any other word would smell as sweet" (2.2.43-44).

- Name the author only in the parenthetical source citation (or the source note) if you want to keep your focus on the topic:
  A second march on Washington followed the first (Whitlock 83).

- Explain for the reader why you have selected and included the material:
  As Serrano's three-year investigation of tragic border incidents shows, the current border policies carry high financial and human costs.

- Interpret what you see as the point or relevance of the material:
  Stein's argument focuses on stem cell research, but his discussion of potential ethical implications (18) also applies to other kinds of medical investigation.

- Relate the source clearly to the paper's thesis or to the specific point it supports:
  Although Robinson analyzes workplace interactions, her conclusions (289–92) suggest the importance of examining these same issues in arenas such as schools.

- Compare or contrast the point of view or evidence of one source with that of another source:
  While Desmond emphasizes the European economic disputes, Lewis turns to the social stresses which also set the stage for World War II.

Often adding transitional phrases or words to guide readers can strengthen your launch statements. Such expressions can relate one source to another (*in addition, in contrast, more recently, in a more favorable view, reflecting a more difficult experience*) or relate a particular source or piece of evidence to your line of reasoning (*next, furthermore, in addition, despite, nevertheless, on the other hand*). Other useful information also can be embedded in a word or two. For example, adding the professional title or affiliation of someone you've interviewed can add authority and increase the credibility of your source (*According to Joan Lewis, an environmental attorney at Saunders and Gonzales, . . .*). Briefly noting relevant experience can do the same (*Recalling events during a three-year tour of duty in Afghanistan, Sergeant Nelson indicated . . .*).

Use the following questions to help you choose precise and varied wording for your launch statements.

WRITING CHECKLIST

Using Transitions and Alternatives for *Said*

☐ Have you scanned the opening words in your launch statements to see if you have fallen into a repetitive pattern such as "X said . . . Y said . . . Z said"?

☐ Have you used your software's Edit-Find option to locate any overused launch words such as *said* or transitions such as *then?*

☐ Have you used your growing vocabulary as a research writer to identify appropriate alternatives for *said,* such as *argued, asserted, claimed, conceded, demonstrated, emphasized, explained, identified, implied, indicated, maintained, noted, observed, responded, speculated,* or *urged?*

☐ In launch statements that show agreement or continuity, have you used appropriate transitions such as *additionally, also, at the same time, equally significant, furthermore, in addition, in the same way, moreover, next, once again, similarly,* or *subsequently?*

☐ In launch statements that show disagreement or difference, have you used appropriate transitions such as *although, despite, even though, from another perspective, however, in contrast, in opposition, instead, nevertheless, on the other hand, rather than, though,* or *unlike?*

☐ In launch statements that introduce examples from sources, have you used appropriate transitions such as *as X illustrates, for example, for instance, in this case, such as,* or *to illustrate?*

☐ In launch statements that show causes or effects, have you used appropriate transitions such as *as a result, because of, consequently, due to, for this reason, in consequence, initially, next,* or *thus?*

Capture Your Source Material Effectively

Often, the ways you have already drawn information from your sources (see Chapter 8) will determine how you integrate that source material into your draft. Your source notes are rich resources, whether they are primarily traditional quotations, paraphrases, and summaries or your own annotations, highlights, and responses on printouts.

As you work source material into your draft, however, you have an opportunity to reconsider its presentation. For example, you may have recorded or highlighted lots of direct quotations in your source notes, perhaps because you weren't sure whether you'd need the exact words of an authority to add credibility or because you were unsure about how to express complex ideas in your own words. In addition, some students mistakenly believe that a paper stuffed with direct quotations will show an instructor how hard they have worked on their research. Ironically, however, many college instructors see the situation the other way around. Instead of being impressed, they think that a string of quotations shows that the writer hasn't taken the next essential step—synthesizing or weaving together the source materials and relating all of them to the writer's own research question and its answer. Consider the following guidelines as you decide how to capture your source material in your draft:

- Quote compelling words, phrases, or sentences exactly.
- Paraphrase connections and details by explaining them in your own words.
- Summarize to convey the gist, essence, or main sense.
- Relate sources by identifying their similarities, differences, and other relationships.
- Connect all of your information from sources to your own points— answering your research question, supporting your thesis, and supplying persuasive reasons and evidence.

Cite Each Source Accurately

In addition to launching and presenting your source material effectively, you should check the accuracy of any hastily written or unclear notes. Match up any questionable quotations especially carefully, checking them word for word against the originals in your research archive. If you don't want to interrupt your drafting to do this or if the original material is not immediately accessible, be certain to write a reminder—right in your draft—so you don't neglect to check for accuracy. Although you may see inaccurate quotations, paraphrases, or summaries as small flaws in your paper, others may interpret them as sloppy work or even plagiarism (see Chapter 7).

Accuracy also requires correct identification of the source of your material, following the style you are using (see Chapter 7 and Chapters 10–13). Although each citation style has its own conventions, all of the styles expect you to accomplish the following things:

- Acknowledge any material from a source—words directly quoted, information or opinions recast in your own words, summaries of ideas or theories, references to research studies and findings,

WRITING CHECKLIST

Distinguishing Quotations from Your Own Words

☐ Have you limited direct quotations to compelling statements?

☐ Have you revised to use strictly your own words and sentence structures if you find any blurry distinctions between your words and your source's?

☐ Have you selected the quotation and written your launch statement so that the two fit together grammatically?

☐ Have you followed your launch statement with appropriate punctuation—a comma (for example, X said, ". . ." or As Y stated, ". . ." or ". . ." according to Z, ". . ."), a colon (following a complete sentence and preceding a free-standing expression), or no punctuation (for words that grammatically follow your own, such as X claims that ". . .")?

☐ Have you placed a pair of quotation marks (" ") around the exact words from your source?

☐ Have you placed a pair of single quotation marks (' ') around a quotation that occurs within another quotation already inside quotation marks?

☐ Have you placed a comma or period before (not after) the second quotation mark of a pair? However, if a short quotation is followed by a parenthetical citation, have you placed the punctuation after the second parenthesis mark?

☐ Have you used an ellipsis mark (. . .)—three spaced dots—to show where you have omitted irrelevant words (for your purposes) from the middle of a direct quotation? Have you added a fourth dot (the sentence period) before an ellipsis that also ends a sentence?

☐ Have you used a pair of brackets—[ ]—to enclose, and thus identify as your own, any words that you have added to a direct quotation, perhaps to clarify its meaning, define a term, supply missing information, or improve its grammatical fit?

☐ If you have added underlining or italics to draw a reader's attention to key wording in a quotation, have you noted "emphasis added" in brackets (within the quotation) or in parentheses (following it)?

☐ Have you added *sic* (Latin for "in the same way" or "thus") in brackets following unusual wording in a quotation if it seems necessary to assure a reader of its accuracy?

☐ If the source itself uses ellipses and you are using MLA style, have you enclosed your own ellipsis marks in brackets to identify them as your addition?

specific reasons or examples, or anything else drawn from that particular resource.

- Identify the source material at the exact moment when you add it to your text, generally by using a short identification form that mentions the author of the source (or its title if the author is not identified) or by adding a number keyed to a later list with that information.

- Supply the specific location of any quotation or paraphrase (usually the page number in the original) so that a reader can easily turn to the exact information you have used.

- Link the short identification in your paper—supplied in your text wording, in parentheses, or through a number linked to a note or a list of sources—to the full description of all of your sources in a list of works cited, a reference list, or a bibliography at the end of your paper.

- Check your text citations against your concluding list of sources to be sure that the two correspond.

Although you may find citing sources a complex or fussy task, you'll find specific models and illustrations showing how to apply these principles in the chapter about the style you are using. In addition, the way everyone learns conventions—for example, what to wear to a wedding or how to speak to a customer at work—is through experience. The more research papers you write—and the more you write using a specific style—the more skillful you'll be. Besides, even well-known faculty who regularly write and publish academic papers don't memorize every detail of these styles. They simply know the secret of correct source citation: When in doubt, look it up!

REVISING AND EDITING

To help you step back from a draft, begin by duplicating your file. (Use a command such as Save As or Versions from the File menu, and give the copy a different name.) This important step will enable you to experiment without losing your existing draft. Your software may also have a useful resource to "track changes" in the Tools or Proof menu. By using colors and cross-outs to highlight text and record comments, this resource allows you to see your text revisions. It can even automatically compare documents so that you can see how much your revision has changed from the previous draft. As you look over your draft, you may find that you need to shift the organization, strengthen your evidence, drop a section, or add a new one. Answering the following questions may help you see how to improve your draft.

WRITING CHECKLIST

Revising Your Draft

☐ Is your focus—your research question and your answer to that question—consistent and clear? Does this focus guide every part of your paper?

☐ Do you state your main idea or thesis clearly for your readers, even if they are not as well informed about the question as you are?

☐ Have you made an outline of your paper—as it is, not as you imagined it to be—in order to check its organization, logic, and balance?

☐ Given the evolution of your paper's sequence of ideas, do you need to add or drop supporting evidence at any point? Does any of your evidence seem feeble, unconvincing, or plainly off the topic?

☐ Have you launched, captured, and cited every bit of your source material as carefully and accurately as possible? If necessary, have you rechecked the exact wording of direct quotations, the page numbers where information appears in the original, or any other pesky details?

Once you have revised your draft as purposefully as you can, you are ready to get a second opinion from a peer reader such as a classmate, a tutor at the writing center, or a friend who will read carefully. Ask this reader to respond to questions such as the following or to your own list of concerns about your paper.

WRITING CHECKLIST

Gathering Peer Responses

☐ Are my research question and my answer to that question clear?

☐ Does the beginning of my paper attract your attention? Do you want to keep reading?

☐ Do you feel satisfied by the conclusion of my paper? Do I persuade you to agree with my main idea or at least to consider its merit?

☐ Which sections do you consider most clearly developed and most strongly supported? Which parts seem a bit weak, fuzzy, or confusing?

☐ Is there any place where I need to launch, capture, or cite my source material differently? Is there any place where I need to clarify which ideas are mine and which are my source's?

☐ Given the due date for my paper, which additional revisions should be my highest priorities?

After you have revised your research paper, edit and proofread it. Carefully check the grammar, word choice, punctuation, and mechanics—and then correct any problems you may find. Allow plenty of time to check your documentation, too—how you identify the sources of information and how you list the works you have cited in your paper. Use the questions at the end of the book (pp. 331-32) to get you started editing and proofreading your paper.

Once your text is corrected and polished, check the format of your paper, following your instructor's directions or the advice in the chapter about the style you are using. If you are submitting a hard copy, make sure that it is clear and easy to read. (Use a new printer cartridge, if necessary, and paper of reasonable quality.) If you are submitting an electronic copy, be certain that you have formatted, attached, or posted it correctly. Either way, keep a backup copy (print, electronic, or both) of your final version in a safe place, just in case your submission is lost or has technical problems. Also keep backup copies of any other materials that accompanied your paper so that you could easily reassemble the entire project.

10

Using MLA Style

This chapter briefly explains and illustrates how to use MLA style, the format for preparing a research paper and crediting sources that is recommended by the Modern Language Association of America. This style is frequently expected in the humanities, especially in courses in composition, literature, comparative literature, languages, and the like. Because studies in these fields often scrutinize the exact wording of sources, this style emphasizes identifying both the source and the exact location of the information from the source. For more extensive advice, turn to the *MLA Handbook for Writers of Research Papers* (6th ed.; New York: MLA, 2003), usually available in your campus bookstore and library.

CITING AND LISTING SOURCES IN MLA STYLE

CITING SOURCES IN MLA STYLE

Who Wrote It?

LISTING SOURCES IN MLA STYLE

UNDERSTANDING MLA STYLE

As the next two sections of this chapter illustrate, MLA style uses a two-part system to credit sources. First, you briefly identify the source in your text, either by mentioning it directly in your discussion or by noting it in parentheses right after you use the information drawn from it. In most cases, the page number in the original source follows this identification. Second, this brief identification, usually the author's last name, leads to a full description of the source in your concluding list, called "Works Cited." The four MLA Source Navigators (pp. 136–43) illustrate how to locate in your source the details necessary to cite and list the source correctly and how to present that information in MLA style. See also pages 132–34 for a directory listing the sample entries supplied here.

MLA style also provides directions for formatting a consistent, easy-to-read paper. If you expect to use this style fairly often, set up an MLA template that you can call up as you begin each new paper. Otherwise use the Page Format options in your software's File menu or the Font and Paragraph options in the Format menu to make any changes needed in your draft. As you complete your paper, refer to the format of the sample MLA paper on pp. 166–73 and the following checklist.

WRITING CHECKLIST

Formatting a Paper in MLA Style

- ☐ Have you selected a common academic typeface such as Times Roman in 12-point size?
- ☐ Have you double-spaced the entire paper, including all quotations and your works-cited list?
- ☐ Have you allowed a one-inch margin on all four sides of the page?
- ☐ Have you positioned a running header, your last name followed by the page number, at the far right side of the page, one-half inch from the top?
- ☐ Have you placed your heading (name, professor, course, and date on separate lines) on the left side of the first page, beginning one inch from the top? Have you centered your title and then immediately begun your paper without any cover page?
- ☐ Have you indented the first line of every paragraph one-half inch (five spaces) and every line of any long quotation (five lines of prose, four lines of poetry, or more of either) one inch (ten spaces) from the left margin?
- ☐ Have you preceded any table with a numbered label—for example, Table 2—followed by its explanatory title on the next line? Have you followed the table with any necessary credit (beginning Source: . . .)?
- ☐ Have you followed any other visual, such as a graph, drawing, chart, or photograph, with a numbered heading—for example, Fig. 1—directly followed by its explanatory title?
- ☐ Have you turned off your software's automatic hyphenation to avoid splitting words with hyphens at the ends of lines? Have you turned off text justification so that you have an even margin on the left but not on the right?
- ☐ Have you continued your page numbering but begun your list of sources on a new page, centering its heading—Works Cited—one inch from the top of the page?
- ☐ Have you begun the first line of each works-cited entry at the left margin but indented each additional line one-half inch (five spaces)? (To do this automatically, check your software for a "hanging" indentation option, possibly through the Format-Paragraph-Indentation-Special menu.)
- ☐ Have you followed any specific directions from your instructor about format or electronic submission?
- ☐ Have you printed a clear, readable final copy and kept a backup copy of your file in case the printed copy gets lost?

SOURCE NAVIGATOR: An Article from a Periodical

I The complete name of the author (beginning with the last name)
2 The title of the article (placed in quotation marks)
3 The title of the journal (underlined)
4 The number of the journal volume
5 The date of the issue
6 The article's page numbers, including the last two (or more for clarity) of the concluding page

Text Citation with Specific Location
    ①   ⑥
(Salamone 735)

Works Cited Entry
    ①   ②
Salamone, Frank A. "Jazz and Its Impact on European
    Classical Music." Journal of Popular Culture 38
    (2005): 732–43.   ③   ④
      ⑤   ⑥

② Jazz and Its Impact on European Classical Music

① FRANK A. SALAMONE

> You Americans take jazz too lightly.
> —Maurice Ravel

ROM THE LATE NINETEENTH CENTURY THROUGH THE 1930S, THERE WAS A cult of the primitive in Europe, exalting traditional art while reinterpreting that art in a European manner. Europe's love affair with all things African extended to African American creative arts as well. There was a long period between the origin of the glorification of the primitive and Africa, and the true coming of jazz to Europe. Picasso began to put into operation the lessons he learned from the exhibit of African art at the Musée de l'homme in Paris, as his *Demoiselles d'Avignon* (1907) and other Cubist masterpieces demonstrate. Stravinsky's *Rite of Spring* (1913) and *Les Noces* (1923) applied those lessons in evoking primitive Russia, and other composers followed.

The emergence of the Harlem Renaissance movement simply intensified that interest and found willing collaborators among many African American artists. Duke Ellington disliked the term "jungle music"; however, he not only lived with it, but he also fostered and profited from its use. He employed sounds that evoked images of the exotic and played at the Cotton Club, where dancers dressed in pseudo-African costumes for the pleasure of the white audience. Josephine Baker also played to the image of the primitive, wearing outrageous costumes, walking wild animals through Paris's streets. Both mocked the image while seemingly embracing it, making their bows to show business and transcending those demands at the same time.

④ ⑤
③ *The Journal of Popular Culture*, Vol. 38, No. 4, 2005
© 2005 Blackwell Publishing, 350 Main Street, Malden, MA 02148, USA, and PO Box 1354, 9600 Garsington Road, Oxford OX4 2DQ, UK

⑥ 732

SOURCE NAVIGATOR: An Article from a Database

1 The complete name of the author (beginning with the last name)
2 The title of the article (placed in quotation marks)
3 The title of the journal (underlined)
4 The number of the journal volume
5 The year of the issue
6 The printed article's original page numbers, as available
7 The name of the database (underlined) and database service (not underlined)
8 The name and location (city and state, if needed) of the library you used
9 The access date, when you used the source (from your printout or your notes)
10 The Internet address (URL, or Uniform Resource Locator) or your search path

Text Citation
①
(Rusciano)

Works Cited Entry
  ①   ②
Rusciano, Frank Louis. "James Baldwin: America's
    Native Son." Academic Exchange Quarterly ③
④⑤⑥ 7 (2003): 311-. Expanded Academic ASAP. InfoTrac. ⑦
    ⑧ Boston Public Lib., Boston, MA. 9 May 2005
    ⑩ <http://infotrac.galegroup.com>.   ⑨

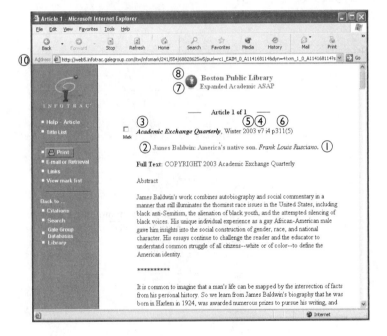

SOURCE NAVIGATOR: A Book

1 The complete name of the author (beginning with the last name)
2 The title of the book (underlined)
3 The name of the translator (beginning with the first name)
4 The place of publication
5 The name of the imprint used by the publisher
6 The shortened name of the publisher
7 The date of publication

Text Citation with Specific Location
①
(Allende 65)

Works Cited Entry
①   ②
Allende, Isabel. My Invented Country: A Memoir. Trans.
③ Margaret Sayers Peden. New York: Perennial-
    HarperCollins, 2003.   ④   ⑤
        ⑥   ⑦

② MY

INVENTED

COUNTRY

A Memoir

① Isabel Allende

Translated from the Spanish
③ by Margaret Sayers Peden

⑤ Perennial
⑥ *An Imprint of* HarperCollins*Publishers*

First published as *Mi País Inventado* in Spain in 2003 by Areté.

⑦ The first U.S. edition of this book was published in 2003 by
HarperCollins Publishers.

SOURCE NAVIGATOR: A Page from a Web Site

I The complete name of the author (beginning with the last name)
2 The title of the page (placed in quotation marks)
3 The name of the site (underlined)
4 The date of creation or last update
5 The name of the sponsoring organization
6 The access date, when you used the source (from your printout or your notes)
7 The Internet address (URL, or Uniform Resource Locator)

Text Citation
　①
(Laskin)

Works Cited Entry
　①　　　　　　　　②　　　　　　　　③
Laskin, David. "Tolstoy's War with Love." Masterpiece
④　　Theater. 2002. PBS Online. 3 May 2005 ⑤ ⑥
　　　<http://www.pbs.org/wgbh/masterpiece/anna/ ⑦
　　　ei_war.html>.

③

⑦

Tolstoy's War with Love ②
by David Laskin ①

Leo Tolstoy waited until he was 34 years old to marry, but once he had settled on 17-year-old Sofia Behrs, "Sonya," as his bride, he saw that events moved very quickly. At his insistence, but a single week elapsed between his proposal and their wedding on September 23, 1862 -- and in the course of that week Tolstoy asked, really required, his fiancée to read the intimate diaries he had kept for much of his life.

Copyright

④ This Web site was produced for PBS Online by WGBH.
Web site ©2002 WGBH Educational Foundation.

⑤ The Masterpiece Theatre and American Collection Web sites are produced by the WGBH Educational Foundation.

CITING SOURCES IN MLA STYLE

The core of an MLA citation is the author of the source. That person's last name links your use of the source in your paper with its full description in your list of works cited. The most common addition to this name is a specific location, such as a page number, identifying where the material appears in the original source. When you supply both in parentheses, do not add any punctuation: (Valero 231). This basic form applies whatever the type of source—article, book, or Web page.

On the other hand, how you decide to integrate that core name—and whether you need to accompany it with a page number—can vary with your purposes as a writer, the nature of the material you are crediting, and the type of source you have used. Whether you are jotting source reminders to yourself in your first draft or editing to correct your use of MLA style in your final draft, keep in mind these three questions:

- Who wrote it?
- What type of source is it?
- How are you capturing the source material?

Who Wrote It?

Naming the author of a source in your text is part of your ethical obligation as a researcher. As a writer, however, you can decide where and how to do so—whether to tuck that name away in parentheses or emphasize it in your discussion. In each instance, whatever the number of authors or other complications that arise in citing a source correctly, you will need to make this same decision as a writer so that you also cite the source effectively.

INDIVIDUAL AUTHOR NOT NAMED IN SENTENCE

Placing the author's last name in parentheses, right after the information from your source, can help keep readers focused on the sequence and content of your sentences.

One approach to the complex politics of Puerto Rican statehood is to return to the island's colonial history (Negrón-Mutaner 3).

INDIVIDUAL AUTHOR NAMED IN SENTENCE

Naming the author in your sentence, perhaps with pertinent credentials or experience, may allow you to capitalize on the persuasive value of the author's "expert" status.

Frances Negrón-Mutaner's analysis connects Puerto Rican history and politics with cultural influences, including the physical features of well-known entertainers (xvii).

TWO OR THREE AUTHORS

Include each author's last name either in your sentence or in parentheses.

As magazines and newspapers multiplied in eighteenth-century Europe, these publications supplied new knowledge while popularizing old folk traditions (Davies and de Blécourt 6).

FOUR OR MORE AUTHORS

Name all the authors, or follow the name of the first author with the abbreviation "et al." (Latin for "and others"). Identify the source the same way in your list of works cited.

Between 1870 and 1900, the nation's cities grew at an astonishing rate (Roark et al. 422).

ORGANIZATION AUTHOR

If a source is sponsored by a corporation, professional society, or other group, name the sponsor as the author if no one else is specified.

Each year, the Kids Count program (Annie E. Casey Foundation) alerts children's advocates about the status of children in their state.

AUTHOR OF AN ESSAY FROM A READER OR COLLECTION

Cite the author of the essay, not the editor of the collection in which it appears. For example, suppose you consulted Amy Tan's essay "Mother Tongue," which appeared in a collection edited by Wendy Martin. You'd cite Tan as the author, not Martin, and also begin your Works Cited entry with her name (see p. 156).

Amy Tan explains the "Englishes" of her childhood and family (32).

UNIDENTIFIED AUTHOR

For a source with an unknown author, supply the complete title in your sentence or the first main word or two of the title in parentheses.

According to a recent study, drivers are 42% more likely to get into an accident if they are using a wireless phone while driving ("Driving Dangerously" 32).

SAME AUTHOR WITH MULTIPLE WORKS

If you are citing several of an author's works, the author's name alone won't identify which one you mean. To ensure clarity, add the title, or identify it with a few key words. For example, you would cite two books by Ann Charters, *Major Writers of Short Fiction* and *The Story and Its Writer,* as follows.

One observer notes the flood of magazine fiction which carries with it "stories of real distinction" (Charters, Major Writers 1408). In fact, Charters believes that "the range and quality of the writer's mind are the only limitations on a story's shape" (Story 3).

DIFFERENT AUTHORS OF MULTIPLE WORKS

If you cite more than one source in parentheses, separate the works with a semicolon. To keep your paper easy to read, favor shorter, separate references, not long strings of sources.

Ray Charles and Quincy Jones worked together professionally for many years and maintained a strong friendship throughout Charles's life (Lydon 386; Jones 58–59).

What Type of Source Is It?

Because naming the author is the core of your citation, the basic form applies to any type of source. Even so, a few types of sources may present complications. (For examples showing how to cite quotations from literary sources, see pp. 148–50.)

A MULTIVOLUME WORK

After the author's name, add the volume number, a colon, and then the specific page.

Malthus has long been credited with this conservative shift in population theory (Durant and Durant 11: 400–03).

INDIRECT SOURCE

If possible, locate and cite the original source. If you do not have access to that source, add "qtd. in" to indicate that the material was "quoted in" the secondary source you cite.

Zill says that, psychologically, children in stepfamilies, even those living in a two-parent household, most resemble children in single-parent families (qtd. in Derber 119).

VISUAL MATERIAL

Many visuals, like other copyrighted materials, cannot be reproduced without the permission of the copyright holder. (Web sites often state their policies and supply contact information on the site.) Ask your instructor for advice whenever you are uncertain about how to handle such material or about whether the "fair use" provision of the copyright law applies, allowing use of a small amount of copyrighted material for purposes such as research.

Whenever you include a visual in your paper, help your reader connect it to your text. In your discussion, identify the artist or the art work, and refer to its figure number.

Eastman Johnson's painting Life in the South is a sentimental depiction of American blacks after the Civil War (see fig. 1).

Below the visual, supply a figure number and title, including the source.

Fig. 1. Eastman Johnson, Life in the South, 1870, High Museum of Art, Atlanta.

How Are You Capturing the Source Material?

The way you have captured source material—whether in your own words or in a short or long quotation—also affects how you present and credit it. Always identify any words taken directly from a source by setting them off with quotation marks or using the indented form for a long "block" quotation. (See p. 110 for a general checklist for quotations.)

When you quote, do so exactly. If the material, quoted or not, comes from a specific place in your source, add a page number or other location, such as a paragraph or screen number from an electronic source or a chapter or line from a literary work (see pp. 149–50). No page number is needed if the material is general (such as an overall theme or concept), the source has only one page, or the source—such as a Web site, film, recording, or performance—lacks page numbers.

OVERALL SUMMARY OR IMPORTANT IDEA

Terrill's recent study Malcolm X: Inventing Radical Judgment takes a fresh look at the rhetorical power and strategies of Malcolm X's speeches.

SPECIFIC SUMMARY OR PARAPHRASE

One analysis of Malcolm X's 1964 speech "The Ballot or the Bullet" concludes that it exhorts listeners to a specific form of radical action — changing vantage point as the foundation for a new unity (Terrill 129-31).

Should you paraphrase from a one-page article, no page number is needed because it will be supplied in your list of works cited.

Vacuum-tube audio equipment is making a comeback, with aficionados praising the warmth and glow from the tubes, as well as the sound (Patton).

BLENDED PARAPHRASE AND QUOTATION

When your words are blended with those of your source, clearly distinguish the two. Use quotation marks to set apart the words of your source and supply the page number in the original.

Some less than perfect means have been used to measure television viewing habits, including a sensor that scans rooms for "hot bodies" (Larson 69).

BRIEF QUOTATION WITH FORMAL LAUNCH STATEMENT

Arthur Frank opens his essay with a powerful claim: "Suffering has always animated life writing" (174).

BRIEF QUOTATION INTEGRATED IN SENTENCE

Pain, illness, and disability all contribute to the heartache that "has always animated life writing" (Frank 174).

"Suffering," according to Arthur Frank, "has always animated life writing" (174).

In "Moral Non-fiction: Life Writing and Children's Disability," Frank maintains, "Suffering has always animated life writing" (174).

LONG QUOTATION

When a quotation is longer than four typed lines, indent the entire quotation one inch, or ten spaces. Double-space it, but don't place quotation marks around it. If the quotation is one paragraph or less, begin its first line without any extra paragraph indentation. Use ellipsis marks (. . .) to show where you omit anything from the middle of the quotation. Place your citation in parentheses after the punctuation that ends the quotation. (See also the checklist on p. 135.)

> Cynthia Griffin Wolff comments on Emily Dickinson's incisive use of language:
>
> Language, of course, was a far subtler weapon than a hammer. Dickinson's verbal maneuvers would increasingly reveal immense skill in avoiding a frontal attack; she preferred the silent knife of irony to the strident battering of loud complaint. She had never suffered fools gladly. . . . Scarcely submissive, she had acquired the cool calculation of an assassin. (170-71)

QUOTATION FROM THE BIBLE

Instead of the page number, note the version, book, and chapter and verse numbers.

> Once again, the author alludes to the same passage: "What He has seen and heard, of that He testifies" (New American Bible, John 3.32).

QUOTATION FROM A NOVEL OR SHORT STORY

Give the page number from your own copy first. If possible, include further location information, such as the section or chapter where the passage can be found in any edition.

> In A Tale of Two Cities, Dickens describes the aptly named Stryver as "shouldering himself (morally and physically) into companies and conversations" (110; bk. 2, ch. 4).

QUOTATION FROM A PLAY

For a verse play, list the act, scene, and line numbers, separated by periods.

> "Love," Iago says, "is merely a lust of the blood and a permission of the will" (Oth. 1.3.326).

QUOTATION FROM A POEM

When quoting poetry, add a slash mark to show where each new line begins. Use the word "line" or "lines" in the first reference but only numbers in subsequent references, as in the following examples from William Wordsworth's "The World Is Too Much with Us." The first reference:

"The world is too much with us; late and soon / Getting and spending, we lay waste our powers" (lines 1-2).

The subsequent reference:

"Or hear old Triton blow his wreathed horn" (14).

If a poem has multiple parts, include the part and line numbers, separated by a period. Do not include the word "line."

In "Ode: Intimations of Immortality," Wordsworth ponders the truths of human existence, "Which we are toiling all our lives to find, / In darkness lost, the darkness of the grave" (8.116-17).

WRITING CHECKLIST

Citing Sources in MLA Style

☐ Have you double-checked to be sure that you have acknowledged all material from a source?

☐ Have you placed your citation right after your quotation, paraphrase, summary, or other reference to the source?

☐ Have you identified the author of each source in your text or in parentheses?

☐ Have you used the first few words of the title to cite a work without an identified author?

☐ Have you noted a page number or other specific location whenever needed?

☐ Have you added any necessary extras, whether volume numbers or poetry lines?

☐ Have you checked your final draft to be sure that every source cited in your text also appears in your list of works cited?

LISTING SOURCES IN MLA STYLE

In MLA style, your paper concludes with a list of the sources from which you have cited material. Center the title "Works Cited" at the top of a new page, and double-space the entire list. Arrange the entries alphabetically by author's last name or, for works with no author, by title. Begin the first line at the left margin; indent any following lines one-half inch. (Use the menu in your software—Format-Paragraph-Indentation—to set up this special "hanging" indentation.) Include only the sources that you cite in your paper unless your instructor has requested a format such as Works Consulted (including every source you read) or an annotated bibliography (describing each source; see pp. 302–08).

Use the MLA Source Navigators (pp. 136–43) to help you get started. They illustrate how to find the necessary information in four types of sources and how to prepare the corresponding text citation and works-cited entry for each source. Refer also to the Works Cited in the sample student paper (p. 173) so that you can see how your final product should look. To a great extent, listing sources correctly depends on following patterns and paying attention to details such as capitalization and punctuation. For example, the basic MLA pattern places a period after each of an entry's three main parts: (1) author, (2) title, and (3) publication details. In addition, MLA style favors simplifying details in the following ways:

- Abbreviate months, state names, and terms common in scholarly writing.
- List only the first of several cities where a publisher has offices.
- List only the first name (without initials) of a publishing company.
- Drop "Inc.," "Co.," and "Press" from the company name, and abbreviate "University Press" as "UP".
- Use the most recent copyright date for a book, and abbreviate the month of publication for a periodical or Web site.

As you prepare your own entries, begin with the author: first things first. The various author formats apply no matter what your source—article, book, Web page, or other material. Then select the format for the rest of the entry depending on the type of work you have used. Find that type in this section, and match your entry to the example, supplying the same information in the same order with the same punctuation and other features. If you can't find an example that exactly matches your source, consult the *MLA Handbook* itself, ask your instructor for advice, or model your entry on the form that seems the closest match. As you work on your list, keep in mind these two key questions, which are used to organize the sample entries that follow:

Who wrote it?

What type of source is it?

Who Wrote It?

INDIVIDUAL AUTHOR

Hazzard, Shirley. The Great Fire. New York: Farrar, 2003.

TWO OR THREE AUTHORS

Name the authors in the order in which they are listed on the title page.

Phelan, James R., and Lewis Chester. The Money: The Battle for Howard Hughes's Billions. New York: Random, 1997.

FOUR OR MORE AUTHORS

Name all the authors, or follow the name of the first author with the abbreviation "et al." (Latin for "and others"). Identify the source in the same way you cite it in the text.

Roark, James L., et al. The American Promise. Boston: Bedford, 1998.

SAME AUTHOR WITH MULTIPLE WORKS

Arrange the author's works alphabetically by title. Use the author's name for the first entry only; for the other entries, replace the name with three hyphens.

Gould, Stephen Jay. Full House: The Spread of Excellence from Plato to Darwin. New York: Harmony, 1996.

---. Triumph and Tragedy in Mudville: A Lifelong Passion for Baseball. New York: Norton, 2003.

ORGANIZATION AUTHOR

Name the organization as author, omitting any initial article ("a," "an," or "the"). (The name may reappear as the publisher.)

Student Conservation Association. *The Guide to Graduate Environmental Programs.*
    Washington: Island, 1997.

AUTHOR AND EDITOR

If your paper focuses on the work or its author, cite the author first.

Marx, Karl, and Frederick Engels. The Communist Manifesto. 1848. Ed. John E.
    Toews. Boston: Bedford, 1999.

If your paper focuses on the editor or the edition used, cite the editor first.

Toews, John E., ed. The Communist Manifesto. By Karl Marx and Frederick Engels.
    1848. Boston: Bedford, 1999.

AUTHOR AND TRANSLATOR

Hoeg, Peter. Tales of the Night. Trans. Barbara Haveland. New York: Farrar, 1998.

If your paper focuses on the translation, cite the translator first.

Haveland, Barbara, trans. Tales of the Night. By Peter Hoeg. New York: Farrar,
    1998.

UNIDENTIFIED AUTHOR

"Showtime at Amazon." Newsweek 29 Nov. 2004. 17 Feb. 2005 <http://
    www.msnbc.com/id/6539282/site/newsweek>.

What Type of Source Is It?

Once you have found the format that fits the author, look for the type of
source and the specific entry that best matches yours. Mix and match the
patterns illustrated as needed. For example, a two-volume printed book
in its second edition might send you to several examples until you have
covered all of its identifying elements.

Printed or Electronic Book

PRINTED BOOK

Volkan, Vamik. Blind Trust: Large Groups and Their Leaders in Times of Crisis and
    Terror. Charlottesville, VA: Pitchstone, 2004.

ONLINE BOOK

For an online book, supply what you would for a printed book. Then add the name of the site, the electronic publication date, your access date, and the URL.

Wharton, Edith. The Age of Innocence. New York: Appleton, 1920. Bartleby.com:
    Great Books Online. 2000. 8 May 2004 <http://www.bartleby.com/1005/>.

MULTIVOLUME WORK

To cite the full work, include the number of volumes ("vols.") after the title.

Who Built America? Working People and the Nation's Economy, Politics, Culture,
    and Society. 2 vols. New York: Worth, 2000.

To cite only one volume, give its number after the title. If you wish, you then can add the total number of volumes after the date.

Who Built America? Working People and the Nation's Economy, Politics, Culture,
    and Society. Vol. 1. New York: Worth, 2000. 2 vols.

REVISED EDITION

Volti, Rudi. Society and Technological Change. 4th ed. New York: Worth, 2001.

BOOK PUBLISHED IN A SERIES

After the title, add the series name as it appears on the title page, followed by any series number.

Berlin, Jeffrey B., ed. Approaches to Teaching Mann's Death in Venice and Other
    Short Fiction. Approaches to Teaching World Lit. 43. New York: MLA, 1992.

BOOK WITH CO-PUBLISHERS

If a book has more than one publisher, list this information in the order given on the title page, separated by a semicolon. (If the publisher uses an imprint name for a line of books, simply identify both, with the imprint first: AltaMira-Rowman.)

Hiatt, Alfred. The Making of Medieval Forgeries: False Documents in Fifteenth
    Century England. London: British Library; Toronto: U of Toronto P, 2004.

BOOK WITHOUT PUBLISHER, DATE, OR PAGE NUMBERS

When this information is not indicated, provide as much as you can. Use brackets to identify anything that does not come from the source itself. Use "c." (meaning "around" from the Latin *circa*) to indicate an approximate date: c. 1995; show uncertainty about the estimate with a question mark. If the date is unknown, use "n.d." (no date).

Plath, Sylvia. Winter Trees. New York: Harper, [1972?].

If the publisher's name or location is not found in the book, use "n.p." (no publisher or no place), or simply omit the publisher's name if the work is pre-1900: New York, 1882. If pages are not numbered, use "n. pag." (no pagination) which will clarify why you have omitted page references.

Rosholt, Malcolm. Days of the Ching Pao: A Photographic Record of the Flying Tigers-14th Air Force in China in World War II. N.p.: n.p., 1978.

Part of a Printed or Electronic Book

When citing part of a book, give the author of that part first. Add the editor of the book after its title and the page numbers of the selection after the publication information.

SELECTION FROM A PRINTED BOOK

Burke, Kenneth. "A Grammar of Motives." The Rhetorical Tradition: Readings from Classical Times to the Present. Ed. Patricia Bizzell and Bruce Herzberg. Boston: Bedford, 2001. 1298–324.

SELECTION FROM AN ONLINE BOOK

Webster, Augusta. "Not Love." A Book of Rhyme. London, 1881. Victorian Women Writers Project. Ed. Perry Willett. Apr. 2003. Indiana U. 28 Jan. 2005 <http://www.indiana.edu/~letrs/vwwp/webster/bookrime.html#p11>.

PREFACE, INTRODUCTION, FOREWORD, OR AFTERWORD

Godwin, Mike. Foreword. High Noon on the Electronic Frontier. Ed. Peter Ludlow. Cambridge: MIT P, 1996. xiii–xvi.

ESSAY, SHORT STORY, OR POEM FROM AN EDITED COLLECTION

Rothman, Rodney. "My Fake Job." The Best American Nonrequired Reading. Ed.
Dave Eggers. Boston: Houghton, 2002. 117–32.

TWO OR MORE WORKS FROM THE SAME EDITED COLLECTION

If you list more than one selection from an anthology, you can prepare an entry for the collection (instead of repeating it for each selection). Then you can simply refer to it from the entries for the separate readings.

Cisneros, Sandra. "Only Daughter." Martin 10–13.

Martin, Wendy, ed. The Beacon Book of Essays by Contemporary American Women.
Boston: Beacon, 1996.

Tan, Amy. "Mother Tongue." Martin 32–37.

ARTICLE FROM A PRINTED REFERENCE WORK

It is not necessary to supply the editor, publisher, or place of publication for well-known references such as *Webster's, The Random House Dictionary, World Book Encyclopedia,* and *Encyclopaedia Britannica.* No volume and page numbers are needed when a reference book is organized alphabetically. If an article's author is identified by initials, check for the book's list of contributors, which should supply the full name.

Binder, Raymond C., et al. "Mathematical Aspects of Physical Theories." The New
Encyclopaedia Britannica: Macropaedia. 15th ed. 1993.

Turner, V. W. "Divination." A Dictionary of the Social Sciences. Ed. Julius Gould
and William L. Kolb. New York: Free, 1964.

ARTICLE FROM AN ONLINE REFERENCE WORK

"Harlem Renaissance." Britannica Concise Encyclopedia. 2005. Encyclopaedia
Britannica. 23 June 2005 <http://concise.britannica.com/ebc/
article?tocId=9366619>.

Article in a Printed or Electronic Periodical

ARTICLE FROM A JOURNAL PAGINATED BY VOLUME

For an article from a journal in which page numbers run continuously through all issues of a volume, give only the volume number, year, and page numbers.

Daly, Mary E. "Recent Writing on Modern Irish History: The Interaction between
Past and Present." Journal of Modern History 69 (1997): 512–33.

ARTICLE FROM A JOURNAL PAGINATED BY ISSUE

For an article from a journal that starts each issue with page 1, provide
the issue number as well as the volume number, separated by a period.

Ferris, Lucy. " 'Never Truly Members': Andre Dubus's Patriarchal Catholicism."
South Atlantic Review 62.2 (1997): 39–55.

ARTICLE FROM AN ONLINE JOURNAL

Supply the same information that you would for a print article; end with
your access date and the URL. If you are citing an abstract, add
"Abstract" before the access date.

Eagleton, Mary B. "Making Text Come to Life on the Computer: Toward an
Understanding of Hypermedia Literacy." Reading Online 6.1 (2002). 25 Feb.
2005 <http://www.readingonline.org/articles/
art_index.asp?HREF=eagleton2/index.html>.

ARTICLE ACCESSED THROUGH AN ONLINE LIBRARY OR SUBSCRIPTION SERVICE

If you find a source through a library subscription service, include the library name and location.

Sataline, Suzanne. "Charter Schools Could Hit Ceiling." Boston Globe 31 Mar.
2004: B1. NewsBank. Boston Public Lib., Boston, MA. 5 May 2004 <http://
infoweb.newsbank.com>.

If you search a subscription service with keywords or topic choices, note
the keyword or path that you followed.

"Echocardiography." Merriam-Webster Medical Dictionary. 13 Oct. 1995. America
Online. 8 June 2004. Keyword: Medical Dictionary.

ARTICLE FROM A PRINTED MAGAZINE

Give the month and year of the issue, or its specific date, after the title
of the magazine.

Rushin, Steve. "Don't Mess with the Ballpoint Pen." Sports Illustrated 15 Mar.
        2004: 15.

If the article's pages are not consecutive, add a + after its initial page.

Hooper, Joseph. "The New Diet Danger." Self July 2003: 128+.

ARTICLE FROM AN ONLINE MAGAZINE

Douthat, Ross. "The Truth about Harvard." Atlantic Online Mar. 2005. 25 Feb.
        2005 <http://www.theatlantic.com/doc/prem/200503/douthat>.

ARTICLE FROM A PRINTED NEWSPAPER

If the newspaper has different editions, indicate the one where the article can be found.

Kolata, Gina. "Men and Women Use Brain Differently, Study Discovers." New York
        Times 16 Feb. 1995, natl. ed.: A1+.

"Plague Researcher Gets Two Years in Fraud Case." Boston Globe 11 Mar. 2004: A2.

ARTICLE FROM AN ONLINE NEWSPAPER

Austen, Ian. "Internet: It's the New TV." New York Times on the Web 24 Feb.
        2005. 25 Feb. 2005 <http://www.nytimes.com/2005/02/24/technology/
        circuits/24data.html>.

EDITORIAL FROM A PRINTED PERIODICAL

Jacoby, Jeff. "When Jerusalem Was Divided." Editorial. Boston Globe 8 Jan.
        2001: A11.

"Taking the Initiatives." Editorial. Nation 13 Nov. 2000: 3–4.

EDITORIAL FROM AN ONLINE PERIODICAL

"Two Messages on Education." Editorial. Washingtonpost.com 25 Feb. 2005. 28
        Feb. 2005 <http://www.washingtonpost.com/wp-dyn/articles/
        A51785-2005Feb24.html>.

LETTER TO THE EDITOR

Cohen, Irving M. Letter. Atlantic Monthly Mar. 2004: 14.

REVIEW

Include the words "Rev. of " before the title of the work reviewed.

Passaro, Vince. "The Unsparing Vision of Don DeLillo." Rev. of Underworld, by

   Don DeLillo. Harper's Nov. 1997: 72–75.

Other Printed or Electronic Document

PRINTED GOVERNMENT DOCUMENT

Generally, the "author" will be the name of the government and the government agency, separated by periods. If the document names an author or editor, that name may be provided either before the title or after it, if you identify the agency as author.

United States. Bureau of the Census. Statistical Abstract of the United States.

   123rd ed. Washington: GPO, 2003.

ONLINE GOVERNMENT DOCUMENT

United States. National Institute of Child Health and Human Development.

   National Institutes of Health. Milk Matters for Your Child's Health! 1999. 2

   Oct. 2003 <http://www.nichd.nih.gov/milk/brochure0105/index.htm>.

ONLINE DOCUMENT

First identify the document; then supply the details about its electronic location.

Carter, Jimmy. "Inaugural Address of Jimmy Carter." 20 Jan. 1977. The Avalon

   Project. 1997. Yale Law School. 14 Feb. 2005 <http://www.yale.edu/lawweb/

   avalon/presiden/inaug/carter.htm>.

PAMPHLET

Metropolitan Life Insurance Company. Metlife Dental. New York: Metropolitan Life

   Insurance, 1996.

DOCTORAL DISSERTATION OR MASTER'S THESIS

If the study is unpublished, place the title in quotation marks; if published, underline the title. Follow the title with "Diss." (for a dissertation) or with an apt master's abbreviation (such as "MA thesis").

Beilke, Debra J. "Cracking Up the South: Humor and Identity in Southern
    Renaissance Fiction." Diss. U of Wisconsin, Madison, 1997.

Internet or Electronic Source

Your list of sources should both identify what you have used and assist
a reader who wishes to find the same material, but the second objective
can be difficult to achieve with Internet materials. Some sources, such
as Web sites, exist only in electronic form and may disappear or change
at random. New electronic forms (such as blogs) can rapidly develop.
Despite such complications, supply the available information that would
assist a reader in accessing material online. (See pp. 142–43 for Source
Navigators showing basic MLA entries for electronic sources. See also
the directory on pp. 132–34 for entries for other electronic sources, including books and periodical articles.)

PERSONAL WEB PAGE

If no title is available, include an identification such as "Home page."

Tannen, Deborah. Home page. 20 June 2005. <http://www.georgetown.edu/
    faculty/tannend/>.

ORGANIZATION WEB PAGE

"Research & Statistics." American Library Association. 2005. 19 June 2005
    <http://www.ala.org/alaorg/ors/>.

HOME PAGE FOR A CAMPUS DEPARTMENT OR COURSE

Sociology. Dept. home page. U of California Los Angeles. 8 Oct. 2003 <http://
    www.sscnet.ucla.edu/soc/>.

DOCUMENT ON A WEB SITE WITH A SEARCH PAGE

If the URL you are citing is long, direct your reader to the site's search
page, especially when that page is a simple, standard access route.

URL for article:

<http://links.jstor.org/sici?sici=0002-9831%28199909%2971%3A3%3C529
    %3ANRPAPI%3E2.0.CO%3B2-B>

URL for site's search page:

<http://www.jstor.org/search>

Glass, Loren. "Nobody's Renown: Plagiarism and Publicity in the Career of Jack
    London." American Literature 71 (1999): 529–49. JSTOR. 7 Feb. 2005
    <http://www.jstor.org/search>.

If a site does not have usable URLs for each page or a search page, list
the address of the home page and the path you followed.

Path: Archives; By Author; A-C.

PUBLICATION ON CD-ROM

Sheehy, Donald, ed. Robert Frost: Poems, Life, Legacy. CD-ROM. New York: Holt,
    1997.

COMPUTER SOFTWARE

Electronic Supplements for Real Writing: 1. Interactive Writing Software.
    Diskette. Vers. 1. Boston: Bedford, 2004.

Visual or Audio Source

ADVERTISEMENT

A. G. Edwards. Advertisement. Scientific American Mar. 2004: 17.

COMIC OR CARTOON

Supply the cartoonist's name and identification as a comic strip or cartoon.

McDonnell, Patrick. "Mutts." Comic strip. Atlanta Journal Constitution 2 Feb.
    2005: F5.

PHOTOGRAPH

Supply the place (museum or gallery and city) where the photograph is
housed. If you are citing it from a publication, identify that source.

Stieglitz, Alfred. Self-Portrait. J. Paul Getty Museum, Los Angeles. Stieglitz: A
    Beginning Light. By Katherine Hoffman. New Haven: Yale UP, 2004, 251.

Strand, Paul. Fifth Avenue, New York. Museum of Modern Art, New York.

For a family or personal photograph, identify who took the photograph and when.

Bay Street Food Pantry. Personal photograph by author. 6 Nov. 2005.

WORK OF ART

Botticelli, Sandro. The Birth of Venus. Uffizi Gallery, Florence.

MAP

Supply identification as a chart or map.

The Road Atlas Deluxe: United States, Canada & Mexico. Map. Skokie, IL: Rand,
   2003.

AUDIOTAPE OR RECORDING

Begin with the name of the artist, composer, speaker, writer, or other contributor, based on your interest in the recording. If it is not on a CD, note the format before you identify the label.

Byrne, Gabriel. The James Joyce Collection. Dove Audio, 1996.

PIECE OF MUSIC

If the date of composition is significant, you may add it following the title.

Mozart, Wolfgang Amadeus. The Marriage of Figaro. Mineola, NY: Dover, 2001.

PROGRAM ON TELEVISION OR RADIO

"A Dangerous Man: Lawrence after Arabia." Great Performances. Perf. Ralph
   Fiennes and Siddig el Fadil. PBS. WNET, New York. 6 May 1992.

The Six Wives of Henry VIII. PBS. WGBH, Boston. 6 Mar. 2003.

FILM

Start with the title unless you wish to emphasize the work of a person connected with the film.

Lord of the Rings: The Return of the King. Dir. Peter Jackson. New Line Cinema,
2003.

Jackson, Peter, dir. Lord of the Rings: The Return of the King. New Line Cinema,
2003.

PERFORMANCE

Whale Music. By Anthony Minghella. Dir. Anthony Minghella. Perf. Francie Swift.
Theater Off Park, New York. 23 Mar. 1998.

Conversation or Field Artifact

PERSONAL, TELEPHONE, OR E-MAIL INTERVIEW

Indicate how you conducted the interview: in person, by telephone, or
by e-mail.

Boyd, Dierdre. Personal interview. 5 Feb. 2005.

BROADCAST INTERVIEW

Identify the source by the person interviewed; if you wish, you may also
identify the interviewer (Interview with X).

Bernstein, Richard. Interview. Fresh Air. Natl. Public Radio. WBUR, Boston. 3 Apr.
2001.

PUBLISHED INTERVIEW

Kerry, John. Interview. Newsweek 8 Mar. 2004: 26.

SPEECH OR LECTURE

Wexel, Beth. Address. Fall Convocation. Craig Hall, Wilton College. 29 Aug. 2005.

PERSONAL LETTER

Finch, Katherine. Letter to the author. 15 Nov. 2005.

E-MAIL

Moore, Jack. E-mail to the author. 11 Nov. 2005.

ONLINE POSTING

Use the subject line as the title. Add the word "news" before a newsgroup's name.

Weiss, Phil. "News from Philadelphia Animation Society Meeting." Online
    posting. 16 Mar. 2004. 14 Apr. 2004. <news:rec.arts.anime.fandom>.

Add the name of an e-mail discussion group or forum (if known) after
the posting date. Supply the URL for the group's Web site or the moder-
ator's e-mail address.

Cubbison, Laurie. "Metaphor and Cliché." Online posting. 13 Apr. 2004. H-Rhetor.
    3 May 2004 <http://www.h-net.msu.edu/~rhetor/>.

WRITING CHECKLIST

Listing Sources in MLA Style

☐ Have you begun each entry with the appropriate pattern for the
author's name?

☐ Have you figured out what type of source you have used? Have
you followed the sample pattern for that type as exactly as
possible?

☐ Have you used quotation marks and underlining correctly for
titles?

☐ Have you used the conventional punctuation—periods, commas, colons, parentheses—in your entry?

☐ Have you accurately recorded the name of the author, title, publisher, and so on?

☐ Have you checked the accuracy of the numbers in your entry—
pages, volume, and dates?

☐ Have you correctly typed or pasted in the address of an electronic source (or supplied a simpler address for the source's
search page)?

☐ Have you arranged your entries in alphabetical order?

☐ Have you checked your final list against your text citations so
that every source appears in both places?

A SAMPLE RESEARCH PAPER IN MLA STYLE

In her paper "Is Inclusion the Answer?" Sarah E. Goers grapples with the complex topic of equal access to education for disabled students. By drawing from varied sources, Goers is able to show several sides of the issue while forming her own conclusions. As a result, her paper is more than just a compilation of facts or a string of quotations. Goers asks a question about a problem that troubles her, she provides evidence to support her answer, and she adds her own thoughts to the facts and ideas she has gleaned from her research.

Writer's last name and page number ½" from top

Writer's name, instructor's name, course, date

Title, centered

½" indent (or 5 spaces)

Opening definition of "inclusion," citing sources in parentheses

Thesis established

Brief overview of paper's development following thesis

Double-spacing throughout

Lecturer's name identifies public address

Sarah E. Goers

Professor Day

English 101

28 January 2004

Is Inclusion the Answer?

Inclusion is one of the most passionately debated issues in public education today. Full inclusion, defined as placing all students with disabilities in general education classes, has three main components: the integration of special education students into the mainstream classroom, educational planning and programming, and the clarification of responsibility for appropriate instruction (Heinich 292). Although the intent of inclusion is to provide the best care for all children by treating both special and general education students equally, some people in the field believe that the full inclusion of disabled children in mainstream classrooms may not be in the best interest of either type of student. Disabled children will not benefit from a general education program unless the school is prepared to accommodate their needs; if placed in a school where their needs are not met due to low funding, unprepared teachers, or a lack of necessary resources, they most likely will suffer. For these reasons, the merits of full inclusion over partial inclusion or separate programs are questionable.

Although individual children learn differently, students classified as "special needs" require significantly different types of instruction because of their physical, mental, or emotional state. The degree of differentiated instruction that they require, and how best to provide it, is the basis of the ongoing debate about inclusion. Initially, full inclusion sounds like a wonderful step toward implementing the democratic belief that all people in all environments are to be treated as equals. In her lecture at William Rainey Harper College, however, Barbara Radebaugh explained the positions of the two major national teacher organizations on this issue.

166

Goers 2

The American Federation of Teachers (AFT) disagrees with full
inclusion, believing that special needs students learn best in
separate programs where they can receive the specialized

Different views
contrasted

instruction their disabilities require. On the other hand, the
National Education Association (NEA) favors "appropriate
inclusion," a less extreme approach, in which each special needs
student would receive a combination of general and special
education throughout the school day (Radebaugh). In this way,
students would experience the general classroom while still
receiving some degree of specialized instruction.

While the teacher organizations debate the benefits of
inclusion in terms of how disabled students learn best, other
groups oppose inclusion because of how the changes might affect
them. At a typical school, if a disabled student were to be placed
in general education classrooms, the school would have to
undergo changes including teacher training and a larger staff,
both to assist the special needs child and to aid other students'
adjustment to an inclusive environment (Block 6-7). Some
opponents of inclusion include the parents of non-learning
disabled students who fear that these changes will result in less
attention for their own children and thus slow their academic
progress. Other opponents, such as local taxpayers, cite the cost

No page num-
ber needed for
one-page article

of these changes as reasons against inclusion (Rios).

In response to such arguments, protective laws have been
enacted to ensure disabled persons equal access to appropriate

Point from last
paragraph used
for transition
to new topic

public education, regardless of extra cost or others' fears. The
Education for All Handicapped Children Act of 1975 mandates that
schools must provide free public education to all students with

Source estab-
lishes historical
background

disabilities. The main tenets of the 1975 legislation declare that
all learners with handicaps between the ages of three and
twenty-one have the right to a free public education and an

individualized education program involving both the school and the parents. Also protecting the disabled is the Individuals with Disabilities Education Act (IDEA), which calls for serving children with disabilities in the least restrictive environment possible, and Section 504 of the Rehabilitation Act, which guarantees disabled people access to services provided by any institution that receives federal funding (Heinich 293).

Society has made great strides in protecting the rights of disabled students, and inclusion theoretically upholds their right to free and equal education. There is still concern about the actual implementation of inclusive practices, however. In California, for example, journalist Denise Rios explains a situation whereby, as more parents opt to place children with special needs in regular classrooms, "state and education officials are grappling with several issues that could affect the future of special education. At the top of their list is funding." According to Rios, financially strapped school districts use as much as 25% of their general funds to pay for federally mandated special education programs. Officials explain that this high percentage is a result of the federal government's not fulfilling its monetary promises, costing local districts in California about $600 million a year (Rios). Money must be taken from other scholastic areas to supplement the lack of funding designated for special education.

To help offset the expensive cost of integrating disabled students into the regular classroom, California officials contend that the federal government promised to fund 40% of program costs when federal mandates guaranteeing access for special education students were passed in 1975. However, government contribution has actually averaged only 7% or 8% of program costs (Rios). While money ideally should not be an issue when it comes to the well-being of students, the figures in a situation

Credentials of source author noted

Brief quotation specifies critical issue, followed by paraphrase of source

Facts and data support main point

Goers 4

such as this are troubling. Since special education may demand a large amount of the already tight funds that most districts are working with, schools may be forced to use a high percentage of these limited resources on a minority of students, rather than the entire school. Without proper financial support from the government, money unfortunately does become an issue when it threatens to undermine the well-being of the majority of students.

When inclusive practices are implemented, teachers as well as students are forced to undergo dramatic classroom changes. Teachers feel a great deal of pressure in this debate in that many believe that they are not adequately trained to teach students with disabilities effectively. They are concerned that special needs students will therefore not receive the instruction that they need to succeed, and these teachers may be frustrated by their inability to provide appropriate instruction (Block 7). Without significant help from special education teachers in the regular classroom, teachers fear that inclusion could result in disaster due to their frustrations, lack of appropriate training, and students' distraction levels. Linda Jacobson describes the dilemma of general education instruction: "Because special education teachers often float among classes, regular classroom teachers sometimes are left on their own." She also notes the AFT's criticism of inclusive practices when "teachers are promised resources and training to make inclusion work, but school systems often don't deliver."

Community College of Baltimore County professor Beth Hewett finds that while teachers receive information about a specific student's disability and how to offer fair classroom treatment, this information is usually only cursory. She eloquently echoes Jacobson's concerns through firsthand experience:

Our experiences with these students often are frustrating and unsatisfying because we do not know enough about

Paraphrase of original source, followed by source in parentheses

Only one citation needed for quotations from the same source that appear in sequence in a paragraph

Credentials of source author noted

1" indent (or 10 spaces)

*Direct quota-
tion longer
than four lines
set off from text
without quota-
tion marks, fol-
lowed by page
numbers in
parentheses*

how to help them. Recognizing our limited knowledge
and skills in helping students with disabilities to read
and write well, we often flounder and leave teaching
situations feeling that we have missed a key opportunity
to help a student address a particular challenge. Many of
us would welcome rescue through more practical
knowledge of the problems, better training to recognize
and deal with them, and access to technological tools
that address special needs. We sense that our students
would be equally grateful if we were better prepared. (1-
2)

> After observing the methods of teachers at the Landmark
Institute, a private postsecondary institution renowned for its work
with learning disabled students, Jacob Gaskins notes the
importance of putting students through a battery of diagnostic
testing and then teaching specifically to these diagnoses in a
variety of modalities. In an institution like Landmark, with a
student/faculty ratio of approximately 3 to 1, teachers are able to
tailor their instruction to give students personal attention. The
sheer number of teachers, all of whom have training specific to all
types of learning disabilities, along with access to, and training in
how to use, supplemental learning tools, enables them to meet the
wide range of needs and disabilities they encounter (73). Because
these resources are not often adequately provided in public
schools, however, many teachers wonder if inclusion is truly
beneficial for students who have disabilities that require
specialized instruction.

*Valuable in-
formation
paraphrased
after naming
author earlier
in paragraph
and noting
page number
of original
source in
parentheses*

> Some parents of disabled students and some disabled students
themselves also do not agree with full inclusion. Mary Maushard
explains in her article "Special Schools Fall Victim to 'Inclusion' "
that many disabled students prefer to learn in a special education

Goers 6

school because they like the small class sizes, the nurturing staff specifically trained to teach special needs students, the family atmosphere, and the many available specialized services. The parents of these students do not want to disrupt a system which their children are happy with and are afraid that their children will "fall through the cracks" in the general educational system. Unfortunately, many special education schools are being closed due to low enrollment, mainly because those parents who support inclusion have taken their disabled children out of special schools and placed them in regular education classes. Among parents who do favor inclusion, some nonetheless worry that the country is moving away from special education schools too fast for solid special education programs to be established in the general schools (Maushard).

Possible solution or compromise follows various sides of argument

As a solution, pull-out programs — in which disabled students are in the regular classroom for part of the day and special instruction classes for the remainder of the day — have been suggested. In this way, disabled students would have daily classroom instruction as well as one-on-one instruction. These programs offer a compromise to address the concerns of some educators that the individual needs of disabled students would be neglected when they are integrated into the general classroom

Ideas from source summarized and credited

(Block 7). However, while ensuring that at least part of the students' day will consist of instruction tailored to their needs, these programs do not ensure that the students' time in the general classroom will be productive. These programs are promising, but only to the extent that the students will also be receiving quality instruction in the general classroom; otherwise, they simply shorten

Electronic sources without page numbers cited only by author

the amount of unproductive classroom time. Thus, there is still a need for teacher training and adequate resources to help meet the needs of disabled students when they are not in the special education classes (Urbina).

Conclusion summarizes main points and restates thesis

Despite individual beliefs about which system is best, we can reasonably assume that the majority of society supports efforts to provide all children with the best possible care and education. When considering inclusion, it is necessary to look at the big picture by considering everyone involved. Unless the school is adequately prepared to provide proper services and meet students' individual needs, inclusion truly may not be the best solution for disabled students. If we want our children to be as successful as they possibly can be, each individual should be assessed and placed where he or she will learn most effectively, whether in a general classroom, a special education classroom, or a combination of both. While many people support inclusion because they feel that it is wrong to exclude anyone, they must also look at the potential problems inclusion may cause. Disabled students should receive proper respect for their needs without the intrusion of policy, funding, and what others, particularly those who are uninformed about the issue, decide they want.

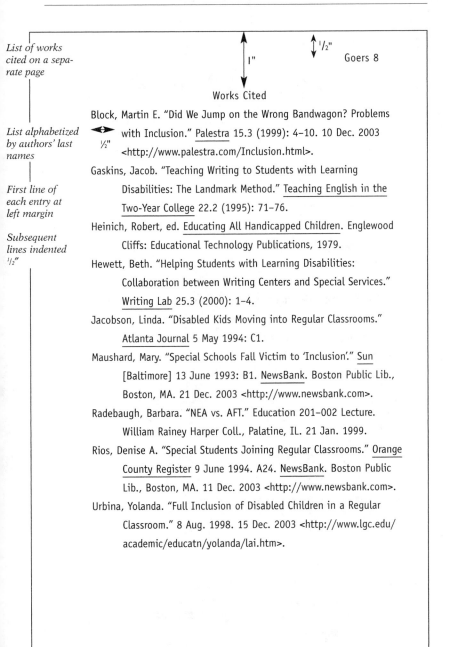

List of works cited on a separate page

1"   ↕ ½"   Goers 8

Works Cited

Block, Martin E. "Did We Jump on the Wrong Bandwagon? Problems

List alphabetized by authors' last names   ½"   with Inclusion." Palestra 15.3 (1999): 4–10. 10 Dec. 2003

<http://www.palestra.com/Inclusion.html>.

Gaskins, Jacob. "Teaching Writing to Students with Learning

First line of each entry at left margin   Disabilities: The Landmark Method." Teaching English in the

Two-Year College 22.2 (1995): 71–76.

Subsequent lines indented ½"   Heinich, Robert, ed. Educating All Handicapped Children. Englewood

Cliffs: Educational Technology Publications, 1979.

Hewett, Beth. "Helping Students with Learning Disabilities:

Collaboration between Writing Centers and Special Services."

Writing Lab 25.3 (2000): 1–4.

Jacobson, Linda. "Disabled Kids Moving into Regular Classrooms."

Atlanta Journal 5 May 1994: C1.

Maushard, Mary. "Special Schools Fall Victim to 'Inclusion'." Sun

[Baltimore] 13 June 1993: B1. NewsBank. Boston Public Lib.,

Boston, MA. 21 Dec. 2003 <http://www.newsbank.com>.

Radebaugh, Barbara. "NEA vs. AFT." Education 201–002 Lecture.

William Rainey Harper Coll., Palatine, IL. 21 Jan. 1999.

Rios, Denise A. "Special Students Joining Regular Classrooms." Orange

County Register 9 June 1994. A24. NewsBank. Boston Public

Lib., Boston, MA. 11 Dec. 2003 <http://www.newsbank.com>.

Urbina, Yolanda. "Full Inclusion of Disabled Children in a Regular

Classroom." 8 Aug. 1998. 15 Dec. 2003 <http://www.lgc.edu/

academic/educatn/yolanda/lai.htm>.

11

Using APA Style

This chapter briefly explains and illustrates how to use APA style, the format for preparing a research paper and crediting sources that is recommended by the American Psychological Association. This style may be expected in many of the social sciences, such as psychology, sociology, and education. Researchers in such fields are likely to be concerned about timely, up-to-date information from credible sources, so this style emphasizes author and date. For more detailed advice, turn to the *Publication Manual of the American Psychological Association* (5th ed.; Washington, DC: APA, 2001), usually available in your campus bookstore and library.

CITING AND LISTING SOURCES IN APA STYLE

CITING SOURCES IN APA STYLE

Visual or Audio Source
Audiotape or Recording, 201
Program on Television or Radio, 201
Film, 201

Conversation or Field Artifact
Personal Interview, 201
E-mail or Electronic Mailing List
Message, 201

UNDERSTANDING APA STYLE

As the next two sections of this chapter illustrate, APA style uses a two-part system to credit sources. First, you briefly identify the author and date of the source in your text, either by mentioning them in your discussion or by noting them in parentheses right after you refer to the information drawn from the source. APA also requires that you supply the page number or other location in the original source when you quote and recommends that you do so when you paraphrase or mention a key concept. Second, this brief identification leads, through the author's name, to a full description of the source in your concluding list, called "References." The four APA Source Navigators (pp. 180–87) illustrate how to find the details necessary to cite and list a source and how to present that information in APA form. See pages 174–76 for a directory listing the sample entries supplied here.

APA style also provides directions for preparing a consistent, easy-to-read paper. If you expect to use this style often, set up an APA template which you can call up as you begin each new paper. Otherwise use the Page Format options in your software's File menu or the Font and Paragraph options in the Format menu to make any changes needed in your draft. As you complete your paper, refer to the format of the sample APA paper on pages 203–12 and the following checklist.

WRITING CHECKLIST

Formatting a Paper in APA Style

- ☐ Have you selected a common academic typeface such as Times Roman or Courier in 12-point size?
- ☐ Have you double-spaced the entire paper, including all headings, tables, quotations, and entries in your reference list?
- ☐ Have you allowed margins of at least one inch on all four sides of the page?

☐ Have you prepared a title page? Have you supplied a running header, positioned at the far right side of the top of the title page and each subsequent page, using a short title followed by five spaces and then the page number? Have you also supplied a typed line identifying a full running header, as if for publication in a journal? (Begin this line with "Running head:" and then, in capital letters, add a brief title—fifty characters or fewer to preview your topic for a reader.) In mid page, have you centered your title, your name, and your institution (and, if expected, your course number, instructor's name, and date)? (See p. 203 for the title page of the sample APA paper.)

☐ Have you supplied on page 2 an abstract, beginning without any paragraph indentation and summarizing your paper in fewer than 120 words?

☐ Have you begun your text on page 3 with your title, centered?

☐ Have you indented the first line of every paragraph one-half inch (five, six, or seven spaces) from the left margin? Have you indented every line of any long quotation (forty words or more) the same amount, except for an additional one-half inch indentation if the passage has a second paragraph?

☐ Have you added headings to identify the sections of your paper? (The simplest format is to center the first-level headings and then italicize any second-level headings and place them at the left margin.)

☐ Have you used letters in a pair of parentheses—(a)—to introduce each item in a list within a sentence? Have you used numbers, indented like a paragraph and followed by a period—1.— to introduce each item in a list consisting of a series of paragraphs?

☐ Have you preceded any table with a numbered label—for example, Table 2—followed by its explanatory title (in italics) on the next line? Have you followed the table with an explanation if needed to clarify the table or your data analysis (beginning *Note.*) or to credit your source (beginning From . . .)?

☐ Have you followed any other visual, such as a graph, drawing, chart, or photograph, with a numbered heading in italics—for example, Figure 1.—directly followed by its explanatory title?

☐ Have you turned off your software's automatic hyphenation to avoid splitting words with hyphens at the ends of lines? Have you turned off text justification so that you have an even margin on the left but not on the right?

☐ Have you continued your page numbering but begun your list of sources on a new page, centering its heading—References—at the top of the page?

☐ Have you begun the first line of each References entry at the left margin but indented each additional line one-half inch? (To do this automatically, check your software for a "hanging" indentation option, possibly following the Format-Paragraph-Indentation-Special menu.)

☐ Have you added an appendix (or several) after your reference list for items such as your survey form?

☐ Have you followed any specific directions from your instructor about format or electronic submission?

☐ Have you printed a clear, readable final copy and kept a backup copy of your file in case the printed copy gets lost?

CITING SOURCES IN APA STYLE

The core of an APA citation is the author of the source. That person's last name links your use of the source in your paper with its full description in your list of references. Next comes the date of the source, which often establishes its currency or its classic status for readers. (Within a paragraph, you don't need to repeat this date if you refer to the source again unless a reader might mix up the sources under discussion.) A common addition is a specific location, such as a page number (using "p." for "page" or "pp." for "pages"), that tells where the material appears in the original source. Unless the source does not have page numbers or other locators, this information is required for quotations and recommended for paraphrases and key concepts. When you supply these elements in parentheses, separate them with commas: (Westin, 2005, p. 48). This basic form applies whatever the type of source—article, book, or Web page.

You may supply the citation information in your sentence, in parentheses, or some combination of the two. How you decide to integrate the core name, in particular, can vary with your purposes as a writer, the type of source you have used, and the nature of the material credited. As you check your APA style, keep in mind these three questions:

• Who wrote it?
• What type of source is it?
• How are you capturing the source material?

Who Wrote It?

Naming the author of a source in your text is part of your ethical obligation as a researcher. As a writer, however, you can decide in each instance whether to tuck that name away in parentheses or emphasize it in your discussion.

INDIVIDUAL AUTHOR NOT NAMED IN SENTENCE

Some experts feel that adolescent boys who bully are not merely aggressive but are depressed and acting out in an aggressive manner (Pollack, 2000).

INDIVIDUAL AUTHOR NAMED IN SENTENCE

Pollack (2000) contends that boys tend to contain their pain for fear of appearing vulnerable and inviting ridicule.

TWO AUTHORS

List the last names of coauthors in the order in which they appear in the source. Join the names with "and" if you mention them in your text and with an ampersand (&) if the citation is in parentheses.

A group's cultural development enhances its chance for survival, providing both physical and psychological protection (Anderson & Ross, 1998).

Anderson and Ross (1998) maintain that the development of a group's culture provides both physical and psychological protection.

THREE OR MORE AUTHORS

For three to five authors, include all the last names in your first reference. In any later references, identify only the first author and add "et al." (for "and others"), whether in the text or in parentheses. For six authors or more, simply use the name of the first author with "et al." for all citations.

The discipline of conservation biology has developed in response to the accelerating rate at which species are being lost (Purves, Orians, & Heller, 1999). Purves et al. specifically explore the consequences of human activities in relation to this acceleration.

ORGANIZATION AUTHOR

Important as nutrition is for healthy people, it is even more critical for cancer patients who may have specific dietary needs such as more protein (American Cancer Society, 2003, p. 7).

(text continues on p. 188)

SOURCE NAVIGATOR: An Article from a Periodical

1 The names of the coauthors (each beginning with the last name followed by the initials) in the order listed in the source
2 The date of the issue (placed in parentheses)
3 The title of the article (without any quotation marks or italics)
4 The title of the journal (italicized)
5 The number of the periodical volume (also italicized)
6 The article's complete page numbers

Text Citation with Specific Location
    ①   ②   ⑥
(Areni & Sparks, 2005, p. 508)

References Entry
    ①   ②   ③
Areni, C. S., & Sparks, J. R. (2005). Language power
    and persuasion. *Psychology & Marketing, 22,*
    507–525.   ④   ⑤
    ⑥

③ Language Power and Persuasion

Charles S. Areni
University of Sydney
①

John R. Sparks
University of Dayton

ABSTRACT

Powerless language involves the use of various linguistic markers (i.e., hedges, intensifiers, deictic phrases, overly polite language, tag questions, and verbal and nonverbal hesitations), which signify relatively low social status in a given communication context. Powerful language suggests higher social status and is characterized largely by the absence of these markers. The results of a laboratory experiment indicated that language power influenced attitudes toward a hypothetical new consumer electronics product, regardless of whether the communication was presented in print versus videotape. For both print and video modalities, speakers using powerful language were more persuasive than speakers using powerless language. However, powerless language had the additional effect of generating more thoughts about the speaker. These results are discussed in terms of the multiple roles postulate of the elaboration-likelihood mode. © 2005 Wiley Periodicals, Inc.

The idea that language reflects social power is a not a new one. Over three decades ago Lakoff (1975) explored language and gender, and proposed that certain patterns of speech constituted a "female register," which was associated with low social power. Subsequent research on language and social power examined how particular language markers convey the impression of speaker social power, and the subsequent effects

④   ⑤ ⑥   ②
Psychology & Marketing, Vol. 22(6): 507–525 (June 2005)
Published online in Wiley InterScience (www.interscience.wiley.com)
© 2005 Wiley Periodicals, Inc. DOI: 10.1002/mar.20071

SOURCE NAVIGATOR: An Article from a Database

1 The names of the coauthors (each beginning with the last name followed by the initials) in the order listed in the source
2 The date of the issue (placed in parentheses)
3 The title of the article (without quotation marks or italics)
4 The title of the journal (italicized)
5 The number of the journal volume (also italicized)
6 The printed article's original page numbers, as available
7 The access date, when you used the source (from your printout or your notes)
8 The name of the database (without quotation marks or italics)

Text Citation
　　　　　①　　②
(Blumberg & Sokol, 2004)

References Entry
　　①　　　　　　　　②　　　　　③
Blumberg, F. C., & Sokol, L. M. (2004). Boys' and girls' use of cognitive strategy when learning to play video games. *The Journal of General Psychology,*④ ⑤⑥*131*, 151–158. Retrieved May 6, 2005, from ⑦ Expanded Academic ASAP database.
　　　　　⑧

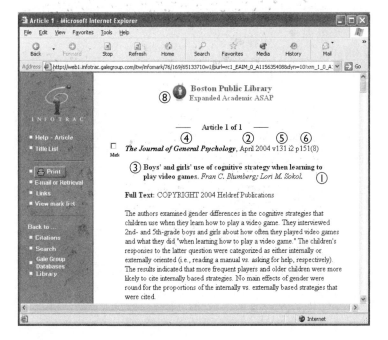

SOURCE NAVIGATOR: A Book

1 The author's last name, followed by first and middle initials
2 The date of publication (placed in parentheses)
3 The title of the book (italicized)
4 The place of publication, using the first city listed
5 The shortened name of the publisher

Text Citation
   ①   ②
(Whybrow, 2005)

References Entry
   ①   ②   ③
Whybrow, P.C. (2005). *American mania: When more is not enough*. New York: Norton.
           ④   ⑤

③ **American**
MANIA
When More Is Not Enough

① **Peter C. Whybrow**

⑤ W. W. NORTON & COMPANY
④ NEW YORK　LONDON

② Copyright © 2005 by Peter C. Whybrow, M.D.

All rights reserved
Printed in the United States of America
First Edition

For information about permission to reproduce selections from this book, write to
Permissions, W. W. Norton & Company, Inc., 500 Fifth Avenue, New York, NY 10110

Manufacturing by R. R. Donnelley, Harrisonburg
Book design by Lovedog Studio
Production manager: Amanda Morrison

LIBRARY OF CONGRESS CATALOGING-IN-PUBLICATION DATA

Whybrow, Peter C.

SOURCE NAVIGATOR: A Page from a Web Site

1 The author's last name, followed by first and middle initials
2 The date of creation or last update (placed in parentheses)
3 The title of the page (without quotation marks or italics)
4 The name of the site (italicized)
5 The access date, when you used the source (from your printout or your notes)
6 The Internet address (URL, or Uniform Resource Locator) without any concluding punctuation

---

Text Citation
  (1)   (2)
(Boeree, 1998)

References Entry
  (1)   (2)   (3)
Boeree, C. G. (1998). Anna Freud: 1895-1982.
  (4) *Personality Theories*. Retrieved May 3, 2005, from (5)
    http://www.ship.edu/~cgboeree/annafreud.html
        (6)

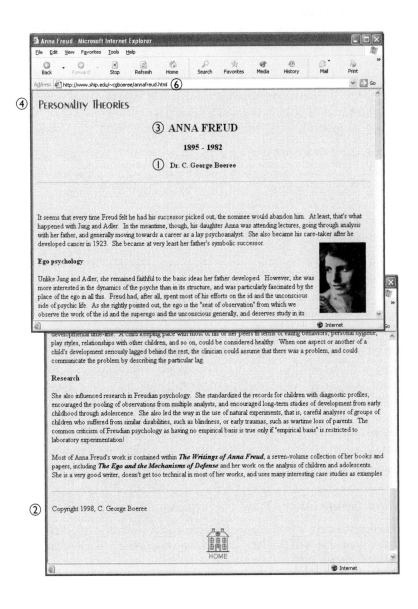

④ **PERSONALITY THEORIES**

③ ANNA FREUD

1895 - 1982

① Dr. C. George Boeree

It seems that every time Freud felt he had his successor picked out, the nominee would abandon him. At least, that's what happened with Jung and Adler. In the meantime, though, his daughter Anna was attending lectures, going through analysis with her father, and generally moving towards a career as a lay psychoanalyst. She also became his care-taker after he developed cancer in 1923. She became at very least her father's symbolic successor.

Ego psychology

Unlike Jung and Adler, she remained faithful to the basic ideas her father developed. However, she was more interested in the dynamics of the psyche than in its structure, and was particularly fascinated by the place of the ego in all this. Freud had, after all, spent most of his efforts on the id and the unconscious side of psychic life. As she rightly pointed out, the ego is the "seat of observation" from which we observe the work of the id and the superego and the unconscious generally, and deserves study in its

developmental time-line. A child keeping pace with most of his or her peers in terms of eating behaviors, personal hygiene, play styles, relationships with other children, and so on, could be considered healthy. When one aspect or another of a child's development seriously lagged behind the rest, the clinician could assume that there was a problem, and could communicate the problem by describing the particular lag.

Research

She also influenced research in Freudian psychology. She standardized the records for children with diagnostic profiles, encouraged the pooling of observations from multiple analysts, and encouraged long-term studies of development from early childhood through adolescence. She also led the way in the use of natural experiments, that is, careful analyses of groups of children who suffered from similar disabilities, such as blindness, or early traumas, such as wartime loss of parents. The common criticism of Freudian psychology as having no empirical basis is true only if "empirical basis" is restricted to laboratory experimentation!

Most of Anna Freud's work is contained within *The Writings of Anna Freud*, a seven-volume collection of her books and papers, including *The Ego and the Mechanisms of Defense* and her work on the analysis of children and adolescents. She is a very good writer, doesn't get too technical in most of her works, and uses many interesting case studies as examples.

② Copyright 1998, C. George Boeree

HOME

AUTHOR OF AN ESSAY FROM A READER OR COLLECTION

Cite the author of the essay; the editor of the collection is identified later in your reference list (see p. 196).

Although rapes occur each year in campus fraternity houses, research studies have yet to investigate why these locations are more likely venues for rape than other college gathering places (Martin & Hummer, 2003).

UNIDENTIFIED AUTHOR

Identify the source with a short title, beginning with the first few words so that it can be located in your alphabetical list of references.

Parents of middle school students are encouraged to monitor their online activities (Safe Kids, 2005).

SAME AUTHOR WITH MULTIPLE WORKS

Five significant trends in parent-school relations have evolved (Grimley, 2005) since the original multi-state study (Grimley, 1985).

DIFFERENT AUTHORS WITH MULTIPLE WORKS

Within a single citation, list the authors of multiple works in alphabetical order (as in your reference list). Separate the works with semicolons.

Several studies have been designed to determine reasons for minority underperformance in educational attainment (Bowen & Bok, 1998; Charles, Dinwiddie, & Massey, 2004; Glazer, 1997).

What Type of Source Is It?

Naming the author is the core of the basic APA citation form, regardless of the type of source you have used. Even so, a few types of sources may present complications.

INDIRECT SOURCE

If possible, locate and cite the original source. Otherwise, begin your citation with "as cited in" and name your source.

According to Claude Fischer, the belief in individualism favors "the individual over the group or institution" (as cited in Hansen, 2005, p. 5).

GOVERNMENT OR ORGANIZATION DOCUMENT

If no specific author is identified, treat the sponsoring agency as the author, and give its full name in the first citation in your text. If the name is complicated or commonly shortened, you may add an abbreviation in brackets. In later citations, use just the abbreviation and the date.

The *2005 National Gang Threat Assessment* (National Alliance of Gang Investigators Associations [NAGIA], 2005, pp. vii–viii) identified regional trends that may help to account for the city's recent gang violence.

Next citation:

(NAGIA, 2005)

WEB SITE OR OTHER ONLINE DOCUMENT

When possible, cite a Web resource or online article as you would any other source.

Breast cancer survival rates depend on early detection before the cancer has a chance to spread (Bruckheim, 1998).

For an online source with no author named, use the full title in your text or the first word or two in parentheses. When the date is unknown, use "n.d." ("no date"). When pages are not numbered in the original, add a location such as a paragraph number ("para. 3" or "¶ 3"), chapter number ("chap. 2"), or section heading that will help readers find the material.

Interval training encourages rotation between high-intensity spurts and "active recovery, which is typically a less-intense form of the original activity" (*Interval training*, n.d., para. 2).

A CLASSIC

If the date of a classic is unknown, use "n.d." ("no date"). If the original date is known, show it along with your edition's date: (Burton 1621/1977). For ancient texts, use the year of the translation: (Homer, trans. 1990). The corresponding entry in your reference list will identify the translator, in this case Fagles.

For a quotation from a classic, identify lines, sections, or other standard divisions instead of pages so that a passage could be located in any edition. For Biblical references, you should specify the version in your initial citation but need not add it to your reference list.

> Many cultures affirm the importance of religious covenant in accounts as varied as the Biblical "Behold, I make a covenant" in Exodus 34:10 (King James Version) and *The Iliad* (Homer, trans. 1990), which opens with the cause of the Trojan War, "all because Agamemnon spurned Apollo's priest" (Book 1, line 12).

VISUAL MATERIAL

To refer to your own figure or table, mention its number in your sentence: "As Figure 2 shows, . . ." (See also the checklist on p. 176). Clearly identify a visual cited from a source.

> Teenagers who play video games with a high degree of violence are more likely to show aggressive behavior (Anderson & Bushman, 2001, Table 1).

To include a table or a visual from a source, in either original or adapted form, you may need to request permission from the author or copyright holder. Many sources—from scholarly journals to Web sites—state their permissions policy in the issue or on the site. (Ask your instructor for advice if you are uncertain about how to proceed.) Credit such material in a "From" or "Adapted from" note below it. The journal in this example allows the use of a table but requires adding the concluding credit line.

> *Note.* From "Inequality in Preschool Education and School Readiness," by K. A. Magnuson, M. K. Meyers, C. J. Ruhm, and J. Waldfogel, 2004, *American Educational Research Journal, 41,* p. 125. Copyright 2004 by the American Educational Research Association; reproduced with permission from the publisher.

PERSONAL COMMUNICATION

Personal communications—such as face-to-face interviews, letters, telephone conversations, memos, and e-mail—are not included in the reference list because your readers would not be able to find and use such sources. But in the text of your paper, name your source and the date of the communication.

J. T. Moore (personal communication, November 10, 2005) has made specific suggestions for stimulating the local economy.

How Are You Capturing the Source Material?

The way that you have captured source material—whether in your own words or in a quotation—also affects how you present and credit it. Always identify any words taken directly from a source by using quotation marks or the indented form for a long "block" quotation. Specify the page or other location of quoted words, unless the source lacks clear location information. (See p. 110 for a general checklist about quotations.) If you present in your own words material from a specific place in your source, APA recommends that you add a page number or other location. A citation, but no location, is needed for general information, such as your summary of an overall finding.

The next four examples illustrate how Ross Rocketto varied his presentation of sources in his paper "Robin Hood: Prince of Thieves? An Analysis of Current School Finance Legislature in Texas."

OVERALL SUMMARY OR IMPORTANT IDEA

The resulting educational inequities have become particularly problematic because of technological changes that require higher levels of education for higher paying jobs (Wilson, 1996).

BLENDED PARAPHRASE AND QUOTATION

According to William Julius Wilson (1996), the economic restructuring of the 1970s created what he refers to as "new urban poverty" — "segregated neighborhoods in which a substantial majority of individual adults are either unemployed or have dropped out of the labor force altogether" (p. 19).

BRIEF QUOTATION INTEGRATED IN SENTENCE

According to Castells, the city is the "most efficient and convenient form of collective consumption" (as cited in Savage, 2003, p. 162), that is, the best means of providing public housing, transport, education, and so on.

LONG QUOTATION

If you quote forty words or more, indent the quotation one-half inch and double-space it instead of using quotation marks. After it, add your

---

WRITING CHECKLIST

Citing Sources in APA Style

☐ Have you double-checked to be sure that you have acknowledged all material from a source?

☐ Have you placed your citation right after your quotation or reference to the source?

☐ Have you identified the author of each source in your text or in parentheses?

☐ Have you used the first few words of the title to cite a work without an identified author?

☐ Have you noted the date (or added "n.d." for "no date") for each source?

☐ Have you added a page number or other location whenever needed?

☐ Have you checked your final draft to be sure that every source cited in your text also appears in your list of references?

---

citation with no additional period, including whatever information you have not already mentioned in your launch statement.

This phenomenon is explained further by Hoxby (1998):

> First, districts that are good, efficient providers of schooling tend to be rewarded with larger budgets. This fiscal reward process works because a district's budget nearly always depends on property taxes, which in turn depend on home prices within the district, which in turn depend on how the marginal home buyers value the local schools. (p. 48)

LISTING SOURCES IN APA STYLE

In APA style, your list of sources appears at the end of your paper. Begin a new page with the title "References" centered. Double-space your list, and organize it alphabetically by authors' last names (or by titles for works without an identified author). If you need to list several works by the same author, arrange these by date, moving from earliest to most recent. Should an author have written two works published in the same year, arrange these alphabetically, and add a letter after each date (2004a, 2004b) so that the date in your text citation leads to the correct entry. (See pp. 194–95) Format each entry with a "hanging indent": the first line is not indented, but subsequent lines are indented one-half inch (about five to seven spaces), just as a paragraph is. (Use the menu in your software—Format-Paragraph-Indentation—to set up this hanging or special indentation.) Include only sources that you actually cite in your paper unless your instructor has requested otherwise.

Use the APA Source Navigators (pp. 180–87) to help you get started. They illustrate how to find the necessary information in four types of sources and how to prepare the corresponding entry for each source for your reference list. Refer also to the References in the sample student paper (p. 212) so that you can see how your final product should look. To a great extent, listing sources correctly depends on following patterns and paying attention to details such as italics, capital letters, and punctuation. APA style favors simplifying details in the following ways:

- Supply only initials for an author's first and middle names.
- Use an ampersand (&), not "and," before the name of the last of a series of authors (even though you would write "and" in your paper except in a citation in parentheses).
- Spell out names of months (used for the dates of newspapers, magazines, and newsletters), but abbreviate terms common in academic writing (such as "p.m.," "Vol." for "Volume," or "No." for "Number").
- Capitalize only the first word, proper names, and the first word after a colon in the title of a book, article, or Web site (but capitalize all main words in the title of a journal or other periodical).
- Do not use quotation marks or italics for an article title in your reference list (even though you would use quotation marks if you mentioned it in your paper).
- Italicize the title of a Web site, book, or periodical (as well as its volume number).
- List only the first of several cities where a publisher has offices.
- Include only the city's name for well-known publishing centers, but add the abbreviated state (or country) name for other locations (unless the name of a university press includes the state).
- Shorten the name of a publisher, but include "Press."
- Use "Author" instead of the publisher's name if the two are the same.
- Omit the concluding period after the URL or address for an electronic source.

As you prepare your own entries, begin with the author. The various author formats apply whatever your source—article, book, Web page, or other material. Then select the format for the rest of the entry depending on the type of source you have used. Find that type in this section, and follow its pattern in your entry, supplying the same information in the same order with the same punctuation and other features. If you can't find an exact match, consult the APA manual itself, get your instructor's advice, or model your entry on the most similar sample. Keep in mind these two key questions, which are used to organize the sample entries that follow:

Who wrote it?

What type of source is it?

Who Wrote It?

INDIVIDUAL AUTHOR

Pollack, W. (2000). *Real boys' voices*. New York: Random House.

TWO AUTHORS

Anderson, R., & Ross, V. (1998). *Questions of communication*. New York: St. Martin's Press.

THREE OR MORE AUTHORS

Provide names for three to six authors; for seven or more, simply use "et al." ("and others") instead of adding more names.

Evans, B., Joas, M., Sundback, S., & Theobald, K. (2005). *Governing sustainable cities*. London: Earthscan.

SAME AUTHOR WITH MULTIPLE WORKS

Arrange the titles by date, the earliest first. If some share the same date, arrange them alphabetically and letter them after the date.

Gould, S. J. (1996). *Full house: The spread of excellence from Plato to Darwin*. New York: Harmony.

Gould, S. J. (2003a). *The hedgehog, the fox, and the magister's pox: Mending the gap between science and the humanities*. New York: Harmony.

Gould, S. J. (2003b). *Triumph and tragedy in Mudville: A lifelong passion for baseball.* New York: Norton.

ORGANIZATION AUTHOR

American Red Cross. (2004). *CPR/AED for the professional rescuer.* Washington, DC: Author.

AUTHOR OF EDITED WORK

Bolles, E. B. (Ed.). (1999). *Galileo's commandment: 2,500 years of great science writing.* New York: Freeman.

AUTHOR AND TRANSLATOR

Ishinomori, I. (1998). *Japan inc.: Introduction to Japanese economics* (B. Schneiner, Trans.). Berkeley: University of California Press. (Original work published 1986)

UNIDENTIFIED AUTHOR

Findings. (2005, April). *Harper's Magazine, 310,* 100.

What Type of Source Is It?

Once you have found the appropriate author format, look for the type of source and the specific entry that best matches yours. Mix and match the patterns illustrated as needed. For example, the second edition of an edited collection of articles might send you to several examples until you have identified all of its elements.

Printed or Electronic Book

PRINTED BOOK

Rosenthal, A. (2004). *Heavy lifting: The job of the American legislature.* Washington, DC: CQ Press.

ONLINE BOOK

Oblinger, D. G., & Oblinger, J. L. (Eds.) (2005). *Educating the Net generation.* Retrieved May 27, 2005, from www.educause.edu/educatingthenetgen/

MULTIVOLUME WORK

Friedman, H. S. (Ed.). (1998). *Encyclopedia of mental health* (Vols. 1-3). San Diego, CA: Academic Press.

REVISED EDITION

Volti, R. (2001). *Society and technological change.* (4th ed.). New York: Worth.

BOOK WITHOUT A DATE

Reade, T. (n.d.). *American originals.* Wichita, KS: Midtown Press.

Part of a Printed or Electronic Book

SELECTION FROM A PRINTED BOOK

Martin, P. V., & Hummer, R. A. (2003). Fraternities and rape on campus. In
M. Silberman (Ed.), *Violence and society: A reader* (pp. 215-222). Upper
Saddle River, NJ: Prentice Hall.

SELECTION FROM AN ONLINE BOOK

Brown, M. (2005). Learning spaces. In D. G. Oblinger & J. L. Oblinger (Eds.),
Educating the Net generation (chap. 12). Retrieved May 27, 2005, from
http://www.educause.edu/educatingthenetgen/

PREFACE, INTRODUCTION, FOREWORD, OR AFTERWORD

Godwin, M. (1996). Foreword. In P. Ludlow (Ed.), *High noon on the electronic
frontier* (pp. xiii-xvi). Cambridge: MIT Press.

ARTICLE FROM A REFERENCE WORK

Norman, C. E. (2003). Religion and food. In *Encyclopedia of food and culture*
(Vol. 3, pp. 171–176). New York: Charles Scribner's Sons.

Article in a Printed or Electronic Periodical

ARTICLE FROM A JOURNAL PAGINATED BY VOLUME

If the pages in all the issues for the year's volume are numbered consec-
utively, no issue number is needed. Italicize the volume number as well
as the title of the journal.

Martin, J. (1997). Inventing sincerity, refashioning prudence: The discovery of
the individual in Renaissance Europe. *American Historical Review, 102,*
1309–1342.

ARTICLE FROM A JOURNAL PAGINATED BY ISSUE

If each issue begins with page 1, add the issue number in parentheses with no space after the volume number.

Lipkin, S. N. (1999). Real emotional logic: Persuasive strategies in docudrama. *Cinema Journal, 38*(4), 68–85.

ARTICLE FROM AN ONLINE JOURNAL

If the article also appears in a printed journal, include "Electronic version" in brackets after the title instead of supplying the URL. If there is no printed version of the article or the content of the online version differs from that of the printed one, include your date of access and the URL.

Loker, W. M. (1996). "Campesinos" and the crisis of modernization in Latin America [Electronic version]. *Journal of Political Ecology, 3,* 69–88.

Rothfleisch, J. (2001). Mid-dermal elastolysis. *Dermatology Online Journal, 7.* Retrieved June 8, 2001, from http://dermatology.cdlib.org/DOJvo17num1/NYUcases/elastolysis/rothfleisch.html

ARTICLE ACCESSED THROUGH A LIBRARY OR SUBSCRIPTION SERVICE

If you access only an abstract for the article, add "Abstract" in brackets after the title.

Allison, S. (2004). On-screen smoking influences young viewers. *Youth Studies Australia 23*(3), 6. Retrieved May 6, 2005, from Expanded Academic ASAP database.

ARTICLE FROM A PRINTED MAGAZINE

Lankford, K. (1998, April). The trouble with rules of thumb. *Kiplinger's Personal Finance Magazine, 52,* 102–104.

ARTICLE FROM AN ONLINE MAGAZINE

Chandler, K. (2005, June 18). Anger management. *Salon.com.* Retrieved June 23, 2005, from http://www.salon.com

ARTICLE FROM A NEWSLETTER

Anti-evolution teachings gain in U.S. schools. (2005, January). *Newsletter on Intellectual Freedom, 54*(3), 27–28.

ARTICLE FROM A PRINTED NEWSPAPER

Stein, R. (2004, March 11). Breast-cancer drug changes suggested. *The Boston Globe*, p. A4.

ARTICLE FROM AN ONLINE NEWSPAPER

Grady, D. (2005, June 23). Studies lead to big changes in lung cancer treatments. *The New York Times*. Retrieved June 23, 2005, from http://www.nytimes.com

EDITORIAL FROM A PRINTED PERIODICAL

Taking the initiatives. (2000, November 13). [Editorial]. *The Nation, 272*, 3–4.

LETTER TO THE EDITOR

Yusuf, S. (2000, November 4). Pakistan's choice [Letter to the editor]. *The Economist, 357*, 6.

REVIEW

Rose, T. (1998, February 24). Blues sisters [Review of the book *Blues legacies and black feminism: Gertrude "Ma" Rainey, Bessie Smith, and Billie Holliday*]. *The Village Voice*, pp. 139–141.

Printed or Electronic Report or Other Document

Many research reports and similar documents are collaborative products, prepared under the auspices of a government, academic, or other organizational sponsor. Start with the agency name if no specific author is identified. In parentheses, add any report number assigned by the agency right after the title, but add any number from a document service (such as ERIC, Educational Resources Information Center, or NTIS, National Technical Information Service) after the entire entry, without any period at the end.

PRINTED GOVERNMENT DOCUMENT

U.S. Bureau of the Census. (2003). *Statistical abstract of the United States* (123rd ed.). Washington, DC: U.S. Government Printing Office.

ONLINE GOVERNMENT DOCUMENT

U.S. Federal Trade Commission. (2002). *The mobile wireless web, data services and beyond: Emerging technologies and consumer issues.* Retrieved January 31, 2005, from http://www.ftc.gov/bcp/reports/wirelesssummary.pdf

RESEARCH REPORT

Liu, J., Allspach, J. R., Feigenbaum, M., Oh, H.-J., & Burton, N. (2004). *A study of fatigue effects from the new SAT* (RR-04-46). Princeton, NJ: Educational Testing Service.

ONLINE RESEARCH REPORT

National Institute on Drug Abuse. (2005). *Inhalant abuse* (NIH Publication No. 00–3818). Retrieved June 23, 2005, from http://www.nida.nih.gov/PDF/RRInhalants.pdf

ONLINE RESEARCH REPORT FROM A DOCUMENT SERVICE

Berger, S. (1995). Inclusion: A legal mandate, an educational dream. *Updating School Board Policies, 26*(4), 1-4. Retrieved February 15, 2001, from ERIC database. (ERIC Document Reproduction Service No. ED386789)

REPORT FROM AN ACADEMIC INSTITUTION

Bunn, M., Wier, A., & Holdren, J. P. (2003). *Controlling nuclear warheads and materials: A report card and action plan.* Cambridge, MA: Harvard University, Belfer Center for Science and International Affairs.

PAMPHLET

Label the source in brackets as a brochure.

U. S. Department of the Interior. (2002). *Lewis and Clark Trail: National historic trail, Illinois to Oregon* [Brochure]. Washington, DC: Author.

DOCTORAL DISSERTATION

Richter, P. (2004). *Improving nursing in the age of managed care.* Unpublished doctoral dissertation, University of Wisconsin, Madison.

Internet or Electronic Source

Your reference list should both identify what you have used and assist a reader who wishes to find the same material, but Internet sources can complicate the second objective. Some sources, such as Web sites, are available only in electronic form and may disappear or change at random. New electronic forms (such as blogs) can rapidly evolve. Despite such complications, try to cite a specific document (not a general home page), make sure each URL is correct, and supply information to help a reader access the material. (See pp. 180–87 for Source Navigators showing the basic APA entries for electronic sources. See also the directory on pp. 174–76 for other entries for electronic sources, including books and periodical articles.) For any updates on online formats, visit the APA Web site at www.apastyle.org.

SECTION OR PAGE FROM A WEB DOCUMENT

Instead of referring to an entire Web site, whenever possible identify the specific material that you have used by supplying its section number or its own URL.

Detweiler, L. (1993). What is the future of privacy on the Internet? In *Identity,*
privacy, and anonymity on the Internet (sec. 2.12). Retrieved February 1,
2005, from http://eserver.org/internet/Identity-Privacy-Anonymity.txt

National Eating Disorders Association. (2002). *Anorexia, bulimia, & binge eating*
disorder: What is an eating disorder? Retrieved February 1, 2005, from
http://www.nationaleatingdisorders.org/
p.asp?WebPage_ID&=;286&Profile_ID&=;41145

DOCUMENT FROM A CAMPUS WEB SITE

Identify the university and sponsoring program or department (if applicable) before giving the URL for the specific page or document.

Allin, C. (2004). *Common sense for college students: How to do better than you*
thought possible. Retrieved April 23, 2005, from Cornell College,
Department of Politics Web site:http://www.cornellcollege.edu/politics/
common-sense_cwa.shtml

COMPUTER SOFTWARE

Microsoft Office Excel 2003 [Computer software]. (2003). Redmond, WA: Microsoft.

Visual or Audio Source

AUDIOTAPE OR RECORDING

Ellis, A. (Writer/Producer). (1995). *Helping students develop their IEPs* [Audiotape]. Washington, DC: National Dissemination Center for Children with Disabilities.

PROGRAM ON TELEVISION OR RADIO

Clark, L. (Writer/Director/Producer). (2004). Descent into the ice. [Television series episode]. In P. Aspell (Executive Producer), *Nova*. Boston: WGBH.

FILM

Lustig, B., Molen, G., & Spielberg, S. (Producers). (1993). *Schindler's list* [Motion picture]. Los Angeles: Universal.

Conversation or Field Artifact

PERSONAL INTERVIEW

Omit a personal interview from your reference list because it is not accessible to readers. Instead, mention it in your paper as a personal communication. (See pp. 190–91.)

E-MAIL OR ELECTRONIC MAILING LIST MESSAGE

Because these messages are difficult or impossible for readers to retrieve, cite them only in your text as personal communications. (See pp. 190–91.)

WRITING CHECKLIST

Listing Sources in APA Style

☐ Have you started each entry with the appropriate pattern for the author's name? Have you left spaces between the initials for each author's name?

☐ Have you used "&," not "and," to add the last co-author's name?

☐ Have you included the date in each entry?

☐ Have you followed the sample pattern for the type of source you have used?

☐ Have you used capitalization and italics correctly for the various titles in your entries?

☐ Have you included the conventional punctuation — periods, commas, colons, parentheses — in your entry?

☐ Have you accurately recorded the name of the author, title, publisher, and so on?

☐ Have you checked the accuracy of numbers such as dates and pages?

☐ Have you correctly typed or pasted in the address of an electronic source? Have you split a long URL only before a period or after a slash?

☐ Have you arranged your entries in alphabetical order?

☐ Have you checked your final list of references against your text citations so that every source appears in both places?

A SAMPLE RESEARCH PAPER IN APA STYLE

In her paper "Japanese: Linguistic Diversity," Stephanie Hawkins investigates the historical complexities and cultural implications of the Japanese language. She wrote her paper for an independent study course as she prepared for a trip to Japan. The APA manual recommends a sequence of sections for a paper reporting an author's experimental or field research: introduction, method, results, and discussion. However, when a paper reviews pertinent literature or theory about a topic, its sections and headings generally evolve from the study's content, as Stephanie's do. She traces the development of spoken and written Japanese, examining how their growth has reflected traditional cultural assumptions and how changes continue to address contemporary issues.

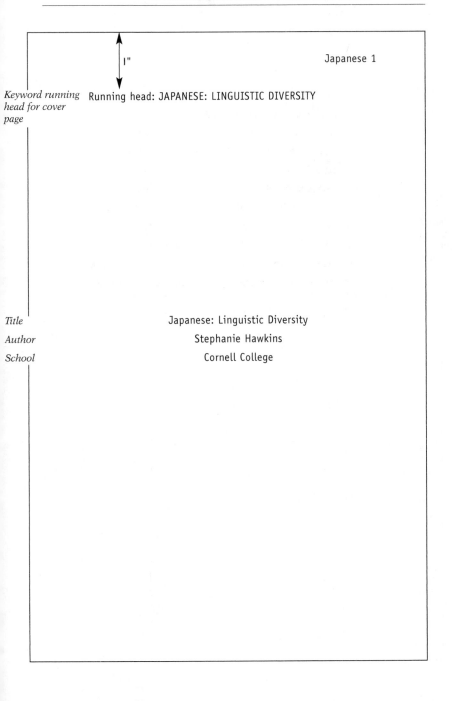

Japanese 1

1"

Keyword running   Running head: JAPANESE: LINGUISTIC DIVERSITY
head for cover
page

Title   Japanese: Linguistic Diversity

Author   Stephanie Hawkins

School   Cornell College

Heading, centered

No paragraph indentation

Main ideas summed up in no more than 120 words

Abstract

With ancient Asian roots and contemporary European influences, the Japanese language has continued to change and to reflect cultural change as well. Japanese has developed a sophisticated structure full of honorifics and gender-specific terms that express the respect required within the society. It also has heavily borrowed words that reflect the society's technological adaptation. Despite the complexity of a language that contains two alphabets and continuously incorporates foreign words, many steps during the last century have helped those whose disabilities keep them at odds with language. In such ways, the history of the language remains the history of the country, its culture, and its people.

Japanese 3

Title, centered   Japanese: Linguistic Diversity

Japanese, like any other language, has continued to develop for centuries. New vocabulary, pronunciation, spellings, and dialects increasingly flourish in Japanese. In addition, Japanese has developed honorifics and gender-specific terms to express the respect required within the society and has borrowed words to respond to technological innovation from the outside. During the last hundred years, other changes have begun to help those with disabilities that affect language facility.

Japanese is rooted in the archaic languages found throughout Asia (Hall, 1968), derived from at least two of the three sections of Mongoloid languages. The linguistic patterns of the Altaic

Double-spaced throughout

Date not repeated for clear second reference in same paragraph

languages, formed in the northern regions of Asia, can still be seen in Japanese. In addition, the origin of Japanese may also lie in the Malay languages which include native Australian and Polynesian (Hall). Similarities between Japanese and both Korean and Polynesian include sentence structure, pronunciation, and classic vocabulary for body parts and nature (Komatsu, 1962). Despite their variety, these archaic languages are not the only ones to influence modern Japanese.

First-level heading, centered   Systems for Written Language

Although Korean is most closely related to Japanese today, Chinese has had the most influence in the development of the written language. China had a written language as early as 4000

Specific page noted

BCE (Komatsu, 1962, p. 47) and began keeping written records regarding Japan around the 3rd century. The Japanese continued these Chinese records through the 8th century as they developed their own official written language, Manyo-kana, whose sole purpose was to give already used Chinese characters Japanese meanings (Komatsu).

Japanese 4

Because common people were not educated enough to read Chinese, by the 9th century the Japanese had developed two writing systems and also continued the use of Chinese characters. Hira-kana, consisting of more than 40 characters, was originally for writing Japanese poetry because of its attractive lettering. Kata-kana, a separate system with an equivalent letter for each in hira-kana, was used for transcribing Chinese words that had no Japanese equivalent (Komatsu, 1962). As the two writing systems developed, hira-kana began to be used for writing any native Japanese words and kata-kana for any non-Japanese words (Komatsu). This dual writing system allowed more people to read Chinese characters, otherwise known as kanji, and to write on their own.

Numbers in figures if 10 or above and if grouped with others in figures

Both writing systems consist of more than 40 sounds with 27 consonants and 5 vowels (Komatsu, 1962). Words are composed of one or more combinations of consonant and vowel; however, a word never ends on a consonant (Komatsu). Sentence elements are divided by particles, single hira-kana designated as position markers such as *in* or *at*. These particles are also used in the honorific structure of the language (Komatsu), which reflects the respect required within the society.

First-level heading, centered

Expressions of Respect

Both honorifics and women's language convey respect, yet both have recently evolved to express insults and sarcasm through overly polite language.

Second-level heading, italicized at margin

Honorifics

The extremely complex system of honorifics in Japanese uses prefixes, suffixes, and dual vocabulary to convey different levels of politeness in speech. While, in English, one is taught to say "please" and call a friend's parent "Mr." or "Mrs." So-and-so, the

Japanese 5

Japanese have different familial terms for anyone else's family. A prefix of "O" to begin a name or verb deepens the respect and appreciation for the person spoken to. Another way to imply more respect is to end a statement with a formal "masu" verb suffix (Komatsu, 1962). These extensive honorifics must be used when talking to a person who is older than oneself, better educated, or not well acquainted (Okamoto, 2002). Such people include one's parents, parents of others (with their own honorific names), teachers, family friends, and people one meets on the train. In all other situations, such as speaking to close friends, younger people, and students, honorifics are not necessary.

With its concern for politeness and respect, Japanese includes few insults or ill-mannered statements. Surprisingly, in the last several decades, excessive use of honorifics and overly polite speech has been commonly perceived as sarcasm, insults, or insincerity (Kristof, 1995; Okamoto, 2002). This overuse of politeness is also seen in what is called "women's language."

Multiple citations grouped in alphabetical order

Women's Language

Japanese women are taught at an early age that they are female, not male. Beginning in kindergarten, young girls are told to use a softer, less insistent version of the language. This development, however, is not new. The use of extreme politeness by women is a traditional part of the Japanese heritage, documented as far back as AD 400 (Inoue, 2002). It stems from the belief that men and women were cosmologically created differently and thus used different forms of language. Soft-spoken women used subtler particles and more feminine forms of words (Abe, 1995). In written language, women used far more hira-kana than men in order to avoid harsh Chinese words (Komatsu, 1962).

Not only does women's speech differ from men's in terms of vocabulary, but in phonology, syntax, and pitch (Inoue, 2002). Certain words are considered feminine, usually referring to household items and jobs. However, women's language extends beyond this, making it nearly impossible for a woman to utter an insult or to make a definitive statement. Mostly, women ask implying questions, which men are able to confirm, instead of making direct statements (Rudolph, 1991). This unique form of speech also affects the way that women are viewed in society, often putting them in a negative light, seen as weak and uneducated (Abe, 1995).

The history of women's speech is just as intriguing as its modern use. During the 13th century, as Buddhism challenged the Shinto religion, women's language was used to avoid Buddhist terms in and near Shinto temples (Abe, 1995). As religious perspectives shifted, women's language, or lack of language, expanded as well. Eventually, this dialect avoided all antagonistic and dishonorable words, leaving women with a submissive and self-degrading vocabulary (Abe). During the Meiji restoration, when Japan opened its gates to outside influence after centuries of seclusion, women received a secondary education. However, instead of learning mathematics and science, they were taught under the "good wife, wise mother" strategy (Abe). Writings from this time portray quiet, obedient housewives and sturdy, pleasant mothers, images that have consistently represented women for decades.

Nevertheless, contemporary women are beginning to dispose of these binding language formalities. As more and more women take on official roles in society, the "good wife, wise mother" foundation is starting to crack. Young women are beginning to use less formal structures when speaking with close friends and

Date not repeated, for clear subsequent references in same paragraph

Japanese 7

family (Rudolph, 1991). Inoue (2002) says that more women see and hear women's language on television and in magazines than actually speak it. As the effects of this language are seen more clearly, this demeaning form of speech is being modified, and usage has begun to decline.

Borrowed Words

The Japanese have had their own independent language for thousands of years, but as in any language, an influx of technology leads to a necessity for new words. Influences on Japanese at the time of its earliest development included Chinese, Korean, and Sanskrit (Tomoda, 1999). But the borrowing of words did not stop there. In fact, the Japanese have borrowed so many words that the kata-kana writing system is a designated alphabet just for spelling words from other languages.

All of the words borrowed from other languages, except Chinese, are known as *gairaigo*. Gairaigo make up nearly 10% of the Japanese language, while Chinese words make up just under 50% of the language (Tomoda, 1999). Some feel that borrowing so many words is dangerous for the longevity of Japanese itself and may also be a sign of globalization. Others, however, are not worried about the continuing scrounging for words and say that those that aren't needed will be dropped in due time (Tomoda). Despite so many mixed feelings about borrowed words, studies show that only 13% of words spoken regularly are gairaigo (Tomoda), though borrowed words present a much larger problem for those who face learning disabilities.

Language and Learning Disabilities

People who are dyslexic, deaf, or blind have disabilities that create language challenges. For such individuals, the complexities of Japanese pose special difficulties.

Writing system (from p. 4) reviewed to aid reader

Numbers in figures with percent sign

End of one section leads into next section

Dyslexia

Dyslexia is a common cross-cultural learning disability. This condition creates difficulty reading, writing, and comprehending because symbols often appear backwards or are misinterpreted. In Japanese this can be a crippling problem. Due to the number of characters, over 2,000, and the minuscule dissimilarities between some of them, the language is a challenge even for those without a learning disability. A study of one young boy showed that semantic, visual, and meaning selection errors were prominent in extreme dyslexia (Yamada, 1995). Often, this boy had trouble deciphering kanji, the Chinese characters, and he mixed up hira-kana with kata-kana. Fortunately, dyslexia is not as prevalent a disability in Japan as in other places.

Deafness

Hearing impairment and deafness, on the other hand, are just as common in Japan as elsewhere, and unfortunately not much was done in the past to incorporate people who are deaf into Japanese society. The first school for the deaf was not opened until 1878 (Nakamura, 2002), and a sign language was not created until shortly after that. While other countries have strong sign language programs, Japan has regional versions of sign language, not one language that spans the entire nation (Nakamura). Because of the complexity of Japanese sign language (JSL), which uses different grammar rules than spoken Japanese and includes facial expressions (Nakamura), finger spelling and air writing are far more common than a standard sign language. JSL also is not recognized as an independent language and therefore is not taught in most schools, though there is some progress in teaching a standard JSL. However, the Japanese have another option: simultaneous communication. This process, not yet widely used, is usually reserved for translating and television, similar to America's captions ("For an independent," 1998).

Findings of specific study summarized

Abbreviation introduced and used in place of full phrase

No-author source cited by title

Blindness

Blindness is also a familiar ailment around the world, eased for many by Braille. In Japanese culture, reading is extremely important, distinguishing one's social and educational standing. Japanese Braille, or Tenji, originated as a distinct writing system in 1890 (Kalyan, 2002) but did not distinguish between hira-kana and kata-kana, making it extremely hard for readers to differentiate meanings. No Braille form of the Chinese characters existed until the recent Hasegawa project created "Tenkanji," a form of Tenji that could incorporate kanji and differentiate hira-kana from kata-kana (Kalyan). Nevertheless, this breakthrough comes at a time when many people who are seeing impaired prefer to use a voice synthesizer with a computer instead of learn the new Tenkanji. Unfortunately, this one-way communication can set one back in social status, as reading and writing are vital for maintaining public standing. With time, however, people who are blind may not be as separated from society as they have been in the past.

Conclusion

Final section sums up main points

The Japanese have proliferated for centuries, becoming an extremely well-populated and technologically advanced nation. As the country has changed, the language has also. With linguistic roots in ancient Asian and contemporary European languages, Japanese has developed a sophisticated structure full of honorifics, borrowed words, and gender-specific terms. Despite the complexity of the language, steps have been made, in the last hundred years, to help those with disabilities that keep them at odds with language. Although it is difficult to understand a language that contains two alphabets and continuously incorporates foreign words, the history of the language remains the history of the nation, its culture, and its people.

References

Page numbering continues

Heading, centered

Abe, H. (1995). From stereotype to context: The study of Japanese

First line at margin; additional lines indented ¹/₂"

women's language. *Feminist Study 21*(3). Retrieved September

27, 2004, from EBSCOhost database.

For an independent Japanese sign language: Harumi kimura.

(1998, April-July). *Integrator 8*(2). Retrieved October 1, 2004,

from http://www.dpa.org.sg/DPA/publication/dpa_apr_jun_98/

URL split only before a period or after a slash

p22.html

Hall, J. W. (1968). *Japan from prehistory to modern times*. New York: Dell.

Inoue, M. (2002). Gender, language and modernity: Toward an

effective history of Japanese women's language. *American

Ethnologist, 29*(2), 392–422.

Entries alphabetized

Kalyan, D. (2002). Brailled kanji: The Hasegawa project. *Journal of

Visual Impairment and Blindness, 96*(10). Retrieved September

27, 2004, from EBSCOhost database.

Komatsu, I. (1962). *The Japanese people: Origins of the people and

language*. Tokyo: Kokusai Bunka Shinkokai.

Kristof, N. (1995, September 24). On language: Too polite for words.

The New York Times Magazine, pp. SM22-SM23.

No period after URL

Nakamura, K. (2002). *About Japanese sign language*. Retrieved October

1, 2004, from http://www.deaflibrary.org/jsl.html

Okamoto, S. (2002). Politeness and the perception of irony: Honorifics

in Japanese. *Metaphor and Symbol 17*(2). Retrieved September

27, 2004, from EBSCOhost database.

Rudolph, E. (1991, September 1). Women's talk. *The New York Times

Magazine*, p. SM8.

Tomoda, T. (1999). The impact of load-words on modern Japanese.

Japan Forum 11(2), 231–254. Retrieved September 27, 2004,

from EBSCOhost database.

Yamada, J. (1995). Kanji not easier to learn: A case study of

developmental dyslexia in Japan. *Dyslexia 1*(2), 120–123.

Retrieved September 27, 2004, from EBSCOhost database.

12

Using *Chicago* Style

This chapter briefly explains and illustrates how to use *Chicago* style for a research paper with footnotes or endnotes and a bibliography. This style, often favored in art, history, and other fields in the humanities, allows a writer to cite sources inconspicuously while still fully identifying and crediting them. The style is explained in *The Chicago Manual of Style* (15th ed.; Chicago: University of Chicago Press, 2003), which supplies extensive advice for authors, editors, and publishers. Compact and useful advice for students, based on the *Chicago Manual*, is available in the current edition of *A Manual for Writers of Term Papers, Theses, and Dissertations,* often identified as "Turabian," the name of its original author.

CITING AND LISTING SOURCES IN *CHICAGO* STYLE

UNDERSTANDING *CHICAGO* STYLE

Chicago style is commonly implemented through a three-part system for crediting sources. First, when you refer to source material in your text, add a superscript number, raised about halfway above the bottom of the regular line of text. This number leads a reader to the second part of the system—a note, beginning with the corresponding number, either placed as a footnote at the bottom of the page where the source material appears or grouped as an endnote with all of your other notes on a new page following the conclusion of your text. From there, the author's last name, supplied in the note, leads to the third part of the system—full identification of the source in an alphabetical bibliography on a new page following the notes. Your software probably can add note numbers and position either endnotes or footnotes automatically. Check your software's Help feature for advice about notes; then go to the appropriate menu, such as Insert-Reference-Footnote, Format-Notes, or Format-References.

Because *Chicago* style is widely used in books and journals as well as student papers, its note style is flexible. Your instructor, like a book or journal editor, may have specific ideas about how to implement it. Check your course syllabus or research paper assignment for any directions, or ask your instructor about the preferred style. For example, if you are expected to use the three-part system, the *Chicago* guidelines recommend using brief notes (see p. 230). On the other hand, if you are asked to include only your notes without a bibliography, then the first note for each source must supply its complete identification, but additional citations of that source can be brief notes. An instructor also may have a preference for endnotes or footnotes. The four *Chicago* Source Navigators (pp. 218–25) illustrate how to locate in your source the details necessary to cite it in a note and list it correctly in *Chicago* style. See also pages 213–14 for a directory listing the sample entries supplied here.

The *Chicago Manual* also provides guidelines for formatting a consistent, readable paper. If you expect to use this style fairly often, set up a *Chicago* template which you can call up as you begin each new paper. Otherwise use the Page Format options in your software's File menu or the Font and Paragraph options in the Format menu to make any changes needed in your draft. As you complete your paper, refer to the format of the sample *Chicago* paper on pp. 247–56 and the following checklist.

WRITING CHECKLIST

Formatting a Paper in *Chicago* Style

☐ Have you double-spaced the entire paper, including all quotations, notes, and bibliography entries, unless directed otherwise?

☐ Have you allowed a one-inch margin on all four sides of the page?

☐ Have you added a running header to number the pages, generally placed at the far right side (or centered) at the top of each page?

☐ Have you placed your heading (name, professor, course, and date) and your title on a cover page or at the top of the first page, following your instructor's directions?

☐ Have you indented (typically one-half inch) for the first line of every paragraph, every line of any long quotation (longer than a paragraph of prose or a single line of poetry), and the first line of each note (before its number)?

☐ Have you stuck to a consistent style for headings if you have used them to identify the sections of your paper? (If you use only one level of heading, begin each heading at the left margin, capitalizing its first and main words. If you use several heading levels, select a consistent style such as regular or italic type to identify each level.)

☐ Have you checked that your note numbers in your text are all in superscript, raised above the line, and follow numerical order without skips or duplicates?

☐ Have you preceded any table with a numbered heading—for example, Table 2—directly followed by its concise explanatory title? Have you followed the table with any necessary credit (beginning *Source:* . . .)?

☐ Have you followed any other visual, such as a graph, drawing, chart, or photograph, with a numbered heading—for example, Fig. 1—directly followed by a concise explanatory title?

☐ Have you turned off your software's automatic hyphenation to avoid splitting words with hyphens at the ends of lines? Have you turned off text justification so that you have an even margin on the left but not on the right?

☐ Have you continued your page numbering but begun any list of endnotes and your bibliography each on a new page?

☐ Have you begun the first line of every bibliography entry at the left margin but indented each additional line? (To do this automatically, check your software for a "hanging" indentation option, possibly through the Format-Paragraph-Indentation-Special menu.)

☐ Have you followed any specific directions from your instructor about format or electronic submission?

☐ Have you printed a clear, readable final copy and kept a backup copy of your file in case the printed copy gets lost?

IDENTIFYING SOURCES IN *CHICAGO* STYLE

The core of a *Chicago* citation is the note that identifies the author and title of your source. The note number that you add to your text directs a reader to that information. A full note supplies the detail to identify your source; a brief note uses the author's name to lead to that identification in your bibliography. In addition, your note can specify the location, such as a page number, where the material you have used appears in the original source. Although full notes sometimes may replace a bibliography, the alphabetically arranged bibliography serves readers in another way. It complements your notes by assembling your sources in a list that gives readers a clear overview of your sources and the direction of your research. The *Chicago* system of connection and identification applies whatever the type of source credited—article, book, or Web page.

Beginning on page 218, you will find paired illustrations of full notes and corresponding bibliography entries, grouped to show variations for authors and types of sources. Your instructor may specify whether you should use full notes (essential without a bibliography) or brief notes (an option with a bibliography), position them as footnotes or endnotes, or provide a bibliography in addition to your list of notes. Any requirements, or your own decisions, about format may affect where you supply or repeat information that identifies a source. For example, if you use footnotes, which allow a reader to glance immediately to the note at the bottom of the page, you don't need to state the name of an author or work identified in the text again in the note. On the other hand, if you use endnotes, a reader has to flip to your notes page for

(text continued on p. 226)

SOURCE NAVIGATOR: An Article from a Periodical

1 The complete name of the author
2 The title of the article (placed in quotation marks and abbreviated in a brief note)
3 The title of the journal (italicized)
4 The number of the journal volume
5 The number (no.) of the issue
6 The year of the issue (placed in parentheses)
7 The article's page numbers

Full Note with Specific Location
① ②
1. Edward Tang, "Rebirth of a Nation: Frederick Douglass as Postwar Founder in *Life and Times*," *Journal of American Studies* 39, no. 1 (2005): 22.
③ ④ ⑤ ⑥ ⑦

Brief Note with Specific Location
① ② ⑦
1. Tang, "Rebirth of a Nation," 22.

Bibliography Entry
① ②
Tang, Edward. "Rebirth of a Nation: Frederick Douglass as Postwar Founder in *Life and Times*." *Journal of American Studies* 39, no. 1 (2005): 19-39.
③ ④ ⑤ ⑥ ⑦

③ ④ ⑥ ⑤ ⑦
Journal of American Studies, **39** (2005), 1, 19–39 © 2005 Cambridge University Press
doi:10.1017/S0021875805009230 Printed in the United Kingdom

Rebirth of a Nation: Frederick Douglass as Postwar Founder in *Life and Times* ②

EDWARD TANG ①

In 1875, a year from the upcoming centennial celebrations, Frederick Douglass commemorated the African American presence in the nation's revolutionary past and Reconstruction present. "If … any man should ask me what colored people have to do with the Fourth of July, my answer is ready," he proclaimed to a black audience in Washington, DC. "Colored

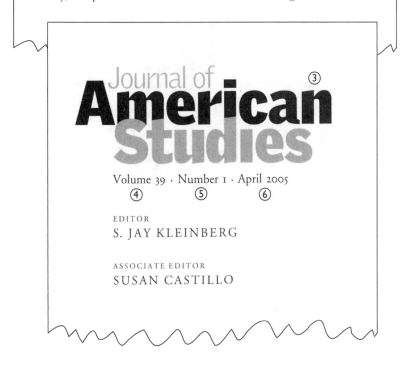

Journal of
**American
Studies** ③

Volume 39 · Number 1 · April 2005
④ ⑤ ⑥

EDITOR
S. JAY KLEINBERG

ASSOCIATE EDITOR
SUSAN CASTILLO

SOURCE NAVIGATOR: An Article from a Database

1 The complete name of the author
2 The title of the article (placed in quotation marks and abbreviated in a brief note)
3 The title of the journal (italicized)
4 The number of the journal volume
5 The number (no.) of the issue
6 The year of the issue
7 The printed article's original page numbers
8 The Internet address (URL, or Uniform Resource Locator)

Full Note with Specific Location
　　①　　　　　　　②
　　2. Marc Egnal, "Rethinking the Secession of the
Lower South: The Clash of Two Groups," *Civil War*　　③
④ *History* 50, no. 3 (2004): 268, http://infotrac
.galegroup.com. ⑤ ⑥　⑦　　　　⑧

Brief Note with Specific Location
　　①　　　②　　　　　　　⑦
　　2. Egnal, "Rethinking the Secession," 268.

Bibliography Entry
　　①　　　　　　②
Egnal, Marc. "Rethinking the Secession of the Lower
　　South: The Clash of Two Groups." *Civil War* ③
④⑤⑥ *History* 50, no. 3 (2004): 261-91. ⑦
　　http://infotrac.galegroup.com.
　　　　⑧

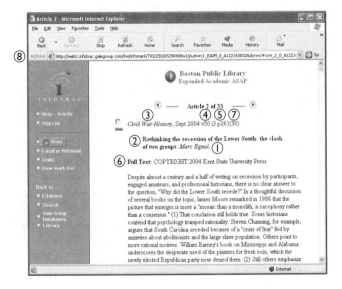

SOURCE NAVIGATOR: A Book

1 The complete name of the author
2 The title of the book (italicized and abbreviated in a brief note)
3 The place of publication
4 The shortened name of the publisher
5 The date of publication

Full Note with Specific Location
     ①   ②
   3. Jared Diamond, *Guns, Germs, and Steel: The Fates of Human Societies* (New York: Norton, 1999), 55.
          ③   ④   ⑤

Brief Note with Specific Location
     ①   ②
   3. Diamond, *Guns, Germs, and Steel*, 55.

Bibliography Entry
     ①   ②
Diamond, Jared. *Guns, Germs, and Steel: The Fates of Human Societies*. New York: Norton, 1999.
         ③   ④   ⑤

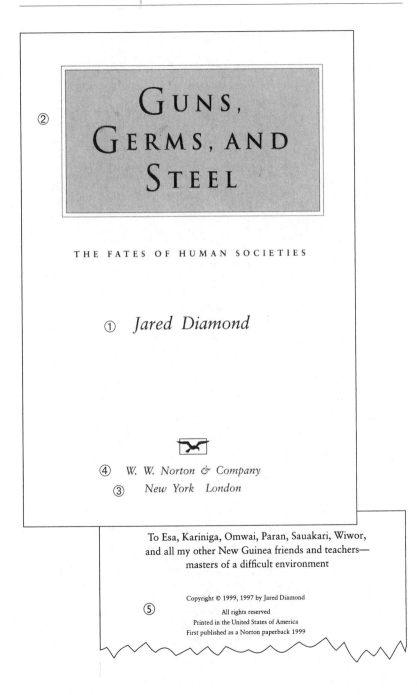

② # GUNS, GERMS, AND STEEL

THE FATES OF HUMAN SOCIETIES

① *Jared Diamond*

④ *W. W. Norton & Company*
③ *New York   London*

To Esa, Kariniga, Omwai, Paran, Sauakari, Wiwor,
and all my other New Guinea friends and teachers—
masters of a difficult environment

SOURCE NAVIGATOR: A Page from a Web Site

1 The complete names of the coauthors in the order listed in the source
2 The title of the page (placed in quotation marks and abbreviated in a brief note)
3 The name of the site (italicized)
4 The name of the sponsoring organization
5 The Internet address (URL, or Uniform Resource Locator) or your search path

---

Full Note

①

    4. Marcella Grendler, Andrew Leiter, and Jill
Sexton, comps., "Guide to Religious Content in ②
③ Slave Narratives," *Documenting the American
South: North American Slave Narratives,* University
Library, University of North Carolina at   ④
Chapel Hill, http://docsouth.unc.edu/neh/ ⑤
religiouscontent.html.

Brief Note

       ①   ②

    4. Grendler, Leiter, and Sexton, "Guide to Religious
Content."

Bibliography Entry

          ①

Grendler, Marcella, Andrew Leiter, and Jill Sexton,
    comps. "Guide to Religious Content in Slave ②
    Narratives." *Documenting the American South:*
  ③*North American Slave Narratives.* University
    Library, University of North Carolina at Chapel ④
    Hill. http://docsouth.unc.edu/neh/
    religiouscontent.html.   ⑤

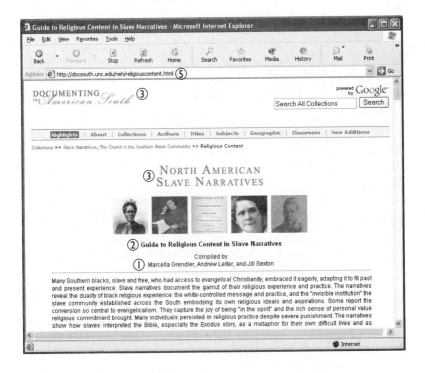

added detail. In this case, you need to reduce the potential for aggravating a reader by supplying the details a second time in the note.

No matter how you implement the *Chicago* system, many decisions are left to you. For example, precisely how you decide to integrate that critical name of the author can vary with your purposes as a writer, your use of your sources, and your reader's needs. As you make such decisions, keep in mind these three questions:

- Who wrote it?
- What type of source is it?
- How are you capturing the source material?

Who Wrote It?

Crediting the author of a source is a necessary part of your ethical obligation as a researcher. As a writer, however, you can decide in each instance whether to emphasize that name by mentioning it in your text or tucking it away in your notes and bibliography. (Sample notes illustrating author variations begin on p. 231.)

AUTHOR NOT NAMED IN SENTENCE

You need not name the author of your source in your text sentence; the note number leads a reader to that information. The entry for an individual author on page 231 identifies the source for this example:

The December 1991 dissolution of the USSR into independent states has been called "the end of an era."[1]

AUTHOR NAMED IN SENTENCE

If you wish to identify an authoritative author, contrast the views of specific authors, or otherwise emphasize the author of your source, name the author in your sentence. In addition, placing the name at the point where information from the source begins will clarify exactly what you are crediting. The entry for an author and a translator on pp. 232–33 identifies the source in this example:

In his discussion about the construction of France's national identity, Morrissey states that "Charlemagne is the quintessential representation of a founding father."[1]

DIFFERENT AUTHORS OF MULTIPLE WORKS

Should you need to credit several sources, all related to a single sentence or all identified in your text by author, combine them in a single note to avoid a string of note numbers. (See p. 244.)

What Type of Source Is It?

Naming the author first is the core of the *Chicago* note form, regardless of the type of source you have used. Even so, some sources, such as visuals, may present complications. (Sample notes illustrating many types of sources begin on p. 228.)

INDIRECT SOURCE

When one source quotes or refers to another, locate the original source if possible. If you do not have access to the original, identify the original source, add "quoted in" to your note, and then identify the secondary source you have used.

Huntington disagrees with sociologist Robert Bellah's argument that "all Americans except the Indians are immigrants or the descendants of immigrants."[1]

1. Robert N. Bellah, *The Broken Covenant: American Civil Religion in a Time of Trial*, 2nd ed. (Chicago: University of Chicago Press, 1992), 88, quoted in Samuel P. Huntington, *Who Are We? The Challenges to America's National Identity* (New York: Simon and Schuster, 2004), 39.

VISUAL MATERIAL

When you use a photograph, chart, or other illustration from a source, add a credit line to identify your source after the numbered heading and the explanatory title. If the visual comes from a published source—printed or electronic—you may need to request permission to incorporate it into your paper. (See pp. 240–42.) If so, add whatever phrasing the copyright holder requests.

Fig. 1. Campus library. (Photograph by Nita Jensen. Reproduced by permission from *The Campus News*.)

How Are You Capturing the Source Material?

The way you have captured source material—whether in your own words or in a short or long quotation—also may affect how you present and credit it. Always identify any words taken directly from a source by setting them off with quotation marks or using the indented form for a long block quotation. (See p. 110 for a general checklist about quotations.) Because most notes refer to specific places in a source, add a page number or other location, such as a numbered paragraph, heading (under "Conclusion"), or chapter number (chap. 3).

The next five examples illustrate how Alexander Poster varied his presentation of sources in his history paper, "The Patterns of Terror in 1965 Indonesia and 1975 East Timor." The corresponding note from his paper follows each example.

OVERALL SUMMARY OR IMPORTANT IDEA

After citing the source in his note, Alex followed it with a clarification that was pertinent but added more detail than he wanted to include in his text.

By 1966, Suharto had displaced Sukarno as Indonesia's head of state; a right-wing regime ruled over the once politically diverse nation.[1]

1. Helen Fein, "Revolutionary and Anti-Revolutionary Genocides: A Comparison of State Murders in Democratic Kampuchea, 1975 to 1979, and in Indonesia, 1965 to 1966," *Comparative Studies in Society and History* 35, no. 4 (1993): 802. Though newspapers asserted Sukarno was in charge immediately after the coup, his power had already begun to slip.

BLENDED PARAPHRASE AND QUOTATION

Soldiers herded villagers into "resettlement camps"; thousands starved as "assimilation" into Indonesian culture progressed.[2]

2. Matthew Jardine, *East Timor: Genocide in Paradise* (Tucson, AZ: Odonian Press, 1995), 57–58.

BRIEF QUOTATION WITH FORMAL LAUNCH STATEMENT

Soe Hok Gie describes the onset of the violence: "Vigilante groups began roaming around dressed in black and armed with swords, knives, cudgels, and even firearms."[3]

3. Soe Hok Gie, "The Mass Killings in Bali," in *The Indonesian Killings 1965–1966,* ed. Robert Cribb, Monash Papers on Southeast Asia, no. 21, 241–58 (Clayton, Victoria: Centre of Southeast Asian Studies, 1991), 256.

BRIEF QUOTATION INTEGRATED IN SENTENCE

The lack of discipline among the incensed soldiers is demonstrated by the looting that occurred in the capital where "cars, items of furniture, cutlery, even windows were taken"[4] from the homes of residents who had been directed to report elsewhere.

4. John Taylor, *Indonesia's Forgotten War: The Hidden History of East Timor* (London: Zed Books, 1993), 69.

LONG QUOTATION

To support his thesis that the two events he investigated were instances of "collective running amok" even though they pursued different objectives, Alex used a long indented quotation to introduce his own definition of that concept.

Robert Cribb defines the concept of "amok" as follows:

> Amok has two classical forms, individual and collective. In the individual form (running amok), a person facing ruin, shame, or social humiliation suddenly breaks into indiscriminate, murderous violence which only ceases when he is killed (or halted) . . . by the appalled bystanders or by the forces of law and order. . . . Collective amok is more calculated and resembles the Viking *berserk:* typically a group of soldiers adopts violent frenzy against opposing odds. Both forms of amok involve the redemption of honour by frenzied violence.[5]

5. Robert Cribb, "Problems in the Historiography of the Killings in Indonesia," in *The Indonesian Killings 1965–1966,* ed. Robert Cribb, Monash Papers on Southeast Asia, no. 21, 1–44 (Clayton, Victoria: Centre of Southeast Asian Studies, 1991), 33.

CITING AND LISTING SOURCES IN *CHICAGO* STYLE

In *Chicago* style, a full note and a bibliography entry supply nearly the same information, but the two are arranged differently. Both are illustrated in the examples paired in this section so that you can easily spot their differences. In the examples, as in your paper, the note begins with the note number that connects it to your quotation or other reference in your text. The bibliography entry begins with the author's last name so that you can readily place it in alphabetical order. A note typically concludes with the specific location, generally a page number, of the information you have used, while a bibliography entry supplies the range of pages for articles or selections from books. If your bibliography provides complete details about each source, you may condense full notes to brief ones, limited to only the author's last name, the work's short title, and the page number or other location. The examples below show full notes, however, in case you are required to provide them, with or without a bibliography.

If you supply footnotes, your software should position them correctly, each falling at the bottom of the page where its corresponding number appears in the text. If you supply endnotes, organize them in numerical sequence on a new page called "Notes." Follow that page with your list of sources, titled "Bibliography," also beginning on a new page. Double-space the list unless directed otherwise. Arrange the entries alphabetically by author's last name or, for works with no author, by title. Begin the first line of each entry at the left margin, and indent any following lines. (Use the menu in your software—Format-Paragraph-Indentation—to set up this "hanging" or special indentation.) Include all the sources that you actually cite in your paper. If you wish, you may add other significant works unless your instructor has requested otherwise.

Use the *Chicago* Source Navigators (pp. 218–25) to help you get started. They illustrate how to find the necessary information in four types of sources and how to prepare the corresponding note and bibliography entry for each source. Refer also to the bibliography in the sample student paper (p. 256) so that you can see how your final product should look. To a great extent, listing sources correctly depends on following patterns and paying attention to details such as capitalization and punctuation. In addition, *Chicago* style favors simplifying details in the following ways:

- List, in most cases, only the first of several cities where a publisher has offices, adding an abbreviated state name except for major cities that do not need further identification.

- Drop "Inc.," "Co.," and similar abbreviations from the name of the publishing company (unless you prefer to cite it in full).
- Use common scholarly abbreviations such as "n.p." for "no place," "n.d." for "no date," "chap." for "chapter," "no." for an issue "number," and "Ibid." for "in the same place" to refer to the preceding note.
- Use only the latest copyright date for a book and the publication date for magazines (without any volume or issue numbers), but identify both volume and issue for journals.
- Supply an electronic access date after the URL only if it is standard in the field, requested by your instructor, or needed to identify the timing of critical changes: (accessed May 3, 2005).
- Drop "The" from the names of publishers, journals, and newspapers.

As you prepare your own notes and bibliography entries, begin with the essential opening information: the name of the author. The various author formats apply whether you have used a book, an article, a Web page, or some other type of source. After that, however, the type of work you have used will determine the rest of the format. Find that type in this section, and match your entry to the example, supplying the same information in the same order with the same punctuation and other features. If you can't find an example that exactly matches your source, consult the *Chicago Manual* itself (or Turabian), ask your instructor for advice, or model your entry on the form that seems the closest match. As you work on your list, keep in mind these two key questions, which are used to organize the sample entries that follow:

Who wrote it?

What type of source is it?

Who Wrote It?

INDIVIDUAL AUTHOR

1. Eric Dorn Brose, *Europe in the Twentieth Century* (New York: Oxford University Press, 2005), 432.

Brose, Eric Dorn. *Europe in the Twentieth Century*. New York: Oxford University Press, 2005.

TWO OR THREE AUTHORS

List the authors' names in the order in which they appear in the source.

1. Naomi Pasachoff and Robert J. Littman, *A Concise History of the Jewish People,* 2nd ed. (Lanham, MD: Rowman & Littlefield, 2005), 269.

Pasachoff, Naomi, and Robert J. Littman. *A Concise History of the Jewish People.* 2nd ed. Lanham, MD: Rowman & Littlefield, 2005.

FOUR OR MORE AUTHORS

In your bibliography, include as many as ten names. If the source has more than ten authors, list seven, and add "et al."

1. Marilyn Osborn and others. *A World of Difference? Comparing Learners Across Europe* (Berkshire, UK: Open University Press, 2003), 5.

Osborn, Marilyn, Patricia Broadfoot, Elizabeth McNess, Claire Planel, Birte Ravn, and Pat Triggs. *A World of Difference? Comparing Learners Across Europe.* Berkshire, UK: Open University Press, 2003.

ORGANIZATION AUTHOR

1. World Bank, *Lifelong Learning in the Global Knowledge Economy: Challenges for Developing Countries* (Washington, DC: World Bank, 2003), 21.

World Bank. *Lifelong Learning in the Global Knowledge Economy: Challenges for Developing Countries.* Washington, DC: World Bank, 2003.

EDITOR AS AUTHOR

If an editor or a compiler (comp.) is named but not an author, supply that name as the author.

1. Toyin Falola, ed., *The Dark Webs: Perspectives on Colonialism in Africa* (Durham, NC: Carolina Academic Press, 2005), 7.

Falola, Toyin, ed. *The Dark Webs: Perspectives on Colonialism in Africa.* Durham, NC: Carolina Academic Press, 2005.

AUTHOR AND TRANSLATOR

1. Robert John Morrissey, *Charlemagne and France: A Thousand Years of Mythology,* trans. Catherine Tihanyi (Notre Dame, IN: University of Notre Dame Press, 2003), 8.

Morrissey, Robert John. *Charlemagne and France: A Thousand Years of Mythology.* Translated by Catherine Tihanyi. Notre Dame, IN: University of Notre Dame Press, 2003.

UNIDENTIFIED AUTHOR

If a work does not name an author or editor, begin with the title. If the author is not listed on the title page but is suspected or identified, include the name in brackets.

1. [George Washington Carleton], *The Suppressed Book about Slavery* (1864).

[Carleton, George Washington]. *The Suppressed Book about Slavery.* 1864.

What Type of Source Is It?

Once you have found the format that fits the author, look for the type of source that best matches yours. Mix and match the patterns illustrated as needed. For example, a collection of essays in its third edition might send you to several examples until you have covered all of its identifying elements.

Printed or Electronic Book

PRINTED BOOK

In this instance, the book reprints its original version.

1. Louis F. Burns, *A History of the Osage People* (Tuscaloosa: University of Alabama Press, 2004), 89–91.

Burns, Louis F. *A History of the Osage People.* Tuscaloosa: University of Alabama Press, 2004. First published 1989 by the author.

ONLINE BOOK

If applicable, include the original date of publication of the work.

1. Charles Dickens, *Great Expectations* (1867; Project Gutenberg, 1998), chap. 47, http://www.gutenberg.org/etext/1400.

Dickens, Charles. *Great Expectations.* 1867; Project Gutenberg, 1998. http://www.gutenberg.org/etext/1400.

MULTIVOLUME WORK

Use the abbreviation "vol." unless a page number comes next. Add any individual title for the volume. Depending on what you used, you may cite a volume or the whole work.

1. Scott Derks, *Working Americans, 1880-1999,* vol. 2, *The Middle Class* (Millerton, NY: Grey House, 2001), 245.

Derks, Scott. *Working Americans, 1880-1999.* Vol. 2, *The Middle Class.* Millerton, NY: Grey House, 2001.

Derks, Scott. *Working Americans, 1880-1999.* 4 vols. Millerton, NY: Grey House, 2000-2002.

REVISED EDITION

Abbreviate terms such as "edition" ("ed.") or "revised" ("rev.").

1. Susan Woodford, *The Art of Greece and Rome,* 2nd ed. (Cambridge: Cambridge University Press, 2004), 116.

Woodford, Susan. *The Art of Greece and Rome.* 2nd ed. Cambridge: Cambridge University Press, 2004.

Part of a Printed or Electronic Book

When citing part of a book, give the author of that part first; add the editor of the book after the title. Supply the page numbers or the chapter number of the selection.

SELECTION FROM A PRINTED BOOK

If the book has an editor, add that name as shown in the entry for an essay or other work in an edited collection (see p. 235).

1. Chris Lamb, "You Should Have Been in the World Trade Center!" in *Drawn to Extremes: The Use and Abuse of Editorial Cartoons* (New York: Columbia University Press, 2004), 1-29.

Lamb, Chris. "You Should Have Been in the World Trade Center!" Chap. 1 in *Drawn to Extremes: The Use and Abuse of Editorial Cartoons.* New York: Columbia University Press, 2004.

PREFACE, INTRODUCTION, FOREWORD, OR AFTERWORD

1. Marian Wright Edelman, afterword to *My Soul Looks Back in Wonder: Voices of the Civil Rights Experience,* by Juan Williams (New York: AARP / Sterling, 2004), 211-14.

Edelman, Marian Wright. Afterword to *My Soul Looks Back in Wonder: Voices of the Civil Rights Experience,* by Juan Williams. New York: AARP / Sterling, 2004.

ESSAY, SHORT STORY, POEM, OR PLAY FROM AN EDITED COLLECTION

1. Jostein Gripsrud, "Broadcast Television: The Chances of Its Survival in the Digital Age," in *Television after TV: Essays on a Medium in Transition,* ed. Lynn Spigel and Jan Olsson, 210-23 (Durham, NC: Duke University Press, 2004), 221.

Gripsrud, Jostein. "Broadcast Television: The Chances of Its Survival in the Digital Age." In *Television after TV: Essays on a Medium in Transition,* edited by Lynn Spigel and Jan Olsson, 210-23. Durham, NC: Duke University Press, 2004.

TWO OR MORE WORKS FROM THE SAME EDITED COLLECTION

You can give publication details for the entire work one time and cross-reference this information in both your notes and your bibliography when you cite other selections.

1. Jostein Gripsrud, "Broadcast Television: The Chances of Its Survival in the Digital Age," in *Television after TV: Essays on a Medium in Transition,* ed. Lynn Spigel and Jan Olsson, 210-23 (Durham, NC: Duke University Press, 2004), 221.

7. Anna Everett, "Double Click: The Million Women March on Television and the Internet," in *Television after TV* (see note 1), 224-41.

Everett, Anna. "Double Click: The Million Women March on Television and the Internet." In Spigel and Olsson, *Television after TV,* 224-41.

Gripsrud, Jostein. "Broadcast Television: The Chances of Its Survival in the Digital Age." In Spigel and Olsson, *Television after TV,* 210-23.

Spigel, Lynn, and Jan Olsson, eds. *Television after TV: Essays on a Medium in Transition.* Durham, NC: Duke University Press, 2004.

ARTICLE FROM A PRINTED REFERENCE WORK

Cite a well-known encyclopedia only in a note. Identify the edition, adding "s.v." (for "sub verbo," meaning "look under the word") before the entry title. For a specialized encyclopedia, you may include full information in a note and bibliography entry.

1. *Encyclopedia Britannica,* 15th ed., s.v. "Crusades."

2. *The Oxford Encyclopedia of Food and Drink in America,* ed. Andrew F. Smith (New York: Oxford University Press, 2004), s.v. "Cooking Contests" (by Becky Mercuri).

Smith, Andrew F., ed. *The Oxford Encyclopedia of Food and Drink in America.* 2 vols. New York: Oxford University Press, 2004.

Article in a Printed or Electronic Periodical

ARTICLE FROM A PRINTED JOURNAL

Supply both the volume and issue numbers, unless the journal supplies only one of these.

1. David Cressy, "Revolutionary England 1640-1642," *Past and Present,* no. 181 (2003): 36.

2. David E. Hogan and Michael Mallott, "Changing Racial Prejudice through Diversity Education," *Journal of College Student Development* 46, no. 2 (2005): 116.

Cressy, David. "Revolutionary England 1640-1642." *Past and Present,* no. 181 (2003): 35-71.

Hogan, David E., and Michael Mallott. "Changing Racial Prejudice through Diversity Education." *Journal of College Student Development* 46, no. 2 (2005): 115-25.

ARTICLE FROM AN ONLINE JOURNAL

1. Bruce Stewart, "Medium and Message: Reflections on Irish Studies in the Informatics Age," *Journal of the Association for History and Computing* 7, no. 3 (December 2004), last paragraph, http://mcel.pacificu.edu/JAHC/JAHCVII3/ARTICLES/stewart.html.

Stewart, Bruce. "Medium and Message: Reflections on Irish Studies in the Informatics Age." *Journal of the Association for History and Computing* 7, no. 3 (December 2004), http://mcel.pacificu.edu/JAHC/JAHCVII3/ARTICLES/stewart.html.

MATERIAL ACCESSED THROUGH AN ONLINE LIBRARY OR SUBSCRIPTION SERVICE

Include either the URL of the main page of the database or a stable URL for the article.

1. Brooke A. Knight, "Watch Me! Webcams and the Public Exposure of Private Lives," *Art Journal* 59, no. 3 (2000): 21. http://links.jstor.org/sici?sici=0004-3249%28200024%2959%3A4%3C21%3AWMWATP%3E2.0.CO%3B2-M.

Knight, Brooke A. "Watch Me! Webcams and the Public Exposure of Private Lives." *Art Journal* 59, no. 3 (2000): 21-25. http://links.jstor.org/sici?sici=0004-3249%28200024%2959%3A4%3C21%3AWMWATP%3E2.0.CO%3B2-M.

Knight, Brooke A. "Watch Me! Webcams and the Public Exposure of Private Lives." *Art Journal* 59, no. 3 (2000): 21-25. http://www.jstor.org/.

ARTICLE FROM A PRINTED MAGAZINE

Identify the article only by the date, not by any volume and issue numbers. In your bibliography, leave out the article's pages because they frequently are not consecutive.

1. Richard Brookhiser, "Orange Parade," *National Review,* March 28, 2005, 52.

2. "Sweeteners Can Sour Your Health," *Consumer Reports on Health,* January 2005, 8.

Brookhiser, Richard. "Orange Parade." *National Review,* March 28, 2005.

"Sweeteners Can Sour Your Health." *Consumer Reports on Health,* January 2005.

ARTICLE FROM AN ONLINE MAGAZINE

1. Jeff Chu, Rita Healy, and Chris Maag, "Fighting Words 101," *Time,* March 14, 2005, http://www.time.com/time/society/article/0,23657,1034711,00.html.

Chu, Jeff, Rita Healy, and Chris Maag. "Fighting Words 101." *Time,* March 14,
    2005. http://www.time.com/time/society/article/0,23657,1034711,00.html.

ARTICLE FROM A PRINTED NEWSPAPER

In your bibliography, you may identify the number of the edition or section in which the article appeared, but leave out its page numbers. Unless the newspaper is well known, add the name of the city if it is not already in its title.

1. Karen W. Arenson, "Bonus Planned for Colleges Whose Students Finish on
Time," *New York Times,* January 26, 2005, late edition, sec. B.

Arenson, Karen W. "Bonus Planned for Colleges Whose Students Finish on Time."
    New York Times, January 26, 2005, late edition, sec. B.

ARTICLE FROM AN ONLINE NEWSPAPER

1. Marcella Bombardieri, "Student Life at Harvard Lags Peer Schools, Poll
Finds," *Boston Globe,* March 29, 2005, http://www.boston.com/news/globe/.

Bombardieri, Marcella. "Student Life at Harvard Lags Peer Schools, Poll Finds."
    Boston Globe, March 29, 2005. http://www.boston.com/news/globe/.

EDITORIAL

1. Editorial, *Los Angeles Times,* March 5, 2005.

Editorial. *Los Angeles Times.* March 5, 2005.

REVIEW

Begin with the name of the reviewer.

1. Maurice Timothy Reidy, "Breaking the Code," review of *The Da Vinci Code,*
by Dan Brown, *Commonweal,* September 12, 2003, 46.

Reidy, Maurice Timothy. "Breaking the Code." Review of *The Da Vinci Code,* by
    Dan Brown. *Commonweal,* September 12, 2003.

PUBLISHED INTERVIEW

1. George H. W. Bush, interview by Jon Meacham, " 'People Are More
Hopeful,'" *Newsweek,* March 14, 2005, 8.

Bush, George H. W. Interview by Jon Meacham. "'People Are More Hopeful.'" *Newsweek,* March 14, 2005.

LETTER TO THE EDITOR

No title or headline is needed.

1. Michael Schlesinger, letter to the editor, *Los Angeles Times,* March 26, 2005.

Schlesinger, Michael. Letter to the Editor. *Los Angeles Times,* March 26, 2005.

Other Printed or Electronic Documents

PRINTED GOVERNMENT DOCUMENT

1. Senate Committee on Foreign Relations, *Anti-Semitism in Europe: Hearing before the Subcommittee on Foreign Affairs,* 108th Cong., 2d sess., April 8, 2004.

U.S. Congress. Senate. Committee on Foreign Relations. *Anti-Semitism in Europe: Hearing before the Subcommittee on European Affairs.* 108th Cong., 2d sess., April 8, 2004.

ONLINE GOVERNMENT DOCUMENT

1. U.S. Department of Education, Federal Student Aid Office, *Funding Your Education: 2005-2006* (Washington, DC: U.S. Department of Education, 2005), 9, http://studentaid.ed.gov/students/attachments/siteresources/fund_ed_high.pdf.

U.S. Department of Education. Federal Student Aid Office. *Funding Your Education: 2005-2006.* Washington, DC: U.S. Department of Education, 2005. http://studentaid.ed.gov/students/attachments/siteresources/fund_ed_high.pdf.

PAMPHLET

1. Susan Valentine, *E-Powering the People: South Africa's Smart Cape Access Project* (Washington, DC: Council on Library and Information Resources, 2004), 5-6.

Valentine, Susan. *E-Powering the People: South Africa's Smart Cape Access Project.* Washington, DC: Council on Library and Information Resources, 2004.

Internet or Electronic Source

Your notes and bibliography should both identify what you have used and assist a reader who wishes to find the same material. However, the second objective can be difficult to achieve with Internet materials that exist only in electronic form and may disappear or change at random.

New electronic forms (such as blogs) can rapidly develop. Despite such complications, supply the available information that would assist a reader in accessing material online. (See pp. 218–25 for Source Navigators showing the basic *Chicago* entries for electronic sources. See also the directory on pp. 213–14 for other entries for electronic sources, including books and periodical articles.)

WEB SITE

1. Symantec Corporation, *Security Response--Hoax Page,* http://www.symantec .com/avcenter/hoax.html.

Symantec Corporation. *Security Response--Hoax Page.* http://www.symantec.com/avcenter/hoax.html.

SECTION OR PAGE FROM A WEB DOCUMENT

1. The Coca-Cola Company, "2004 Annual Report on Form 10-K," *Coca-Cola Investors,* http://www2.coca-cola.com/investors/pdfs/form_10K_2004.pdf.

The Coca-Cola Company. "2004 Annual Report on Form 10-K," *Coca-Cola Investors.* http://www2.coca-cola.com/investors/pdfs/form_10K_2004.pdf.

HOME PAGE FOR A CAMPUS DEPARTMENT OR COURSE

1. Emory University, "Art History Department Home Page," *Emory Art History Department,* http://arthistory.emory.edu.

Emory University. "Art History Department Home Page." *Emory Art History Department.* http://arthistory.emory.edu.

PUBLICATION ON CD-ROM

1. *The Paths Dreams Take: Japanese Art from the Collections of Mary Griggs Burke and the Metropolitan Museum of Art,* CD-ROM, Metropolitan Museum of Art.

The Paths Dreams Take: Japanese Art from the Collections of Mary Griggs Burke and the Metropolitan Museum of Art. CD-ROM. Metropolitan Museum of Art.

Visual or Audio Source

ADVERTISEMENT

Although *Chicago* does not supply an example for this type of source, you might apply its general advice about adapting a similar format—in this case, a magazine article.

1. "Iomega," *PC World,* May 2005, 111.

"Iomega." *PC World,* May 2005, 111.

COMIC OR CARTOON

1. Matt Groening, "Bartzilla," in *Big Bratty Book of Bart Simpson* (New York: HarperCollins, 2004), 78-88, comic.

Groening, Matt. *Big Bratty Book of Bart Simpson.* New York: HarperCollins, 2004.

PHOTOGRAPH

If you refer to several photographs from one source, cite the source in the bibliography, but not the individual items.

1. George Inness, "Two Sisters in the Garden," in *George Inness and the Science of Landscape,* by Rachel Ziady DeLue (Chicago: University of Chicago Press, 2004), 70, figure 13.

DeLue, Rachel Ziady. *George Inness and the Science of Landscape.* Chicago: University of Chicago Press, 2004.

WORK OF ART

Indicate the work's medium—oil, pastel, and so forth—as well as its location.

1. Paul Cézanne, *Portrait of Delacroix after a Photograph by Eugène Durieu,* crayon, 1864-1866, Avignon, Musée Calvet.

Cézanne, Paul. *Portrait of Delacroix after a Photograph by Eugène Durieu.* Crayon, 1864-1866. Avignon, Musée Calvet.

MAP

If you refer to several maps from one source, cite the source in the bibliography, but not the individual items.

1. John Callow, *King in Exile: James II; Warrior, King and Saint, 1689-1701* (Gloucestershire, UK: Sutton, 2004), 83, map 2.

Callow, John. *King in Exile: James II; Warrior, King and Saint, 1689-1701.*
Gloucestershire, UK: Sutton, 2004.

AUDIOTAPE OR RECORDING

Identify the medium (compact disc, audiocassette, and so forth), and use the symbol © for "copyright" and ℗ for "published." List first the name most relevant to your paper—composer, conductor, or performer.

1. George Gershwin, *Our Love Is Here to Stay: Ella & Louis Sing Gershwin,* compact disc, ℗ 1998 Verve. Original sound recording made by Capitol Studios, 1956-1959.

Gershwin, George. *Our Love Is Here to Stay: Ella & Louis Sing Gershwin.* Compact disc. ℗ 1998 Verve. Original sound recording made by Capitol Studios, 1956-1959.

PROGRAM ON TELEVISION OR RADIO

1. *Desperate Housewives,* episode no. 108, ABC, December 12, 2004, directed by Larry Shaw and written by Jenna Bans.

Desperate Housewives. Episode no. 108, ABC, December 12, 2004. Directed by Larry Shaw and written by Jenna Bans.

FILM

1. *Ocean's Twelve,* directed by Steven Soderbergh (Hollywood, CA: Warner Brothers, 2004).

Ocean's Twelve. Directed by Steven Soderbergh. Hollywood, CA: Warner Brothers, 2004.

Conversation or Field Artifact

PRIMARY MATERIAL FROM AN ARCHIVE

Identify the title and date of a specific item only in your note unless it was the only material you used from the archive. Name the collection and the archive that houses the material.

1. Clarence Darrow to Mary Field Parton, 1914, ser. 1, box 1, fol. 5, Mary Field Parton-Clarence Darrow Papers, 1909-1975, Newbery Library, Chicago.

Mary Field Parton-Clarence Darrow Papers, 1909-1975. Correspondence. Newbery
    Library, Chicago.

PERSONAL INTERVIEW

Your own face-to-face, e-mail, or telephone interview, whether your interviewee is named or confidential, should be cited only in your notes or
simply identified in your text.

1. Amy Frame, in discussion with the author, December 4, 2005.

2. Interview with union organizer, December 2, 2005.

3. Barry Welton, e-mail message to author, November 14, 2005.

BROADCAST INTERVIEW

1. David Bennahum, interview by Jeffrey Brown, *The Newshour with Jim
Lehrer,* PBS, June 24, 2004.

Bennahum, David. Interview by Jeffrey Brown. *The Newshour with Jim Lehrer.*
    PBS. June 24, 2004.

SPEECH OR LECTURE

1. Richard B. Freeman, "Can We Improve Worker Well-Being in the New
Global Economy?" (lecture, Georgia State University, Atlanta, GA, April 8, 2005).

Freeman, Richard B. "Can We Improve Worker Well-Being in the New Global
    Economy?" Lecture, Georgia State University, Atlanta, GA, April 8, 2005.

E-MAIL MESSAGE

Include these personal messages only in a note, not your bibliography.
For privacy reasons, do not include the e-mail address of the sender.

1. Elizabeth Winter, e-mail message to author, January 3, 2005.

ONLINE POSTING

If the source has been archived, supply the URL, but identify it only in
a note.

1. David Kent, e-mail to Information Literacy Instruction Listserv, February
22, 2005.

Multiple Sources and Notes

SEVERAL SOURCES IN ONE NOTE

When you consolidate related citations in one note, arrange the sources in the sequence used in your passage; separate them with semicolons. Supply a separate entry for each source in your bibliography.

1. Maurice Timothy Reidy, "Breaking the Code," review of *The Da Vinci Code,* by Dan Brown, *Commonweal,* September 12, 2003, 46; Alvaro Silva, "My Life in Opus Dei," *Commonweal,* February 25, 2005, 12; Brian Bethune, "Cracking the Da Vinci Code," *Maclean's,* December 20, 2004, 36.

SEVERAL NOTES CITING THE SAME SOURCE

Unless you are consistently using brief notes with a full bibliography, supply a full note the first time you identify a source. Should you refer to the same source again, restrict your note to the basics: the author's last name, the work's title in concise form (if more than four words), and the page or other location. If you refer to the same source in two notes in sequence, use "Ibid.," meaning "from the same place."

1. Maurice Timothy Reidy, "Breaking the Code," review of *The Da Vinci Code,* by Dan Brown, *Commonweal,* September 12, 2003, 46.

2. "Museum Puts 'Da Vinci Code' on Trial in Leonardo's Hometown," *New York Times,* February 19, 2005, late edition, sec. A.

3. Brian Bethune, "Cracking the Da Vinci Code," *Maclean's,* December 20, 2004, 36.

4. Reidy, "Breaking the Code," 48.

5. Ibid.

6. "'Da Vinci Code' on Trial."

7. Bethune, "Cracking the Da Vinci Code," 40.

WRITING CHECKLIST

Citing Sources in Notes in *Chicago* Style

- ☐ Have you double-checked to be sure that you have acknowledged all material from a source?
- ☐ Have you placed each note number right after your quotation or after the end of the sentence or clause in which you refer to information from the source?
- ☐ Have you skimmed your note numbers in your text, checking that all are raised above the line, follow numerical order, and refer accurately to a corresponding note?
- ☐ Have you introduced each note with its number, positioned on the regular text line, and a period?
- ☐ Have you begun each note with the author of the source (or the first few words of the title for a work without an identified author)?
- ☐ Have you supplied a page number or other location whenever needed?
- ☐ Have you checked that every source cited in a note that belongs in your bibliography, if you are including one, appears there?

WRITING CHECKLIST

Listing Sources in *Chicago* Style

- ☐ Have you begun each bibliography entry with the appropriate pattern for the author's name?
- ☐ Have you figured out what type of source you have used? Have you followed the sample pattern for that type as exactly as possible?
- ☐ Have you correctly used quotation marks (for titles of articles and Web pages) and italics (for titles of books, journals, and Web sites)?
- ☐ Have you used the conventional punctuation—periods, commas, colons, parentheses—in your entry?

☐ Have you accurately recorded the names of the author, title, publisher, and so on?

☐ Have you checked the accuracy of the numbers—pages, volume, issue, and date?

☐ Have you correctly typed or pasted in the address of an electronic source?

☐ Have you arranged your entries in alphabetical order?

☐ Have you checked your final bibliography against your notes so that no sources have inadvertently been left out?

A SAMPLE RESEARCH PAPER IN *CHICAGO* STYLE

Amanda Zeddy, a history and political science major, investigated the religious environment in the southwestern United States after the Spaniards arrived in the "New World." Her paper, "Pueblo Indian Neophytes during Early Spanish Rule in New Mexico," uses *Chicago* style to identify her sources as she analyzes the situation faced by the Pueblo Indians.

itle

Pueblo Indian Neophytes during
Early Spanish Rule in New Mexico

Author

Amanda Zeddy

Course
information
nd date

Professor Mason

History 100

2 December 2005

Heading with page number

1"   Zeddy 1

Background for research question

    The social atmosphere in Spain during the fifteenth century was one of passionate religious zeal brought about by centuries of Christian-Muslim conflict. The Spanish brought with them this fervor as they colonized the recently discovered "New World." After the triumph of the Protestant Reformation in northern and central Europe, mission work was perceived as a way of restoring the Roman Catholic Church's prominence in the world. The Americas provided an ideal venue as they housed millions of "pagan" natives, supposedly ready and waiting for Catholic salvation.[1] The Pueblo Indians of New Mexico were among the Spaniards' targets for conversion. The Spanish began the conversion of the natives immediately following conquest; they subdued the Indians with "a sword in one hand and a bible in the other." They employed many methods to convert the natives, but a vast number of Indians converted not because of true piety or direct force exerted by the Spanish. Most, like the Pueblos of New Mexico, converted to Catholicism primarily out of necessity, simply to survive in the new environment that the Spanish had created.

1"

1"

Note numbers in text

Thesis stated

Topical presentation of background

    The Pueblo Indians were groups of natives in central New Mexico and northeast Arizona that resided in permanent stone or adobe dwellings. The term "Pueblo" refers to a cultural classification, which disregards the language and tribal lines that separate the various Pueblo groups. The Pueblo were mainly agricultural, growing principally beans and corn along with pumpkins, cotton, and tobacco. Despite the arid weather of the region, the Pueblos were assiduous farmers and thrived agriculturally. The natives did some limited hunting, mostly for jackrabbits. Crafts such as weaving, pottery, and basket production developed with skill and artistry. Women fashioned pots, made

Zeddy 2

bread, and owned the homes and gardens, as familial descent was

Double-spacing
throughout

usually traced through the mother's line. Men and women shared in

activities such as weaving baskets and cloth, building houses, and

farming. Individual "pueblos" were independent identities that had

connections to other pueblos through related customs and

languages.

Pueblo religion consisted in a form of animism. The religion

included various ceremonies that were believed to have powers

over the weather, the harvest, war, and hunting.[2] Religious lore

of the Pueblos expressed ideals and values that they held in high

esteem. These traditions aided in organizing and giving their

society purpose. The Western concept of linear time was foreign

to the Indians. They believed that time was cyclic or "eternally

returned." Particular events were not seen as unique. For example,

a seed that sprouts into a plant, produces fruit, and then dies is

reborn into another seed, and the cycle is repeated.[3]

The history of the Spanish contact with the Pueblo Indians

Chronological
presentation of
events

began in 1539. Rumors of "great cities in the North" enticed the

Franciscan monk Marcos di Niza to make an expedition to the

region of the Zuni Indians. Initially, relations were friendly, but

the Spanish proved capricious. Immediately following Marcos di

Niza, a substantial expeditionary force was organized by Francesco

Vasquez de Coronado to conquer the area. In the summer of 1540

Coronado's forces reached and seized the principal Zuni village. The

party also penetrated the Tiguex province on the Rio Grande, which

held twelve pueblos with a population of approximately eight

thousand.

Native insubordination was overcome with Spanish brutality

that included being burnt at the stake or shot. Genuine campaigns

of conquest did not occur until 1598 and 1599, both led by Juan de Onate of Zacatecas with a force that included four hundred men and ten Franciscans. They quickly organized forms of government in the region that included a priest in each district to control the Indians. The Spanish altered and virtually destroyed the Pueblos' way of life. Abuses of the Indians continued after Juan de Onate; on January 24, 1599, the residents of the cliff village of Acoma were massacred after a Spanish detachment was slain in that locale.[4]

Converting the Indians through mission efforts became an integral goal and desire of Spanish colonization. Indian conversion not only fulfilled the religious fervor of the Spanish but had other goals as well. With few colonists in New Mexico, there was a shortage of labor. The natives were the obvious choice of cheap labor for the Spanish missionaries. The Franciscan missionaries were to convert the Pueblos to Christianity and also to instruct the Indians in Western methods of farming, building, and mechanics.[5]

Most missionaries did not know the native language, which resulted in miscommunication between the Spanish and the Indians. Due to the lack of communication, the Indians did not fully understand or accept the basic tenets of Christianity until the missionaries finally learned their language or, more likely, the natives learned Spanish. Baptism was considered enough to save a native's soul temporarily, even if the "converted" Indian had little or no understanding of Christianity. The natives' temporary salvation through baptism was conditional; the natives were to understand that the "padre" through the Sacrament of Penance ultimately decided whether the Indians would enter heaven or purgatory. This blackmail gave a considerable amount of influence to the padres over their neophytes.[6] By 1617, there were eleven Franciscan churches in New Mexico, and fourteen thousand Indians

Zeddy 4

had been baptized. These figures expanded even further as the
Spanish gained more influence through military force and the
efforts of the missionaries to forty-three churches and thirty-four
thousand natives baptized in 1627.[7]

The arrival of Juan de Onate and the Spanish brought
confusion and chaos into Pueblo society. The Spanish disturbed
agricultural practices and trading networks among the Pueblos of
New Mexico. They seized Pueblo food supplies, which in turn
ruined trade between the Pueblos and the nomadic Apache and
Navajo tribes.[8] In addition, the Pueblos were required to pay
"tributes" to their new Spanish governor in the forms of clothing
and maize. In the arid environment in which the Pueblos lived,
these necessities were not in abundance. Thus, the New Mexican
natives found their culture dependent upon the Spanish for
subsistence, even though the Spanish were the very ones who
threatened their survival.[9] The tribute payments began when Juan
de Onate and his expedition first came to New Mexico. They lacked
their own provisions, so they forced the natives to give them their
own.[10] The brutality that the Spanish displayed when collecting
tribute from the Indians was especially callous and unfeeling, as
recorded by the Spaniard Fray Lope Izquierdo in 1601:

> Our men, with little consideration, took blankets away from the
> Indian women, leaving them naked and shivering with cold.
> Finding themselves naked and miserable, they embraced their
> children tightly in their arms to protect them, without making
> any resistance to the offenses done to them, for they are a
> humble people, and in virtue and morality the best behaved thus
> far discovered.[11]

Worse than the clothing tributes were the food tributes
exacted by the Spanish. Harvests could not be counted on every

*Long quotation
from primary
source aligns
with paragraph
indentation*

Zeddy 5

Effects explained

year to yield the same amount. Drought and natural disasters occurred frequently, which resulted in the Pueblos storing and preserving food each year in expectation of an unfruitful harvest. The Spaniards' demands for the natives' food supplies annihilated the balance that the Pueblos had maintained with their environment for countless generations.[12]

By ruining the Pueblos' harvesting techniques, the Spanish also devastated the trading networks between the Pueblos and other native groups. Trade had been a means of survival when groups suffered poor harvest years. A group would trade its goods for another village's foodstuffs, ensuring survival. When the Spanish seized and demanded provisions, these connections were destroyed.[13] Relations between the Pueblos and the nomadic Navajo and Apache tribes suffered, not only from the disrupted trading patterns, but also from a newly introduced means of raiding the Pueblos: the horse. With the horse, the Apache and Navajo groups were not limited to travel by foot and also gained the advantage of speed and a means of carrying away larger amounts of plunder. The Navajo and Apache bands now attacked the Pueblos with added frequency, more speed, and greater efficiency.[14] The Pueblos became completely dependent on their Spanish invaders for the essentials of life, clothing, food, and protection.

Thesis restated and developed

The Indians were forced to convert to Roman Catholicism in order to survive under the conditions that the Spanish had created for them. Conversion to the Pueblos was simply a practical ploy for survival; they still practiced their traditional religion, though concealing their genuine religious beliefs and practices from the missionaries.[15] In exchange for converting to Christianity, the Indians received food, clothing, and protection from the Spanish.

Zeddy 6

The natives' situation was so desperate that some even gave themselves as servants to the Spanish in hopes of obtaining maize or other foods.[16] The friars realized that the Catholic faith had little appeal to the Indians. Fray Francisco de Zamora describes why:

> [The Spaniards] took away from them by force all the food that they had gathered for many years, without leaving them any for the support of themselves and their children, robbed them of the scanty clothing they had to protect themselves . . . causing the natives much harm and wounding their feelings. This brought great discredit to our teaching, for they said that if we . . . [as] Christians caused so much harm and violence, why should they become Christians?[17]

Loyalty among the natives towards the Spanish was scant due to this hypocrisy and cruelty. Spanish military might drove more Indians to convert for the sake of protection against the Apache and the Navajo. Evidence that conversion was not complete among the Pueblos also emerged in forms of resistance. By maintaining their traditional religious practices in secret, the Indians resisted full acceptance of Western religious thought and belief. Resistance also culminated in violent resistance movements against the missionaries.

The Pueblo Indians of New Mexico faced the decision either to convert to Christianity or to subject themselves to hunger, the elements, and the threat of other hostile native groups. Their choice to convert to Roman Catholicism originated from despair and necessity, not from sincere religious devotion or even directly from Spanish military force. Evidence that the Pueblos were not true Christian converts culminated in 1680 with the Pueblo War of Independence. The Indians revolted against the oppressive missionaries who had stifled their religious practices, seized their

---

Ellipses mark omissions

Brackets mark addition to quotation

Conclusion reinforces thesis

food, demanded their labor, and abused Indian women. The Pueblo population had also plummeted drastically due to the diseases brought by the Spanish. The Pueblos placed the blame for their hardships on the Spanish, who had ended the native religious ceremonies that the Pueblo believed kept the world in balance. The resulting revolt of 1680 returned New Mexico to the Pueblos as well as liberated them from the Spanish for twelve years. With the reconquest of the Pueblos by Diego de Vargas in 1692 came more tolerant relations with the Indians.[18] Though smaller revolts continued to occur, the more lenient treatment made the Indians more apt to accept Spanish religion and customs and culminated in a culture that was a mixture of the two societies, allowing the Pueblos more freedom to practice their traditional and unique religion.

Notes

Initial full note

1. Cleve Hallenbeck, *Spanish Missions of the Old Southwest* (Garden City, NY: Doubleday, Page, 1926), 5.

Double-spaced list in numerical order

2. *The Catholic Encyclopedia,* s.v. "Pueblo Indians" (by James Mooney, transcribed by M. Donahue), http://www.newadvent.org/cathen/12554b.htm (accessed 29 Nov. 2005), 1, 9–11.

3. Ramon A. Gutierrez, *When Jesus Came the Corn Mothers Went Away: Marriage, Sexuality, and Power in New Mexico, 1500–1846* (Stanford, CA: Stanford University Press, 1991), 7–8.

4. *Catholic Encyclopedia,* 3–4.

Subsequent brief notes

5. Hallenbeck, *Spanish Missions,* 11.

6. Ibid., 85–86.

7. *Catholic Encyclopedia,* 4–5.

8. Andrew L. Knaut, *The Pueblo Revolt of 1680: Conquest and Resistance in Seventeenth Century New Mexico* (Norman: University of Oklahoma Press, 1995), 54.

9. Ibid., 57.

"Ibid." used for references to same source

10. Ibid., 58.

11. Ibid., 59.

12. Ibid.

13. Ibid., 61.

14. Ibid., 69.

15. Ibid., 53.

16. Ibid., 65.

17. Quoted in Knaut, *Pueblo Revolt,* 65–66.

18. Colin G. Calloway, *First Peoples: A Documentary Survey of American Indian History* (Boston: Bedford/St. Martin's, 1999), 81.

Bibliography

Calloway, Colin G. *First Peoples: A Documentary Survey of American Indian History*. Boston: Bedford/St. Martin's, 1999.

Specialized encyclopedia included

The Catholic Encyclopedia. http://www.newadvent.org/cathen/ 12554b.htm (accessed 29 Nov. 2005).

Gutierrez, Ramon A. *When Jesus Came the Corn Mothers Went Away: Marriage, Sexuality, and Power in New Mexico, 1500–1846.* Stanford, CA: Stanford University Press, 1991.

Double-spaced list in alphabetical order

Hallenbeck, Cleve. *Spanish Missions of the Old Southwest.* Garden City, NY: Doubleday, Page, 1926.

Knaut, Andrew L. *The Pueblo Revolt of 1680: Conquest and Resistance in Seventeenth Century New Mexico.* Norman: University of Oklahoma Press, 1995.

13

Using CSE Style

This chapter briefly explains and illustrates how to use CSE style, the format for crediting sources that is recommended by the Council of Science Editors, a professional group that has evolved from the Council of Biology Editors. This style—or a variation on it—is used in many scientific and technical fields. The guidelines for printed sources in this chapter are based on the sixth edition of *Scientific Style and Format*, published in 1994. Until its next edition is published, CSE refers researchers to the *National Library of Medicine Recommended Formats for Bibliographic Citation Supplement: Internet Formats* for advice on citing electronic sources. This chapter's models for electronic sources are based on these guidelines, available at <www.nlm.nih.gov/pubs/formats/internet.pdf>.

CITING AND LISTING SOURCES IN CSE STYLE

CITING SOURCES IN CSE STYLE

LISTING SOURCES IN CSE STYLE

UNDERSTANDING CSE STYLE

CSE recommends two systems for identifying sources: a reference-number system and an author-date system. The reference-number system uses a superscript number, raised above the text line, to refer a reader to the full entry with the same number in a numerical list of sources at the end of the paper. In contrast, the author-date system places the author's last name and the date of publication in parentheses in the text. Then that name leads to the corresponding entry in an alphabetical list of references at the end. (For examples of both formats, see pp. 261–74 for citing sources and pp. 275–85 for listing sources.) Both systems encourage accurate, efficient source citations.

Follow the system assigned by your instructor, expected in your academic field, or implemented in key journals that you have used for your research. If you are asked to follow the style of a specific journal, its directions for authors are likely to implement some version of one of these two CSE styles, and the references in its published articles also illustrate its application. Raise any questions about the format for your paper with your instructor. The four CSE Source Navigators (pp. 262–69) illustrate how to locate in your source the details necessary to cite it in CSE style. They also show, for both CSE formats, how to identify the source in your text and then list it with your other references. See also pp. 257–58 for a directory listing the sample entries supplied here.

The CSE style manual faces the challenge of describing a workable editorial style for all of the many scientific disciplines. For this reason, it tackles topics as varied as punctuation, numbers, and scientific terms, but it does not supply specific directions for preparing student papers. The following general guidelines are based on standard academic conventions as well as CSE recommendations for preparing an article for publication. As you complete your paper, refer to the format of the sample CSE paper on pp. 287–95 and the following checklist.

WRITING CHECKLIST

Formatting a Paper in CSE Style

☐ Have you allowed a one-inch margin on all four sides of the page?

☐ Have you double-spaced the entire paper unless directed otherwise for long quotations and entries in your reference list?

☐ Have you added a running header, generally a short title and a page number positioned at the far right side at the top of each page?

☐ Have you placed your heading (name, course, and date) and your title on a cover page or at the top of the first page, following your instructor's directions?

☐ Have you selected a title that accurately and specifically describes your research (as well as its limits) using standard scientific terms?

☐ Have you begun your paper with a one-paragraph abstract that sums up the main points in your paper?

☐ Have you used consistent indentation (typically one-half inch) for the first line of every paragraph and every line of any long quotation?

☐ Have you stuck to a consistent format for headings, presenting all those at the same level in the same way? (A conventional sequence is to center first-level headings and place second-level headings at the left margin on the line above the next sentence.)

☐ Have you selected headings that reflect your research process—Abstract, Introduction, Methods, Results, and Discussion—or describe the topics covered in your paper?

☐ Have you preceded any table with a numbered heading—for example, Table 2—and, after two spaces, its concise explanatory title? Have you prepared your tables so that they present data simply, clearly, and consistently?

☐ Have you followed any other visual, such as a graph, drawing, map, or photograph, with a numbered heading—for example, Figure 1—and, after two spaces, its concise explanatory title?

☐ Have you turned off your software's automatic hyphenation to avoid splitting words with hyphens at the ends of lines? Have you turned off text justification so that you have an even margin on the left but not on the right?

☐ Have you begun all the entries in your list of sources at the left margin unless directed otherwise?

☐ Have you followed any specific directions from your instructor about format or electronic submission?

☐ Have you printed a clear, readable final copy and kept a backup copy of your file in case the printed copy gets lost?

CITING SOURCES IN CSE STYLE

Either system recommended by CSE, the reference-number system or the author-date system, can efficiently identify your sources. However, each has advantages and disadvantages.

When you use the reference-number system, you add a superscript number, raised above the regular text line, to identify each source to which you refer. Then you use the corresponding number for an entry in your list of references, which is arranged in numerical order and supplies the full details about each of your sources. If you cite a source again in your paper, you simply repeat the original number assigned to it. Check your software's Format-Font menu for a superscript option, or turn to its Help advice about using a sequence of numbers in your text and your list of sources.

When you use the author-date system, you supply in parentheses in your text the author's last name and the work's publication date. Each time you refer to the source, you repeat this citation. The author's name connects the material in your text with your alphabetical list of sources. There, the corresponding entry fully identifies the source.

No matter which system you use to implement CSE style, many decisions are left to you as you consider your purposes as a writer, your use of your sources, and your reader's needs. As you make such decisions, keep in mind these three questions:

- Who wrote it?
- What type of source is it?
- How are you capturing the source material?

Who Wrote It?

Crediting the author of a source is a necessary part of your ethical obligation as a researcher. As a writer, however, you decide in each instance whether to emphasize that name by mentioning it in your sentence or to

(*text continues on p. 270*)

SOURCE NAVIGATOR: An Article from a Periodical

1 The author's last name followed by first and middle initials (without periods)
2 The title of the article (without italics or quotation marks)
3 The title of the magazine (without italics or quotation marks)
4 The date of the issue
5 The article's page numbers

Reference-Number System

. . . as illustrated in Korea[1] . . .
   ①   ②   ③ ④
1. Weisman A. Earth without people. Discover 2005
  Feb:60-5. ⑤

Author-Date System

. . . as illustrated in Korea (Weisman 2005) . . .
  ①   ④   ②
Weisman A. 2005 Feb. Earth without people.
  Discover:60-5.
  ③   ⑤

②

Earth Without People

What would happen to our planet if the mighty hand of humanity simply disappeared?

① By Alan Weisman • Photo illustrations by Glen Wexler

GIVEN THE MOUNTING TOLL OF fouled oceans, overheated air, missing topsoil, and mass extinctions, we might sometimes wonder what our planet would be like if humans suddenly disappeared. Would Superfund sites revert to Gardens of Eden? Would the seas again fill with fish? Would our concrete cities crumble to dust from the force of tree roots, water, and weeds? How long would it take for our traces to vanish? And if we could answer such questions, would we be more in awe of the changes we have wrought, or of nature's resilience?

A good place to start searching for answers is in Korea, in the 155-mile-long, 2.5-mile-wide mountainous Demilitarized Zone, or DMZ, set up by the armistice ending the Korean War. Aside from rare military patrols or desperate souls fleeing North Korea, humans have barely set foot in the strip since 1953. Before that, for 5,000 years, the area was populated by rice farmers who carved the land into paddies. Today those paddies have become barely discernible, transformed into pockets of marsh, and the new occupants of these lands arrive as dazzling white squadrons of red-crowned cranes that glide over the bulrushes in perfect formation, touching down so lightly that they detonate no land mines. Next to whooping cranes, they are the rarest such birds on Earth. They winter in the DMZ alongside the endangered white-naped cranes, revered in Asia as sacred portents of peace.

If peace is ever declared, suburban Seoul, which has rolled ever northward in recent decades, is poised to invade such tantalizing real estate. On the other side, the North Koreans are building an industrial megapark. This has spurred an international coalition of scientists called the DMZ Forum to try to consecrate the area for a peace

⑤ ③   ④

I The author's last name followed by first and middle initials
2 The title of the article (without italics or quotation marks)
3 The title of the journal (abbreviated without italics or quotation marks)
4 The date of the issue
5 The number of the journal volume
6 The number of the issue (optional unless each issue begins on page 1)
7 The printed article's original page numbers
8 The name of the database
9 The publication information for the database
10 The access date, when you used the source (from your printout or your notes)
11 The total number of pages
12 The Internet address (URL, or Uniform Resource Locator) or your search path
13 Article number or other locator

Reference-Number System

. . . the environmental impact of cruise tourism² . . .
     ①   ②
  2. Johnson D. Environmentally sustainable cruise
     tourism: a reality check. Mar Policy 2002;26 ③④⑤
⑥ ⑦ ⑧ (4):261-70. In: Science Direct [database on the
     Internet]. Amsterdam: Elsevier Science; 2002 ⑨
⑩⑪[cited 2005 May 10]. 10 p. Available from: http://
  ⑫www.sciencedirect.com/; DOI:10.1016/S0308-597X ⑬
    (02)00008-8. Subscription required for access.

Author-Date System

. . . the environmental impact of cruise tourism
(Johnson 2002) . . .
  ①   ④   ②
Johnson D. 2002. Environmentally sustainable cruise
③⑤ tourism: a reality check. Mar Policy 26(4):261-70.⑥⑦
  ⑧ In: Science Direct [database on the Internet].
  ⑨ Amsterdam: Elsevier Science [cited 2005 May 10]. ⑩
  ⑪ 10 p. Available from: http://www.sciencedirect ⑫
    .com/; DOI: 10.1016/S0308-597X(02)00008-8.⑬
    Subscription required for access.

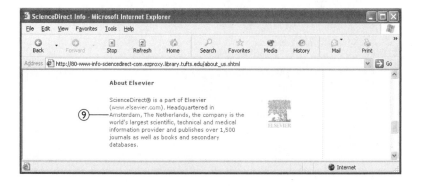

SOURCE NAVIGATOR: A Book

1 The author's last name followed by first and middle initials (without periods)
2 The title of the book (without underlining or italics)
3 The place of publication
4 The shortened name of the publisher
5 The date of publication
6 The total number of pages in the book

Reference-Number System

As Greene[3] observes, . . .
      ①   ②
   3. Greene B. The fabric of the cosmos: space, time,
      and the texture of reality. New York: AA Knopf;
      2004. 570 p.   ③   ④
      ⑤   ⑥

Author-Date System

As Greene (2004) observes, . . .
    ①   ⑤   ②
Greene B. 2004. The fabric of the cosmos: space, time,
      and the texture of reality. New York: AA Knopf.
      570 p.   ③   ④
      ⑥

② THE FABRIC
OF THE COSMOS

SPACE, TIME, AND THE TEXTURE OF REALITY

① BRIAN GREENE

④ ALFRED A. KNOPF ③ NEW YORK ⑤ 2004

THIS IS A BORZOI BOOK
PUBLISHED BY ALFRED A. KNOPF

SOURCE NAVIGATOR: A Page from a Web Site

1 The name of the organization acting as author
2 The title of the document (without underlining or italics)
3 The place of publication
4 The name of the publisher or sponsor
5 The date of creation
6 The access date, when you used the source (from your printout or your notes)
7 The Internet address (URL, or Uniform Resource Locator)

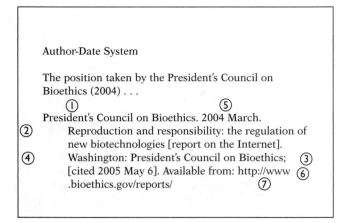

Reference-Number System

The position taken by the President's Council on Bioethics[4] . . .
    ①   ②
    4. President's Council on Bioethics. Reproduction
       and responsibility: the regulation of new biotech-
       nologies [report on the Internet]. Washington: ③
    ④ President's Council on Bioethics; 2004 March ⑤
    ⑥ [cited 2005 May 6]. Available from:
       http://www.bioethics.gov/reports/ ⑦
       reproductionandresponsibility/fulldoc.html

Author-Date System

The position taken by the President's Council on
Bioethics (2004) . . .
    ①   ⑤
    President's Council on Bioethics. 2004 March.
② Reproduction and responsibility: the regulation of
       new biotechnologies [report on the Internet].
④ Washington: President's Council on Bioethics; ③
       [cited 2005 May 6]. Available from: http://www ⑥
       .bioethics.gov/reports/ ⑦

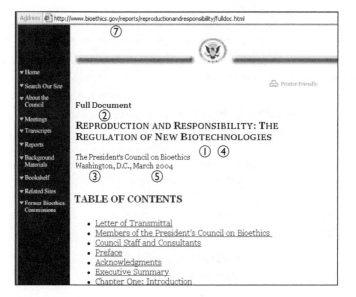

Address http://www.bioethics.gov/reports/reproductionandresponsibility/fulldoc.html

⑦

▼ Home
▼ Search Our Site
▼ About the
   Council
▼ Meetings
▼ Transcripts
▼ Reports
▼ Background
   Materials
▼ Bookshelf
▼ Related Sites
▼ Former Bioethics
   Commissions

Printer Friendly

Full Document

②

**REPRODUCTION AND RESPONSIBILITY: THE
REGULATION OF NEW BIOTECHNOLOGIES**

The President's Council on Bioethics   ① ④
Washington, D.C., March 2004

③   ⑤

TABLE OF CONTENTS

- Letter of Transmittal
- Members of the President's Council on Bioethics
- Council Staff and Consultants
- Preface
- Acknowledgments
- Executive Summary
- Chapter One: Introduction

tuck it away in your list of sources. The following examples show how the two CSE systems appropriately credit an author.

AUTHOR NOT NAMED IN SENTENCE

The reference-number system makes for easy reading because the text numbers are unobtrusive. On the other hand, it deemphasizes the author's name because a reader typically has to turn to the reference list to discover the author's name.

Studies over the past 10 years have shown that eating soy as part of a low-fat diet helps reduce cholesterol.[1] Although a wide variety of soy-based food is available, soy products vary in nutritional value and health benefits.[2] However, soy-based foods, such as tofu and soymilk, once could be purchased only in health food stores but today can be found on mainstream grocery stores' shelves.[1]

Once your reader turns to your concluding list of sources, the corresponding entries there identify the authors you need to credit.

1. Lewandowski J. Science of soy: the latest word on this versatile bean. Better Nutrition 2005 Apr:20-2.

2. Erdman Jr. JW, Badger TM, Lampe LW, Setchell KDR, Messina M. Not all soy products are created equal: caution needed in interpretation of research results. J Nutr 2004;134:1229S-1233S.

The author-date system gives more visibility to the author's name and also establishes the currency of the study. However, a long string of citations in the text or a series of long names for organization authors may interfere with easy reading.

Studies over the past 10 years have shown that eating soy as part of a low-fat diet helps reduce cholesterol (Lewandowski 2005). Although a wide variety of soy-based food is available, soy products vary in nutritional value and health benefits (Erdman and others 2004). However, soy-based foods, such as tofu and soymilk, once could be purchased only in health food stores but today can be found on mainstream grocery stores' shelves (Lewandowski 2005).

When a reader turns to your list of sources, the entries there expand the identification of the authors you need to credit.

Erdman Jr. JW, Badger TM, Lampe LW, Setchell KDR, Messina M. 2004. Not all soy products are created equal: caution needed in interpretation of research results. J Nutr 134:1229S-1233S.

Lewandowski J. 2005 Apr. Science of soy: the latest word on this versatile bean. Better Nutrition:20-2.

AUTHOR NAMED IN SENTENCE

If you wish to name the author in your text, add the note immediately after the name in the reference-number system.

According to Lewandowski[1], studies over the past 10 years have shown that eating soy as part of a low-fat diet helps reduce cholesterol.

In the author-date system, you can move the author identification from parentheses to your sentence to vary your emphasis.

As Lewandowski (2005) has demonstrated, studies over the past 10 years have shown that eating soy as part of a low-fat diet helps reduce cholesterol.

MORE THAN ONE AUTHOR

In the reference-number system, the names of multiple authors are supplied only in your list of sources unless you wish to mention them in your text sentence. In the author-date system, however, join the names of two authors with "and": (Quan and Cabot 2004). For more than two authors, follow the first author with "and others": (Quan and others 2005).

DIFFERENT AUTHORS OF MULTIPLE WORKS

Each system also allows you to group citations of different authors who have all contributed to your understanding of a specific point.

Recent studies[1,2] have concentrated on soy's contributions to healthy living.

Arrange the citations in alphabetical order in the author-date system.

Recent studies (Erdman and others 2004; Lewandowski 2005) have concentrated on soy's contributions to healthy living.

What Type of Source Is It?

Crediting the author is crucial for a CSE source reference, whether your text leads to that name using the reference-number system or you supply it in parentheses, connecting it with your list of sources using the author-date system. These systems apply regardless of the type of source you have used. Even so, some types may present complications.

INDIRECT SOURCE

If possible, locate and cite the original source. Otherwise, first identify the original source and then the source you used: (Benton 1836, cited in Murray 1998). List both with your other references; conclude your entry for the original by identifying the source you used.

VISUAL MATERIAL

Number the visuals you use in consecutive order as you introduce them in your text. Refer to each figure or table by number in your sentence: "As Figure 2 shows, . . ." or "In Table 3, . . ." To include a visual from a source, in either original or adapted form, you may need to request permission from the author or copyright holder. (Many sources—from scholarly journals to Web sites—state their permissions policy in the issue or on the site. Ask your instructor for advice if you are uncertain about how to proceed.) In addition to requesting permission, if needed, follow each table from a source with appropriate credit, citing its number or name from your reference list: "Source: Adams 2004," "Source: Adapted from Table 2 in Adams (2004)," or "Source: Reference 3." Follow a figure with a source credit (see p. 291).

PERSONAL COMMUNICATION

Personal communications (such as face-to-face interviews, letters, telephone conversations, discussions at a meeting, memos, and e-mail) are inaccessible unless they have been archived or published. For this reason, do not list them with your other sources, but do ask permission of your source before citing them in your paper. Then simply identify them in the text of your paper in parentheses, adding that they are "unreferenced": "(2005 e-mail from LT Hall to me; unreferenced)."

How Are You Capturing the Source Material?

The way that you capture source material—whether in your own words or in a short or long quotation—also may affect how you present and credit it. Although many scientific papers use no or few quotations from sources, be sure to identify any passages that you do quote directly. Set off any words taken directly from a source with quotation marks or with the indented form for a long quotation. (See p. 110 for a general checklist about quotations). CSE recommends these additional guidelines:

- Follow the capitalization used in your source for the first letter of the quotation.

- If you wish to emphasize specific words in the quotation by using italics, note your change in brackets: ". . . Despite this *claim* [italics mine] . . ."

- Place commas and periods that do not reflect the punctuation of the source outside a closing quotation mark, following British convention, unless your instructor prefers that you follow American convention and place these marks inside (as recommended by the other documentation styles in this book).

- In a long quotation, indent the first sentence (within the indented block) if it begins a paragraph in your source.

- In the reference-number system, identify the author and title of the source of a long quotation either in the text as you introduce it or in parentheses, without any concluding period—"(Lewandowski, *Science of Soy)"*—at the end of the quotation along with the reference number.

The following examples illustrate how Jonathan Lindbloom incorporated sources in his biology paper, "Isolations of *Millepora complanata* Somatic Tissue for RAPD, AFLP or Other Genetic Fingerprint Analysis." Jon wrote his paper for "Biological Problems," an independent research project required of all biology majors at his college. Following a trip to the Bahamas with a geology class, accompanied by both geology and biology faculty, Jon began research to determine the genetic relationships of various types of coral. His paper uses the author-date system. For a paper using the reference-number system, see pp. 287–95.

REVIEW OF PAST STUDIES

Other studies have utilized both morphological and genetic data to determine species boundaries in Coral elucidation of species boundaries on the sibling species of *Montastrea annularis*. Such studies have been attempted with protein electrophoresis (Knowlton and others 1992), multiple genetic loci (Lopez and Knowlton 1997), AFLP analysis (Lopez and others 1999; Lopez and Knowlton 1997), as well as a morphological analysis (Lopez and others 1999).

REVIEW OF METHODS

The isolation based on the Rowan and Powers (1991) protocol resulted in the isolation of DNA between 480 and 528 μg as determined by spectrophotometry (Figure 3).

SPECIFIC INFORMATION

Fire coral (Hydrocoral) exhibit the same life cycle as the other hydrozoans but create their own calcareous skeleton (Barnes 1990).

WRITING CHECKLIST

Citing Sources in CSE Style

☐ Have you double-checked to be sure that you have acknowledged all material from a source?

☐ Have you checked that every source cited in your text appears in your source list?

☐ Have you placed the reference number or the citation in parentheses right after the term or expression to which it applies, not after a sentence pause or at the end of the sentence?

☐ If you are using the reference-number system, have you made sure that your note numbers are all in superscript, raised above the line, and follow numerical order without skips or duplicates? Have you separated two sequential note numbers with a comma ([1,2]) and used a hyphen between more than two ([3-5]) when multiple citations appear at one place in your text?

☐ If you are using the author-date system, have you identified the author of each source in your text sentence or in parentheses? Have you noted the date for each source?

LISTING SOURCES IN CSE STYLE

Whether you use the reference-number system or the author-date system, your paper concludes with a list of sources titled "References" for the sources cited in your paper; you may add an alphabetical list, titled "Additional References" or "Bibliography," for other sources used to investigate your research question. Depending on your instructor's directions, use one of these common formats: (1) double-space the list, beginning the first line of each entry at the margin and indenting the following lines to leave the numbers or alphabetical sequence visible or (2) single-space the entries and run all lines to the left margin, using an extra line to separate each entry from the next. The entries in your reference list will look different depending on whether you have used the citation-sequence or name-year system to cite references in your paper.

- If you have used the reference-number system, number and list your sources in the sequence in which they first appeared in your paper. The examples in this section that illustrate this system begin with numbers.
- If you have used the author-date system, list the unnumbered references in alphabetical order by the first author's last name. The date follows the name, preceding the rest of the entry. The examples in this section that illustrate this system begin with authors' names, not with numbers.

Use the CSE Source Navigators (pp. 262–69) to help you get started. They illustrate how to find the necessary information in four types of sources and how to cite and list the entry for the source. Refer also to the reference list in the sample student paper (p. 294) so that you can see how your final product might look. To a great extent, listing sources correctly depends on following patterns and paying attention to details such as capitalization, spacing, and punctuation. In addition, CSE style recommends simplifying details in the following ways:

- Supply only initials for the first and middle names of authors.
- Omit periods after all these cases: author initials (except to conclude the list of names), "page" or "pages" abbreviated as "p" and "number" as "nr," "circa" ("about") abbreviated with dates as in "c2004," revised editions (Rev ed, 4th ed), and three-letter abbreviations of months (Apr, Jun).
- Skip any italics or quotation marks for titles.

- Abbreviate (without periods) a journal title of more than one word.
- Shorten a span of dates (1996-98) or pages (141-5, 139-58, 198-214) for an article or selection; provide only the total number of pages for a book (348 p).
- List only the first of several cities where a publisher has offices (or the one most convenient for readers), adding an abbreviated state name if needed to be clear.
- Drop abbreviations such as "Inc." or "Co." from the publisher's name; abbreviate "University Press" (Univ Pr) and common terms in group names such as "Society" (Soc) or "Institute" (Inst).
- Omit "The" from the names of publishers, journals, and newspapers.
- Use common scientific abbreviations familiar to general readers; if you frequently use a less familiar term, spell it out when you first use it, supply the abbreviation in parentheses, and use the abbreviation when you mention it again.

As you prepare your own entries, begin with the essential opener: the name of the author. The various author formats apply whether you have used a book, an article, a Web page, or some other type of source. After that, however, the system you are using determines the placement of the date. (As you refer to the examples in this chapter, stick either to the numbered entries that show the reference-number system or the un-numbered entries that show the author-date system.) Then, the type of source you have used determines the rest of the format. Find that type in this section, and match your entry to the example, supplying the same information in the same order with the same punctuation and other features. If you can't find an example that exactly matches your source, consult *Scientific Style and Format* itself, use the reference lists in a journal following the same CSE system as a model, ask your instructor for advice, or pattern your entry on the form that seems the closest match. As you work on your list, keep in mind these two key questions, which are used to organize the sample entries that follow:

Who wrote it?

What type of source is it?

Who Wrote It?

INDIVIDUAL AUTHOR

1. Childress JF. Human stem cell research: some controversies in bioethics and public policy. Blood Cells Mol Dis 2004;32:100-5.

Childress JF. 2004. Human stem cell research: some controversies in bioethics and public policy. Blood Cells Mol Dis 32:100-5.

TWO AUTHORS

1. Huey RB, Ward PD. Hypoxia, global warming, and terrestrial Late Permian extinctions. Science 2005 15 Apr;308:398-401.

Huey RB, Ward PD. 2005 Apr 15. Hypoxia, global warming, and terrestrial Late Permian extinctions. Science;308:398-401.

THREE OR MORE AUTHORS

List up to ten authors; for more, add "and others" after the tenth.

1. Carroll SB, Grenier SK, Weatherbee SD. From DNA to diversity: molecular genetics and the evolution of animal design. 2nd ed. Malden (MA): Blackwell; 2005. 258 p.

Carroll SB, Grenier SK, Weatherbee SD. 2005. From DNA to diversity: molecular genetics and the evolution of animal design. 2nd ed. Malden (MA): Blackwell. 258 p.

ORGANIZATION AUTHOR

Begin an author-date entry with the same abbreviation used to simplify the corresponding text citation in brackets.

1. Organisation for Economic Co-operation and Development. Assessing microbial safety of drinking water: improving approaches and methods. Paris: Organisation for Economic Co-operation and Development; 2003. 295 p.

[OECD] Organisation for Economic Co-operation and Development. 2003. Assessing microbial safety of drinking water: improving approaches and methods. Paris: OECD. 295 p.

AUTHOR OF EDITED WORK

1. Fitzpatrick SM, Bruer JT, editors. Carving our destiny: scientific research faces a new millennium. Washington: JH Pr; 2001. 320 p.

Fitzpatrick SM, Bruer JT, editors. 2001. Carving our destiny: scientific research
faces a new millennium. Washington: JH Pr. 320 p.

AUTHOR AND TRANSLATOR

1. Martínez IM, Arsuaga JL. Green fire: the life force from the atom to the mind.
Miller MB, translator. New York: Thunder's Mouth Pr; 2004. 420 p. Translation
of: Amalur, del átomo a la mente.

Martínez IM, Arsuaga JL. 2004. Green fire: the life force from the atom to the
mind. Miller MB, translator. New York: Thunder's Mouth Pr. 420 p. Translation
of: Amalur, del átomo a la mente.

UNIDENTIFIED AUTHOR

1. [Anonymous.] Asthma emerges as significant problem for elderly. Clin Resour
Manag 2001;2(11):170-3, 161.

[Anonymous.] 2001. Asthma emerges as significant problem for elderly. Clin
Resour Manag 2001;2(11):170-3, 161.

What Type of Source Is It?

Once you have found the appropriate author format, look for the type of
source and the specific entry that best matches yours. Mix and match the
patterns illustrated as needed.

Printed or Electronic Book

PRINTED BOOK

Add the total number of pages in a book at the end of the entry.

1. Forbes N. Imitation of life: how biology is inspiring computing. Cambridge:
MIT; 2004. 171 p.

Forbes N. 2004. Imitation of life: how biology is inspiring computing.
Cambridge: MIT. 171 p.

ONLINE BOOK

1. National Research Council, Committee on Research Standards and Practices to
Prevent the Destructive Application of Biotechnology, Development, Security,

and Cooperation. Biotechnology research in an age of terrorism [Internet]. Washington: National Acad Pr; 2004 [cited 2005 Jul 3]. 164 p. Available from: http://www.nap.edu/books/0309089778/html

National Research Council, Committee on Research Standards and Practices to Prevent the Destructive Application of Biotechnology, Development, Security, and Cooperation. 2004. Biotechnology research in an age of terrorism [Internet]. Washington: National Acad Pr; [cited 2005 Jul 3]. 164 p. Available from: http://www.nap.edu/books/0309089778/html

REVISED EDITION

1. Pita DD. Addictions counseling: a practical and comprehensive guide to counseling people with addictions. Rev ed. New York: Crossroad; 2004. 188 p.

Pita DD. 2004. Addictions counseling: a practical and comprehensive guide to counseling people with addictions. Rev ed. New York: Crossroad. 188 p.

Part of a Printed or Electronic Book

SELECTION FROM A PRINTED BOOK

To cite a chapter or part with a separate title but written by the same author as the book, add its description after that of the book as a whole.

1. Malarkey LM, McMorrow ME. Saunders nursing guide to laboratory and diagnostic tests. Philadelphia: Elsevier Saunders; 2005. Part 1, Nursing responsibilities in laboratory tests and diagnostic procedures; p 1-41.

Malarkey LM, McMorrow ME. 2005. Saunders nursing guide to laboratory and diagnostic tests. Philadelphia: Elsevier Saunders. Part 1, Nursing responsibilities in laboratory tests and diagnostic procedures; p 1-41.

SELECTION FROM AN EDITED COLLECTION

To cite a chapter or part written by someone other than the author of the entire work, identify it first, and then identify the book as a whole.

1. Humphries CJ, Ebach MC. Biogeography on a dynamic earth. In: Lomolino MV, Heaney LR, editors. Frontiers of biogeography: new directions in the geography of nature. Sunderland (MA): Sinauer; 2004. p 67-86.

Humphries CJ, Ebach MC. 2004. Biogeography on a dynamic earth. In: Lomolino
MV, Heaney LR, editors. Frontiers of biogeography: new directions in the
geography of nature. Sunderland (MA): Sinauer. p. 67-86.

ARTICLE FROM A REFERENCE WORK

1. Walsh B. Artificial selection. In: Pagel M, editor. Encyclopedia of evolution.
Oxford (England): Oxford Univ Pr; 2002. p 79-83.

Walsh B. 2002. Artificial selection. In: Pagel M, editor. Encyclopedia of
evolution. Oxford (England): Oxford Univ Pr. p 79-83.

Article in a Printed or Electronic Periodical

ARTICLE FROM A JOURNAL PAGINATED BY VOLUME

Include the volume number and pages for the article; although some science styles include the month (after the year) and the issue number (in parentheses after the volume), they are optional in CSE.

1. Bradshaw WE, Zani PA, Holzapfel CM, Fry J. Adaptation to temperate climates.
Evolution 2005;58:1748-63.

Bradshaw WE, Zani PA, Holzapfel CM, Fry J. 2005. Adaptation to temperate
climates. Evolution 58:1748-63.

ARTICLE FROM A JOURNAL PAGINATED BY ISSUE

Add the issue number in parentheses after the volume and before the pages.

1. Kates RW, Parris TM, Leiserowitz AA. What is sustainable development?
Environment 2005;47(3):8-22.

Kates RW, Parris TM, Leiserowitz AA. 2005. What is sustainable development?
Environment 47(3):8-22.

ARTICLE FROM AN ONLINE JOURNAL

If the article does not have page numbers, calculate its length using, for example, the number of screens ("about 3 screens") or paragraphs ("about 10 paragraphs").

1. Pattinson SD, Caulfield T. Variations and voids: the regulation of human cloning around the world. BM Med Ethics [Internet]. 2004 [cited 2005 Apr 1];5 (9): [8 p.]. Available from: http://www.biomedcentral.com/1472-6939/5/9

Pattinson SD, Caulfield T. 2004. Variations and voids: the regulation of human cloning around the world. BM Med Ethics [Internet]. [cited 2005 Apr 1];5(9): [8 p.]. Available from: http://www.biomedcentral.com/1472-6939/5/9

ARTICLE ACCESSED THROUGH A LIBRARY OR SUBSCRIPTION SERVICE

1. Sothern MS. Obesity prevention in children: physical activity and nutrition. Nutrition 2004;20:704-8. In: Science Direct [database on the Internet]. New York: Elsevier; 2005-[cited 2005 Apr 29]. 5 p. Available from: http://www.sciencedirect.com/; DOI: 10.1016/j.nut.2004.04.007. Subscription required for access.

Sothern MS. 2004. Obesity prevention in children: physical activity and nutrition. Nutrition 20:704-8. In: Science Direct [database on the Internet]. New York: Elsevier; 2005-[cited 2005 Apr 29]. 5 p. Available from: http://www.sciencedirect.com/; DOI: 10.1016/j.nut.2004.04.007. Subscription required for access.

ARTICLE FROM A PRINTED MAGAZINE

If the magazine has a volume and issue number, include these as you would for a journal. Otherwise, give its date.

1. Ruddiman WE. How did humans first alter global climate? Scientific Am 2005;292(3):46-54.

Ruddiman WE. 2005. How did humans first alter global climate? Scientific Am 292(3):46-54.

1. Burnham R. The man who remade the universe. Astronomy 2005 Feb:38-46.

Burnham R. 2005 Feb. The man who remade the universe. Astronomy:38-46.

ARTICLE FROM A PRINTED NEWSPAPER

1. Wade N. The uncertain science of growing heart cells. New York Times 2005 Mar 14; Sect A:1(col 2).

Wade N. 2005 Mar 14. The uncertain science of growing heart cells. New York Times;Sect A:1(col 2).

ARTICLE FROM AN ONLINE NEWSPAPER

1. Grady D. Mysterious viruses as bad as they get. New York Times on the Web [Internet]. 2005 Apr 26 [cited 2005 Apr 27]:[about 38 paragraphs]. Available from: http://www.nytimes.com/2005/04/26/health/26viru.html. Registration required for access.

Grady D. 2005 Apr 26. Mysterious viruses as bad as they get. New York Times on the Web [Internet]. [cited 2005 Apr 27]:[about 38 paragraphs]. Available from: http://www.nytimes.com/2005/04/26/health/26viru.html. Registration required for access.

Printed or Electronic Report or Other Document

PRINTED GOVERNMENT DOCUMENT

1. National Institutes of Health (US) [NIH]. Improving health through discovery. Bethesda (MD): NIH; 2004. Report nr 04-5449. 6 p.

[NIH] National Institutes of Health (US). 2004. Improving health through discovery. Bethesda (MD): NIH. Report nr 04-5449. 6 p.

ONLINE GOVERNMENT DOCUMENT

1. National Center for Chronic Disease Prevention and Health Promotion. Targeting tobacco use: the nation's leading cause of death [Internet]. Atlanta (GA): Centers for Disease Control and Prevention; 2005 [cited 2005 Apr 27]. Available from: http://www.cdc.gov/nccdphp/aag/pdf/aag_osh2005.pdf

National Center for Chronic Disease Prevention and Health Promotion. 2005. Targeting tobacco use: the nation's leading cause of death [Internet]. Atlanta (GA): Centers for Disease Control and Prevention; [cited 2005 Apr 27]. Available from: http://www.cdc.gov/nccdphp/aag/pdf/aag_osh2005.pdf

RESEARCH REPORT

For a report available on the Internet, see page 268.

1. Barton PE. Meeting the need for scientists, engineers, and an educated citizenry in a technological society. Policy information report. Princeton (NJ): Educational Testing Service; 2002 May. 39 p.

Barton PE. 2002 May. Meeting the need for scientists, engineers, and an educated citizenry in a technological society. Policy information report. Princeton (NJ): Educational Testing Service. 39 p.

PAMPHLET

1. Cullen V. The research fleet: University-National Oceanographic Laboratory System. Woods Hole (MA): Woods Hole Oceanographic Institution; 2000. 33 p.

Cullen V. 2000. The research fleet: University-National Oceanographic Laboratory System. Woods Hole (MA): Woods Hole Oceanographic Institution. 33 p.

Internet or Electronic Source

Although your reference list should identify your sources so that a reader could find the same material, Internet sources may complicate this task. Some sources, such as Web sites, are available only in electronic form and may disappear or change at random. New electronic forms (such as blogs) can rapidly evolve. Help a reader to access your sources by making sure each URL is correct and by supplying available information including the work's vehicle and type in brackets: for example, [Internet], [serial on the Internet], or [homepage on the Internet]. (See pp. 262–69 for Source Navigators showing the basic CSE entries for electronic sources. See also the directory on pp. 257–58 for other electronic sources, including books and periodical articles.)

WEB SITE

1. ActionBioscience.org [Internet]. Washington: American Inst of Biological Sciences; c2000-05 [cited 2005 Jun 25]. Available from: http://www.actionbioscience.org/

ActionBioscience.org [Internet]. 2000-05. Washington: American Inst of Biological Sciences [cited 2005 Jun 25]. Available from: http://www.actionbioscience.org/

SECTION OR PAGE FROM A WEB DOCUMENT

1. Davis LM, Blanchard JC. Are local health responders ready for biological and chemical terrorism? [report on the Internet]. Santa Monica (CA): RAND; 2002 [cited 2005 Mar 31]. 15 p. Available from: http://www.rand.org/publications/IP/IP221/IP221.pdf

Davis LM, Blanchard JC. 2002. Are local health responders ready for biological and chemical terrorism? [report on the Internet]. Santa Monica (CA): RAND; [cited 2005 Mar 31]. 15 p. Available from: http://www.rand.org/publications/IP/IP221/IP221.pdf

COMPUTER SOFTWARE

1. Bodyworks [computer program]. Version 6.0. Boulogne (France): Mindscape; 2002. 1 CD-ROM. Accompanied by: 1 troubleshooting guide. System requirements: Windows 95/98 or higher; 486 DX/66 MHz processor or faster; 16 MB RAM required; 256-color SVGA display or higher; 12 MB hard disk space required; 2x CD-ROM drive.

Bodyworks [computer program]. 2002. Version 6.0. Boulogne (France): Mindscape. 1 CD-ROM. Accompanied by: 1 troubleshooting guide. System requirements: Windows 95/98 or higher; 486 DX/66 MHz processor or faster; 16 MB RAM required; 256-color SVGA display or higher; 12 MB hard disk space required; 2x CD-ROM drive.

Visual or Audio Source

AUDIOTAPE OR RECORDING

In the reference-number system, begin with the title.

1. Astronomy: stars, galaxies, and the universe [sound recording]. Kater JB. Prince Frederick (MD): Recorded Books; 2004. 7 sound discs: digital, 4-3/4 in. (Modern Scholar series). Accompanied by: 1 guide, 104 p.

Kater JB. 2004. Astronomy: stars, galaxies, and the universe [sound recording]. Prince Frederick (MD): Recorded Books. 7 sound discs: digital, 4-3/4 in. (Modern Scholar series). Accompanied by: 1 guide, 104 p.

Conversation or Field Artifact

PERSONAL COMMUNICATION

Personal communications (such as personal interviews, letters, telephone conversations, discussions at a meeting, memos, and e-mail) are not listed with your other references (see p. 272.)

WRITING CHECKLIST

Listing Sources in CSE Style

☐ Have you titled your list "References," "Additional References," "Bibliography," or as directed in your assignment?

☐ If you are using the reference-number system, have you listed your references in numerical order, following the sequence of their first appearance in your text?

☐ If you are using the author-date system, have you correctly alphabetized your entries based on the author's last name? Have you arranged multiple sources by the same author in date order, ending with the most recent?

☐ Have you begun each entry with the appropriate pattern for the author's name?

☐ Have you figured out what type of source you have used? Have you followed the sample pattern for that type as exactly as possible?

☐ Have you used the conventional punctuation — periods, commas, colons, parentheses — and capitalization in your entry?

☐ Have you accurately recorded the names of the author, title, publisher, and so on?

☐ Have you checked the accuracy of the numbers — pages, volume, issue, and date?

☐ Have you correctly typed or pasted in the address of an electronic source?

☐ Have you checked your final list against your text citations to ensure that no sources have been left out?

A SAMPLE RESEARCH PAPER IN CSE STYLE

In "Contaminant Residues in Least Tern (*Sterna antillarum*) Eggs Nesting in Upper Newport Bay," Susanna Olsen proposes a biology research project to study shorebirds in a marine salt marsh in southern California. She begins her paper on the first page, following the format for an article submitted to a journal; if your instructor prefers a cover page, supply one with the paper title, your name, course number, and date. Her paper follows the reference-number system and uses conventional sections—Abstract, Introduction, Methods, and Discussion—to present her proposal. (Were she reporting a completed study, she would have added "Results" after "Methods.") Susanna's paper discusses both how the proposed study would be conducted and what it might show—to what extent conservation efforts to keep Newport Bay safe and clean are succeeding.

Least Tern 1

Susanna Olsen

18 February 2005

Biology 132

Specific title begins with key terms

Contaminant Residues in

Least Tern (*Sterna antillarum*) Eggs

Nesting in Upper Newport Bay

Abstract

One-paragraph summary

Many migratory shorebirds nest and breed during winter in Upper Newport Bay. In particular, the endangered least tern breeds on Tern Island in the bay. Terns and other seabirds and shorebirds feed on fish which often contain contaminants such as DDE and PCB. These pollutants are passed on to offspring, and if levels exceed certain levels, survival of chicks is limited. Due to Newport Bay's close proximity to urban areas, I hypothesize mercury and organochlorine levels are high. The levels of pollutants in the environment will be measured by sampling sediment from the bay. However, because metabolic factors affect the absorption and toxicity of these pollutants, eggs and dead hatchlings will be sampled to assess the effects of pollutants on the least tern.

Hypothesis stated

Introduction

Conventional headings supplied

Introduction to study region

Upper Newport Bay is home to many shorebirds year round as well as a nesting site for many migratory birds. The marine salt marsh is one of the last such remaining in southern California. Portions of the upper bay are also home to housing developments, recreational marinas, boat launch sites, and public swimming beaches. The Santa Ana River once fed into the upper bay, but currently it runs to the ocean just northwest of Newport Bay. Now the only "fresh" water to enter Upper Newport Bay comes from several storm drains that snake their way through Orange County.

Least Tern 2

On the way to Upper Newport Bay, the drains pass residential, commercial, and recreational areas such as golf courses.

Past studies of region reviewed

Past studies have shown that Upper Newport Bay contains many pollutants. For example, Dieldrin was found in the waters of

Sources cited using reference numbers

the bay, causing abnormal growth of oyster embryos.[1] Dieldrin is a pesticide used on corn, cotton, and termites; the EPA banned all uses for it in 1987. However, the compound breaks down slowly and binds to soil, being taken in by plants, insects, and birds.[2] Another study[3] assesses the role of storm water runoff and pollution in the back bay, finding that most toxicity is due to organophosphates and carbamates. Diazinon was one of the most popular organophosphates used in the United States, and as of 2005 it is banned for use as a lawn and garden insecticide.[4]

Another dangerous contaminant is PCB, or polychlorinated biphenyl, which was used for coolants, in lubricants, and in fluorescent lighting. The EPA banned use of PCBs in 1977, but their presence in the environment is still evident. Low breeding success of a colony has been linked to high levels of blood PCB.

Plural form of abbreviation with no apostrophe

Levels of PCB congeners vary between colonies despite levels of PCBs in the environment due to different activity levels of specific iso-enzymes.[5] Greater levels of enzymatic induction correlate to colonies of low breeding success.

Past studies of problem reviewed

Of sea birds currently studied, in Chile, Trudeaus' tern lays eggs containing the largest amount of mercury and PCB.[6] PCB is a danger to terns due to its effects on chick survival. Unhatched common tern eggs contain elevated levels of PCBs as compared to eggs sampled at random.[7] Similarly, in the Baltic Sea, PCBs and mercury, as well as DDT metabolites, are found in high concentrations in little tern egg samples.[8] The continued presence of PCB in the environment is one factor affecting egg

Least Tern 3

contamination. The ability of terns to metabolize PCBs as well as other pollutants also dictates the presence of pollutants in eggs and adults.

Accepted scientific abbreviations, used with and without expansion

In all areas of the world, terns have been adversely affected by pollutants. One of the most well known pollutants, DDT or dichlorodiphenyltrichloroethane, caused the same eggshell thinning in terns as in other birds during the late 1960s and 1970s. Another organochlorine known to be harmful to seabirds is DDE. DDE, one of the breakdown products of DDT, is still found in the environment despite the banning of DDT in 1972.[9] In the Baltic Sea, diseased gull chicks contain higher levels of DDE than healthy chicks.[10] Pesticides have a large effect on survival rates of chicks and on overall populations of sea birds.

Rationale for study

Hypothesis stated

Upper Newport Bay is one of the largest shorebird nesting sites of the few remaining in southern California. Housing developments, commercial areas, and golf courses exist adjacent to the ecological nature reserve, and runoff from storm drains and cliff sides ends up in the upper bay. I hypothesize that pesticides are present in moderately high levels in Upper Newport Bay, despite the apparent success of shorebird colonies. The effects of pollutants on the endangered least tern entering the bay should be quantified so that necessary action can be taken to further protect and encourage the species.

Methods

Second-level heading

Collection of Eggs

Indirect source, within another source

Contaminant levels of eggs reflect contamination of the egg-laying female, which results from increased feeding in order to produce costly eggs. Intraclutch variation of contaminants is low;[11(cited in 6)] thus a single egg from each clutch will be collected. The eggs will be collected from Tern Island in the

Least Tern 4

Northeast Portion of Upper Newport Bay. The eggs will be kept frozen at −18°C until they can be analyzed.

Collection of Unhatched Eggs and Dead Hatchlings

In past research, it has been noted that dead hatchlings and unhatched eggs contain higher levels of contaminants than eggs sampled at random. Nesting sites will be surveyed every 3 days in order to collect dead hatchlings as well as unhatched eggs from clutches where most offspring are hatched.

Sediment Collection

During breeding season, the sediment near Tern Island will be sampled weekly. Using a Van Veen grab, as described in Schiff and Bay,[12] the top 2 cm of sediment will be collected 10 meters north, south, east, and west of Tern Island. The sediment will be placed in precleaned containers and frozen at <−4°C. Organisms in the sediment will be filtered out using a screen and relaxed using $MgSO4$. The samples then will be fixed in formalin buffered with 10% borax and preserved using ethanol. The sediment will be analyzed for heavy metal content and organochlorine compounds.

Sediment samples will also be collected after major storm events (>0.25 in) from within a 10-meter radius of the point where a storm drain enters into Upper Newport Bay. A total of four storm drains empty directly into Upper Newport Bay, encompassing a large amount of the Newport Bay Watershed. Sediment samples will be analyzed as described in Schiff and Bay.[12]

Mercury Content Determination

Total mercury (Hg) content of a yolk and white homoginate will be analyzed by CWS Method No. MET-CHEM-AA-03.[13(cited in 14)] Following Braune,[14] mercury samples will be quantified using cold vapor atomic absorption spectrophotometry with a Perkin-Elmer

Numerals used for numbers that show quantity

Source authors identified in text

Source of visual credited

Least Tern 5

Newport Bay Watershed Elevation & Water Use

Drainage Facilities

G00D01	Harbor Dam (Deleted)	G02P01	Irvine-Baycrest Storm Drain
G00D02	Harbor View Dam	G02P02	Westcliff Storm Drain
G00P01	East Newport Heights Storm Drain	G03	Santa Isabel Channel
G00P02	Industrial Storm Drain	G0P01	Costa Mesa Storm Drain
G00P07	Bayside Storm Drain	G0P02	22nd Street Storm Drain
G02	East Costa Mesa Channel		

Figure 1 Newport Bay watershed elevation and water use: drainage facilities (from County of Orange (CA), Watershed and Coastal Resources Division. Newport Bay watershed elevation and water use: drainage facilities. Santa Ana (CA): County of Orange [cited 2005 Feb 1]. Available from: http://www.ocwatersheds.com/watersheds/newportbay_watercourses_elevation_image1.asp)

3030b-AAS equipped with a Varian VGA hydride generator and PCS-55 autosampler.

Organochlorine Content Determination

Organochlorine analysis will include determination of chlorobenzenes, hexachlorobenzenes, DDT, DDD, DDE, mirex, dieldrin, and PCBs. Analysis will be carried out using gas chromatography with electron capture detection.[15(cited in 14)]

Statistical Analysis

In order to compare contaminant levels in randomly sampled eggs, unhatched eggs, and dead hatchlings, a Tukey Test with unequal sample sizes will be used for a multiple comparison of means.[16] ANOVAs will be performed to determine variance between storm drain sites and contaminants in the sediment as well. Also, a 2-sample T-test assuming unequal variance can be used to compare sediment near storm drains to sediment near the breeding site.

Discussion

The least tern is on the federal and state endangered species lists. In southern California, the least tern nests and breeds in Upper Newport Bay of Orange County. Due to the urban surroundings of Newport Bay, pollutants and heavy metals make their way through the watershed and into the estuary.[1] If levels of certain contaminants, such as PCBs, are above tolerable levels in tern eggs, they may reduce survival of hatchlings. However, if hatchlings are healthy in Upper Newport Bay and show low levels of PCB contamination, this situation may not be due to levels of PCB in the environment. The sediment data can indicate whether terns are healthy due to the levels of contaminants or due to their ability, or lack thereof, to metabolize specific pollutants.

If contamination levels are low in tern eggs and in sediment samples from Newport Bay, we can assume that storm drains do

Second citation of source uses its original number

Least Tern 7

Potential significance of study explained

not carry harmful pollutants from Orange County to the bay and that the nearby housing developments on the cliffs are not causing pollution due to runoff from lawns and gardens. If these are the findings of this study, we can assume that Tern Island is a nearly ideal nesting site for the least tern, and conservationists should continue their efforts to make the area safe and clean. On the other hand, if this study finds elevated levels of pollutants, which correlate to reduced fitness, action must be taken in the watershed area to stop the use of recently banned pesticides and to discourage widespread use of pesticides in recreational areas such as golf courses.

*Sources listed
in numerical
order*

References

1. Konar B, Stephanson MD. Gradients of subsurface water toxicity to oyster larvae in bays and harbors in California and their relation to mussel watch bioaccumulation data. Chemosphere 1995;30:165-72.

2. Agency for Toxic Substances and Disease Registry (US) [ATSDR]. ToxFAQs™ for Aldrin/Dieldrin [Internet]. Atlanta (GA): US Department of Health and Human Services, Public Health Service; 2002 [modified 2004 Nov 22; cited 2005 Feb 10]. Available from: http://www.atsdr.cdc.gov/tfacts1.html

3. Taylor SM. Receiving water quality monitoring for assessment of storm water runoff impacts, a case study. Int Water Res Eng Conf Proc 1998;2:1577-82.

4. Environmental Protection Agency (US) [EPA]. Diazinon: Phase out of all residential uses of the insecticide. Pesticides: topical and chemical fact sheets. Washington: EPA; [modified 2005 Feb 1; cited 2005 Feb 9]. Available from: http://www.epa.gov/pesticides/factsheets/chemicals/diazinon-factsheet.htm

5. Van den Brink NW, Bosveld ATC. PCB concentrations and metabolism patterns in common terns (*Sterna hirundo*) from different breeding colonies in the Netherlands. Mar Poll Bull 2001;42:280-5.

6. Munoz Cifuentes J, Becker PH, Sommer U, Pacheco O, Schlatter R. Seabird eggs as bioindicators of chemical contamination in Chile. Environ Poll 2003;126:123-37.

7. Becker PH, Schuhmann S, Koepff C. Hatching failure in common terns (*Sterna hirundo*) in relation to environmental chemicals. Environ Poll 1993;79:207-13.

Least Tern 9

8. Thyen S, Becker PH, Behmann H. Organochlorine and mercury contamination of little terns (*Sterna albifrons*) breeding at the western Baltic Sea, 1978–1996 2000;108:225-38.

9. Environmental Protection Agency (US) [EPA]. DDT. Persistent bioaccumulative and toxic (PBT) chemical program. Washington: EPA; [modified 2004 May 28; cited 2005 Feb 9]. Available from: http://www.epa.gov/opptintr/pbt/ddt.htm

10. Hario M, Hirvi JP, Hollmen T, Rudback E. Organochlorine concentration in diseased cd. Healthy gull chicks from the northern Baltic. Environ Poll 2004;127:411-23.

11. Becker PH, Koepff C, Heidmann WA, Buthe A. Schadstoffmonitoring mit Seevogeln. Forschungsbericht UBA-FP 91-081, TEXTE 2/92, Umwetbundesamt, Berlin, 1991. (Cited in 6)

12. Schiff K, Bay S. Impacts of stormwater discharges on the nearshore benthic environment of Santa Monica Bay. Mar Environ Res 2003;56:225-43.

13. Neugebaur EA, Sans Cartier GL, Wakeford BJ. Methods for the determination of metals in wildlife tissues using various atomic absorption spectrophotometry techniques. 2000. (Cited in 14)

14. Braune BM, Donaldson GM, Hobson KA. Contaminant residues in seabird eggs from the Canadian arctic. II. Spatial trends and evidence from stable isotopes for intercolony differences. Environ Poll 2002;117:133-45.

15. Norstrom RJ, Won HT. Long-term preservation of egg tissue homogenates for determination of organochlorine compounds: freezing versus freeze drying. J Assoc Off Anal Chem 1985;68:129-35. (Cited in 14)

16. Zar JH. Biostatistical analysis. 4th ed. Upper Saddle River (NJ): Prentice Hall, 1999.

*ndirect source
identified*

APPENDIX

Adapting Your Research and Documentation Skills

When you are preparing a major research paper, the preceding chapters in this book will help you to find, incorporate, and credit ideas and evidence drawn from sources. In other instances, however, you may need to adapt your research and source citation skills as you prepare specific parts of a research assignment or other papers that draw on a limited number of sources. The following selections from student papers illustrate how others have applied their research skills and documented their sources in a variety of assignments.

ADAPTING YOUR RESEARCH AND DOCUMENTATION SKILLS

USING AN INFORMAL OUTLINE
WITH SOURCE NOTES

Before writing her research paper "Is Inclusion the Answer?" (pp. 166–73) about educational alternatives for disabled students, Sarah Goers developed an informal topic or keyword outline to help her plan and organize the main sections of her draft. She also added author names in parentheses to identify where she expected to integrate supporting information from her sources. Because Sarah knew that she also would need to prepare a formal outline (pp. 300–01) of her final paper, she followed a conventional outline format. To prepare your own informal outline, you can pattern it on a formal outline or use other methods such as making a numbered list or using software tools such as bullets, numbers, highlighting, or boxing.

SAMPLE INFORMAL OUTLINE

"Is Inclusion the Answer?" by Sarah Goers

Informal Outline for Inclusion Paper

I. Inclusion debate (Heinich; main viewpoints)
   A. Opposition from teacher organizations (Radebaugh on AFT and NEA)
   B. Opposition from mainstream schools (Block, Rios)
      1. Parents of mainstream students
      2. Taxpayers
   C. Support for equal rights of disabled children (1975 legislation, IDEA, Heinich)

II. Consequences of implementing inclusion
   A. Costs for special education (Rios)
      1. Federal funds
      2. General education funds
   B. Preparation of general education teachers for special needs students (Block, Jacobson, Hewett)
      1. Training
      2. Assistance from special education teachers
   C. Resources for specialized instruction (Gaskins on Landmark)
      1. Enough teachers for personalized attention
      2. Supplemental learning tools

III. Opposition of parents of disabled students (Maushard)
   A. Children happy with special education services
   B. Fear of separate schools closing before programs established in general schools

IV. Pull-out programs (Block, Urbina)
   A. Students in a general classroom also receive specialized instruction
   B. Teacher training and resources still needed
   C. Disabled children treated with respect

PREPARING A FORMAL RESEARCH PAPER OUTLINE

Sarah Goers needed to include a formal outline with her research paper "Is Inclusion the Answer?" (pp. 166–73). After she finished writing her paper, she converted her informal outline (p. 298) to a formal outline that accurately reflected her final draft. She expanded the key words and topics in her informal outline to complete sentences in order to develop her outline more specifically. She placed the outline before her paper and submitted both.

A formal outline presents the structure and logic of a paper by identifying its main points and grouping supporting points beneath them. Its labeling system and indentation show which ideas are comparable and which are subordinate. Because Sarah's paper was fairly brief and straightforward, she used only the first three of the four conventional outline levels: roman numerals (I, II, III, IV), capital letters (A, B, C), arabic numerals (1, 2), and lowercase letters (a, b). An outline of an extensive paper, such as a senior thesis, might even require one or two additional levels in parentheses: first arabic numerals—(1), (2)—and then lowercase letters—(a), (b).

When you prepare a formal outline, place your broadest ideas at the first level (roman numerals); work down to your more specific points (capital letters) and subpoints (arabic numbers, lowercase letters, and so forth). Make sure that all of the points at a given level are comparable divisions of the topic. Label them all the same way, indent them the same amount of space, and state them using parallel grammatical structure. Most readers also expect an outline to follow an A with a B and a 1 with a 2 in order to avoid single items which could not adequately develop a level.

SAMPLE FORMAL OUTLINE

Outline
Is Inclusion the Answer?

Thesis: The full inclusion of disabled children into mainstream classrooms may not truly be in the best interest of every student.

I. The practice and degree of inclusion is debated among many groups.

   A. Teacher organizations oppose full inclusion.

      1. The American Federation of Teachers believes that special needs students learn best in separate programs.

      2. The National Education Association favors a combination of general and specialized education.

   B. Some opponents argue that inclusion will negatively affect other groups.

      1. Parents of non-learning disabled students fear that inclusion will result in less academic attention for their children.

      2. Taxpayers argue that inclusion will be too expensive to implement.

   C. Despite the debate, disabled children do have equal rights to free public education.

II. The actual implementation of inclusive practices may have negative consequences.

   A. Without promised federal funding, schools may have to spend general funds on special education, possibly at the expense of other scholastic areas.

   B. General education teachers are often not adequately prepared to accommodate special needs students.

     1. Without proper training, teachers become frustrated, and special education students do not receive the instruction that they need.

     2. General education teachers often do not receive enough assistance from special education teachers.

  C. Resources needed for specialized instruction are often inadequate in public schools.

     1. Public schools often do not employ enough teachers to provide the personalized attention that disabled students need.

     2. Supplemental learning tools are not available in many public schools.

III. Some parents of disabled students and students themselves oppose inclusion.

  A. Children are happy with special education schools, and parents don't want their learning disrupted.

  B. Parents fear that separate schools will close before solid programs are established in general schools.

IV. Pull-out programs have been proposed.

  A. Students experience the general classroom and also receive specialized instruction.

  B. Pull-out programs are subject to the same concerns raised by full inclusion

     1. Teacher training is still needed.

     2. Adequate resources must be available in general classrooms.

  C. Disabled students deserve respect for their individualized needs.

DEVELOPING AN ANNOTATED BIBLIOGRAPHY

Many research assignments require an annotated bibliography, sometimes prepared as the final product of the research, sometimes handed in at intervals during the research process, and often submitted with a final paper. Annotated bibliographies also may be assigned as group projects so that each group member conducts a portion of the research to identify relevant sources, reads and evaluates sources, and writes annotations while everyone in the group or the class gains a deeper understanding of the literature about the topic.

When you build an annotated bibliography, clarify two points from the beginning. First, decide which format you should use to identify the sources in your bibliography. (See chapters 10–13 for the MLA, APA, *Chicago*, and CSE Source Navigators and formats for listing sources.) Next, determine what kinds of information your annotation should emphasize—summary, evaluation, or both. A summary (see pp. 112–113) is a brief, neutral explanation in your own words of the thesis or main points covered in a source. In contrast, an evaluation is a judgment of the source, generally assessing its accuracy, reliability, or relevance in relation to your research question. (See pp. 78–93 for more on evaluating sources.) In either case, your goal is to read critically and to convey clearly your understanding of the source.

Stephanie Hawkins prepared her APA-style paper "Japanese: Linguistic Diversity" (see pp. 203–12) for an independent study and wanted to demonstrate her critical thinking about the topic. As the following examples from her annotated bibliography illustrate, she briefly summarized her sources and added evaluative comments on their contributions, relationships, or usefulness for her study.

SELECTED APA BIBLIOGRAPHY ENTRIES WITH BRIEF ANNOTATIONS

Japanese 12

Annotated Bibliography

Abe, H. (1995). From stereotype to context: The study of Japanese women's language. *Feminist Study 21*(3). Retrieved September 27, 2004, from EBSCOhost database. Abe discusses the roots of Japanese women's language, beginning in ancient Japan and continuing into modern times. I was able to use this peer-reviewed source to expand on the format of women's language and the consequences of its use.

For an independent Japanese sign language: Harumi kimura. (1998, April–July). Retrieved October 1, 2004, from http://www.dpa.org.sg/DPA/publication/dpa_apr_jun_98/p22.html

This brief Web site describes Japanese sign language as well as a second option for deaf Japanese, simultaneous communication. This source was used mostly to confirm information from Karen Nakamura's Web site on the same topic.

Kristof, N. (1995, September 24). On language: Too polite for words. *New York Times Magazine,* pp. SM22-SM23.

Kristof, a regular columnist for the *New York Times Magazine,* briefly describes the use of honorifics as an outlet for sarcasm and insults. Although the article discusses cultures other than Japanese, it provides insight into the polite vulgarity of the Japanese language.

Nakamura, K. (2002). *About Japanese sign language.* Retrieved October 1, 2004, from http://www.deaflibrary.org/jsl.html This Web site is one of the few English resources regarding Japanese sign language (JSL). Nakamura explains the complexity of JSL and the difficulties deaf and hearing impaired Japanese face in their society.

Alan Espenlaub prepared an extensive term paper, "Coming of Age under Sputnik: Teenage Male Anxiety and Uncertainty in 1958 America," for a history course, United States Society and Thought since 1860, offered by Professor Pamela Laird. His assignment required analysis and persuasive argument, supported by both primary (firsthand) and secondary (secondhand) sources, about the era and the life of "Kenny," a typical teenager of the time. Alan organized the sources in his annotated bibliography into these two categories and supplied paragraph-length annotations, as the following selections illustrate. He also heeded the advice in his syllabus to turn to a reliable source for background and included the reference he used to check facts.

SELECTED *CHICAGO* BIBLIOGRAPHY ENTRIES
WITH PARAGRAPH ANNOTATIONS

Espenlaub 25

Annotated Bibliography

Primary Sources

"Common Sense and Sputnik." Editorial. *Life,* October 21, 1957.
This public plea urged Americans not to overreact to the
meaning of Sputnik's launch. This is one of many examples of
the mass media's attempt to lower the public anxiety level and
quell distrust in the government after the launch of Sputnik.
This propaganda effort would make an interesting research
project on its own.

"Idea Home of the Year." *Better Homes and Gardens,* September
1957.
This article is a fascinating time capsule containing what was
considered the state of the art in new suburban homes of the
time, down to the appropriate gender differences that were
assumed to be universal standards when decorating children's
bedrooms. As explained on page 59, the girl's room "goes all
out for feminine whims" with its "tiny check wallpaper" while
the boy's room "has rugged personality in bold" patterns with
a "rough finished oak" bed and "a saddle leather bench." The
boy's room featured shelving over his desk for boy stuff
whereas the girl's had a mirror so she could look at herself
while doing her homework, makeup, or hair. These images were
useful in reconstructing the bedroom of Kenny and his brother.
An interesting study would be to analyze gender stereotype
reinforcement in interior decoration, as portrayed in popular
magazines, over time.

Ford Motor Company. "This Is the EDSEL. The Emphasis Is on Engineering, But the Accent Is on Elegance." *Life,* October 28, 1957.

This double-page full-color advertisement shows a shopping center parking lot full of shining new Edsel cars and happy shoppers.

Palm trees in the background suggest that the southern California lifestyle goes along with the new Edsel lifestyle (1958 was the first year for the Edsel). In the center of the ad is a two-toned blue Edsel Citation two-door hardtop with a poodle in the front seat, even though the windows are rolled down. The ratio of male to female shoppers pictured at the shopping center is one in ten. Many dyads appear to be mother and daughter. No boys are in the picture. Since the ad's target audience was most probably adult male providers, it is possible that including a teenage son in a picture of a new car would be a negative signal in the potential purchaser's mind. On the other hand, males would feel good about being able to provide a new car for "the little woman," Mrs. Consumer.

Killian, James R., Jr. *Sputnik, Scientists, and Eisenhower: A Memoir of the First Special Assistant to the President for Science and Technology.* Cambridge, MA: MIT Press, 1977.

"Sputnik and Its Shock Waves," Chapter 1, offers an insightful discussion of the variety of reactions and motives vibrating through the nation. Chapter 4 covers pre-Sputnik science and technology policy. This book truly offers an insider's view of the significant events surrounding Sputnik.

Secondary Sources

Ambrose, Stephen E. *Eisenhower: Soldier and President.* New York: Touchstone/Simon and Schuster, 1990.

Chapter 18 covers both the events at Little Rock, Arkansas,

and Sputnik (early 1957 to early 1958). The Sputnik launch led
to what can accurately be called a national hysteria of press
coverage, which increased the intensity of mass fear in the
American public and signaled the end of complacency on
the part of officials. Eisenhower's advisers lobbied for an
immediate spending increase for U.S. science education to
address the advanced state of science education in the USSR.
Ike was caught up in a pressure situation, as it was difficult to
find the needed funds during the ongoing recession, yet he
could not fail to respond.

Barson, Michael, and Stephen Heller. *Red Scared: The Commie
Menace in Propaganda and Popular Culture*. San Francisco:
Chronicle Books, 2001.
Chapter 6 ("We Will Bury You!") documents the relationships
among the post–WWII phase of the red scare in America,
Sputnik's launch, the U.S. Vanguard missile failure, the space
race, and popular culture manifestations such as Cold War
movies and board games that reflected the fears and anxieties
of the time.

Baxandall, Rosalyn, and Elizabeth Ewen. *Picture Windows: How the
Suburbs Happened*. New York: Basic Books, 2000.
In chapters 11 and 12 on the 1950s, the authors address the
social dynamics of "fitting in," the concept of female (wife)
isolation in suburban tract housing, the idea of domesticity as
patriotism, the identity construct of "Mrs. Consumer," the
conservative politics of the majority of suburbanites, the rise
of anti-suburban sentiment, the problem of "suburban
malaise," and related racial segregation and class issues.

Boyer, Paul S., ed. *The Oxford Companion to United States History*.
New York: Oxford University Press, 2001.
This well-known reference was used for fact checking.

Hoy, Suellen. *Chasing Dirt: The American Pursuit of Cleanliness.* New York: Oxford University Press, 1995.

In this fascinating book, Hoy describes teenage behaviors regarding "personal hygiene" in the fifties, the "culture of cleanliness," consumerism, and the anti-littering campaign related to the proliferation of packaging, sprawl, and automobility. "Keep America Beautiful" became the catch-phrase for the anti-littering campaign.

Jones, Gerard. *Honey, I'm Home! Sitcoms: Selling the American Dream.* New York: Grove Weidenfeld, 1992.

Chapter 7 analyzes how mid-1950s television sitcoms "invented America" in shows such as *The Adventures of Ozzie and Harriet* and *Father Knows Best*. Jones supplies an especially helpful discussion of the morality lessons and gender role definitions woven into the scripts for these shows. Chapter 9 covers the late 1950s sitcoms *Leave It To Beaver, The Real McCoys* and *My Three Sons,* which, the author argues, were vehicles for processing the social changes of the time. While America was "progressing" toward a new construct of society, it also was "haunted by ancient prejudices, dead ideologies, and infantile selfishness" (p. 133).

INTEGRATING A FEW SOURCES IN A PAPER

In courses across the disciplines, many assignments require "researched" or "documented" papers (integrating and crediting supporting information from the course texts or a few outside sources) rather than full-scale "research papers." Often such papers continue or extend classroom discussion and require the analysis and synthesis of ideas. Because their sources may be familiar to everyone in the class, a less formal citation style may be acceptable. For example, in-text citation of an essay or literary work at first mention, page numbers in parentheses for subsequent citations, and a final Works Cited entry generally would be sufficient for crediting a source in MLA style. Similarly, complete notes in *Chicago* style, without a corresponding bibliography, also might be sufficient. When you write such a paper, always check with your instructor to learn the exact expectations in your course. Even if slightly reducing the repetition of standard forms as you cite or list sources is acceptable, reducing your acknowledgment of sources is not. Be certain to identify and credit all direct quotations and make clear the original sources of the ideas and information that you present. (See pp. 94–104.)

In the following sample paper, written for a philosophy course, Brian Fenoglio compared eastern and western thought about the self. He supplied *Chicago*-style footnotes and page references for all quotations but was not expected to supply a two-book bibliography as well.

SAMPLE PAPER CREDITING A FEW SOURCES

Brian Fenoglio   PHI 358

04-26-02   Prof. White

Western and Eastern Thoughts: Tying Them Together

In considering the ideas of self in western philosophy, one cannot help but be amazed by related (although simultaneously differing) ideas in specific eastern philosophies and religions. For example, John Locke and Derek Parfit--in their discussions of the self--put forth the ideas of the sameness of memory or psychology and the continuity of consciousness. In the eastern religion (although some consider it a philosophy rather than a religion) of Buddhism, self can be described in much the same manner, but at the same time in a very different way. Possibly more interesting than either of these two ideas individually is the thought of somehow combining east and west into a coherent account of the self and ultimately the mind. In the end, this new hybrid of east and west could someday lead us to the truth about the self and the mind.

The Western Ideas

John Locke

In the ideas of western philosophy, Locke presents an account of self: it is impossible for anyone to perceive without perceiving that he does perceive. When we see, hear, smell, taste, feel, meditate, or will anything, we know that we do so. Thus it is always as to our present sensations and perceptions, and by this everyone is to himself that which he calls *self*. . . .[1]

According to Locke's account, then, self is nothing more than us being aware of our sensations and perceptions. The entire quantity of events and actions that occur to me at a specific time all unite in one experience and define who I am. Certainly this is not all

---

[1] Cooney, Brian, ed. *The Place of Mind*, (Belmont, CA: Wadsworth, 2000), 429-30.

that accounts for self; after all, could it not be the case that both James and I are in an emergency room and receive the same shot in the same place, thereby both of us being the same self? Locke responds to this unlikely, but still possible, scenario: "And as far as this consciousness can be extended backwards to any past action or thought, so far reaches the identity of that *person:* it is the same *self* now it was then, and it is by the same *self* with this present one that now reflects on it, that that action was done."[2] According to Locke here, in the same way that the entire quantity of events and actions makes my experience at one particular instance, so does the multitude of events and actions of my past (i.e. in my memory) make up my entire experience and therefore fully define who I am. Unfortunately Locke neglects the various problems of amnesia, false "memory," and ordinary forgetfulness. For instance, in the case of false "memory," Locke's position would hold that if I "remember" being President of the United States, then I am that person; however, it is certainly not the case that I am President of the United States.

Derek Parfit

In order to get around these sorts of problems, Derek Parfit fixes Locke's idea of the sameness of memory or psychology by introducing into Locke's theory the idea of continuity of consciousness:

> The Psychological Criterion: (1) There is *psychological continuity* if and only if there are overlapping chains of strong connectedness. X today is one and the same person as Y at some past time if and only if (2) X is psychologically continuous with Y, (3) this continuity has the right kind of cause, and (4) there does not exist a different person who is

---

[2] Ibid., 430.

also psychologically continuous with Y. (5) Personal identity over time just consists in the holding of facts like (2) to (4).[3]

In other words, instead of insisting that one's memory is the sole defining aspect of self--as Locke did--Parfit expands upon that idea to conclude that the true definition of self is the continuous psychology of an individual. That is to say, I ^{now} am one and the same as I ^{past} provided that I ^{now} am psychologically continuous with I ^{past}, this continuum is of the right cause (i.e. the events that I ^{now} remember actually did happen to I ^{past}), and I ^{now} am the only "now" continuous with I ^{past}.

The Eastern Ideas

Buddhist Thought

In studying the western ideas of Locke and Parfit, one notices a similarity between them and the eastern religions, Buddhism in particular. Within Buddhism is the idea of reincarnation of each living thing. One's mind endures many earthly lives. For example, the body sitting here typing this paper is one body among many past bodies that have been the shell for my mind, and this process will continue until the cycle is ended by attainment of Nirvana. This idea suggests that with proper thought and the right sorts of mental exercises, one can remember his or her past lives. Although, these ideas seem completely compatible with the ideas of Parfit and Locke, the similarities stop there.

The most well-known Buddhist theories developed from the Madhyamika School, believing that everything, in essence, is sunyata (emptiness). For the Madhyamika, the self is not absolute and is not substantial on its own, yet it is responsible for everything:

---

[3] Ibid., 447.

the Madhyamikas as a whole realized that it is impossible to have a metaphysics which asks whether ideas expressed in such a system are true "'of reality," because there is no relation between this system of thought and a reality outside it. Consequently they insisted on coherence and self-consistency, rather than on correspondence, especially since we can only be aware of anything to the extent that we know it through the interpretive forms of our experience.[4]

Using the principle of sunyata, the experience of everything in our lives is defined by the self; for nothing is something within itself because everything is really just the self's interpretation of it. Thus, self is all there really is for each person. But in the same way that our experiences are defined by interpretations of the self, so is our self. My self is nothing until it is defined by the interpretations of others' selves (that is, I, Brian Fenoglio, am defined as the son of Terry and Cindy, friend of James and Liz, student of Professor White, and so forth).

Tying It Together

The problem concerning us now is to consider whether an accurate and coherent account can be found in combining the ideas of the east (that is, Buddhism) and the west (that is, Parfit and Locke). One can reasonably imagine an account of the workings of the universe where the theory of reincarnation is true. If this is hard, simply think of the countless people who--while under hypnosis--can recall being someone else; furthermore, these people can give accurate information about their former lives without having any prior knowledge of who these past people were.

---

[4] Guenther, Herbert V., *Buddhist Philosophy in Theory and Practice* (Berkeley, CA): Shambhala, 1971), 126-127.

Is it now the case that my self is nothing on its own, yet is responsible for everything? This claim may appear absurd at first, but let us first consider the possibility that my self is responsible for everything. Is it not true that my interpretations of experiences really become those experiences? Take, for example, the idea of the tree falling in the woods: Does it make a sound if nothing is there to experience it? Of course not, for it is our interpretations of experiences that make them real. The falling tree makes no sound if it is not experienced by anything. Now the claim can be reasonably made that my self is responsible for everything--at least to me; but can my self be nothing on its own? Simply put, since nothing is there to experience my self, then I truly am nothing--unless I can experience myself. However, experiencing yourself in any true way is impossible. My self is defined by the interpretations of other selves (and I am the only self to interpret me). I cannot define myself--for example, I, Brian Fenoglio, am Brian Fenoglio--because it would be the same as defining a can of pop as pop in a can. Therefore, it can now be reasonably put that my self is nothing on its own.

Incorporating Parfit's idea of the continuity of consciousness, one ends up with the idea that reincarnation holds true, and if it is possible to remember our past lives and experiences, then each of our selves is a complex interpretation of all of the history of living things; each new interpretation of history is defined by other interpretations and defines all other interpretations. Humanity is then varying perspectives and experiences within the continuing history of every living thing.

CITING PASSAGES FROM A LITERARY WORK

When you write a paper that analyzes or interprets a literary work, you often will closely examine features such as its themes, characters, plot, setting, point of view, or use of language. Generally you will support your thesis about the novel, poem, play, or other work by quoting, paraphrasing, and summarizing evidence from the work itself. A reader is likely to expect a compelling literary analysis to identify exactly where such evidence appears in the literary work. Although such a paper may not require you to track down any sources, it certainly will require that you carefully select, launch, capture, and cite material from a source (see pp. 124–29). As chapter 10 on MLA style explains, passages in literary works are often best cited by chapter, book, line, scene, or other divisions used in all editions rather than by the page number, which might differ from edition to edition. If you are writing a literary analysis, follow your instructor's directions and the MLA guidelines carefully (see pp. 144–50 or the *MLA Handbook* itself). If a specific text or anthology is used by everyone in your class, your instructor may or may not require a list of works cited.

When Cindy Keeler wrote the paper from which the following selection comes, she compared two literary works. She added a bibliographic note at the end to specify her use of the class text and two additional texts for her comparison. The selection includes her opening paragraphs and this concluding note. It also illustrates complications that may arise in papers that quote from literary sources or use words from languages other than English.

In her discussion, Cindy cited the conventional book and line numbers from the *Aeneid* and the stanza numbers from the assigned version of *Troilus and Criseyde* to identify the location of each quotation or other specific information from each literary work. In addition, because she had a strong classics background, she quoted from the *Aeneid* in Latin when appropriate. MLA style recommends using quotation marks to set off a quotation (whether in English, Latin, or another language) but using underlining (the traditional MLA method of indicating italics) to emphasize a specific term from a language other than English. To distinguish original text from its translation, set off the translation with single quotation marks (or double marks if it appears in parentheses).

MLA also recommends simplifying references to well-known titles. Here, after the title of Chaucer's *Troilus and Criseyde* is introduced, its short form—*Troilus*—is enough to identify it in discussion; the abbreviation *Aen.* and *TC* are sufficient for parenthetical citations. When you write a literary analysis for a literature, comparative literature, or language course, ask your instructor about any conventions that would apply to your assignment, such as the MLA abbreviations for the titles of Shakespeare's plays or other well-known literary works.

SELECTION FROM A LITERARY ANALYSIS

Cindy Keeler
Literature of Transformation

The Effect of the Code of Courtly Love:
A Comparison of Virgil's Aeneid and Chaucer's
Troilus and Criseyde

In the poem Troilus and Criseyde, Geoffrey Chaucer offers a retelling and expansion of the classic story of ill-fated lovers. Within the poem, Chaucer refers to several preceding instances of the same subject; Orpheus and Eurydice, Daphne and Apollo, and Herse and Mercury are all mentioned. Despite the similarities in plot, one crucial difference exists between Troilus and the ancient works: the code of courtly love had not yet been invented for the ancient works. By comparing the Aeneid with Troilus, one can easily see the effects of this code on literature.

One ancient tale describing the plight of lovers is that of Dido and Aeneas. In Book 4 of the Aeneid, Virgil tells a story not unlike that of Troilus and Criseyde. Both stories focus on the subject of love. In each there is a lover; Dido burns with passion for Aeneas, while Troilus burns for Criseyde. This fire imagery itself is pronounced in the description of both loves. Dido "caeco carpitur igni" 'is consumed by unseen flame' (Aen. 4.2), and "inflammavit animum / incensum amore" 'has inflamed her excited mind with love' (Aen. 4.54). Later she is accensa ("inflamed") (Aen. 4.364). All of these words connote some sort of burning. Similarly in Troilus, Chaucer describes Troilus's passion through fire imagery. In Book 1, stanza 64, Troilus discovers that "the flame / More fiercely burnt, the nearer that he came." Stanza 65 continues: "The nearer to the flame, the hotter 'tis." Book 2 contains similar passages, as

in stanza 191: "The more wood and coal, the more the fire; /
Increase of hope, be it what it may, / Will very often bring
increased desire." Thus, Chaucer as well uses flame as a metaphor
for love.

[The paper continues with other similarities and
differences between the two poems.]

Bibliographic Note

In addition to the Nevill Coghill (Penguin Classics) edition of
Troilus and Criseyde, I used Hart and Osborn's 1883 interlinear
Virgil, which contains the Aeneid. As this version for some
unknown reason sometimes alters word order of the Latin, I used
an online text as well. This text (fully in Latin) is available at
http://patriot.net/~lillard/cp/verg.html.

IDENTIFYING COURSE TEXTS AS SOURCES
IN AN EXAMINATION

Sometimes you will be writing a midterm or final exam under pressure and need to identify sources during the exam. Even when you are writing an open-book or take-home exam, the requirements for citing such sources are often less rigorous than they would be in a research paper, partly because the instructor already knows the sources you are expected or likely to mention and partly because time does not allow for formal citation.

The following answers come from the final examination for an ethnic studies course taught by Professor Donna Langston. Students were asked to answer five of eleven questions with short essays, at least two handwritten pages in a large blue book or one typed page. These sample answers illustrate how purposefully the student writers approached their task. When you are writing an essay exam, try their strategies: open your answer by restating or focusing on the question asked, tackle exactly the task required (such as explaining "what is . . ." with a definition or giving several key examples), embed pertinent information from class discussion and lectures, and mention a variety of sources to substantiate your points. Notice how these writers also used different strategies to solve the problem of crediting sources while writing under pressure.

EXAMINATION ANSWERS BASED ON SOURCES

Examination Question: What is manifest destiny?

Answer by Angela Mendy

Manifest destiny was an expression by leaders and politicians in
the 1840s to clarify continental extension and expansion and in a
sense revitalize the mission and national destiny for Americans.
Americans felt that it was their undertaking, or rather duty, to
extend their boundaries of free will to others by imparting their
optimism and beliefs in a democratic society to those who were
capable of independence. It barred those people who were perceived
as being incapable of self-government, such as Native American
people and those of non-European origin. This did not just stop
there though. As the thirteen colonies grew and the U.S. economy
increased, new needs and endeavors to expand into new land
increased. Land at that time represented more income and wealth
and freedom, so expansion into western frontiers presented
opportunities for self-development. Some of the reasons for manifest
destiny were that the U.S. needed the land due to a periodic high birth
rate and increases in population due to immigration, and besides, at
that time, frontier land was inexpensive or, in most cases, free.

Manifest destiny still exists in a way, but probably the greatest
form of manifest destiny by this country was the war with Mexico
which began in 1846 when America proceeded to win much of what
is now the Southwestern United States. Many people have also
agreed that "manifest destiny is as old as America itself and that
this idea came across the Atlantic with Columbus and that it
resided with the spirits of the colonists of Jamestown and it landed
at Plymouth Rock with the Pilgrims. It also traveled with the fire
and brimstone preachers during the Great Awakening and built the
first national road" (Michael L. Lubragge).

This phrase "manifest destiny" was first used by the American journalist and diplomat John Louis O'Sullivan in an editorial column supporting the appropriation of Texas. The phrase first appeared in an 1845 edition of the United States Magazine and Democratic Review (Encarta). The phrase was also later used by expansionists in all political parties to justify the acquisition of California and the Oregon Territory. By the end of the 19th century, the same phrase was being used to justify the proposed occupation of various islands in the Caribbean Sea and the Pacific Ocean. Manifest Destiny was what the United States saw when it looked at places like Asia and the Far East. It has no end. And we will continue to experience this movement through the end of time and in very different ways. Put simply, manifest destiny is everlasting and eternal.

Examination Question: Give several key examples of how educational, health, or economic disparities continue to exist.

Blue Book Answer by Whitney King

Educational, health, and economic disparities continue to exist despite the recognition that all men (and women) really are created equal in this country. Economic disparities continue to persist because minorities are often paid less for the same work than whites and have to pay more for houses, cars, and other big-ticket, negotiable-price items. It is also much harder for minorities to find a job than whites, and they have to do a better job than their white counterparts to keep those jobs. I was listening to an interview on the radio the other day with Reggie Rivers, who used to play for the Broncos, about how racism really persists in sports, specifically the NFL, although stereotypically African Americans are better athletes than whites. There are very few coaches in the NFL who are African Americans, no team owners, and very few quarterbacks. These are the positions that get a lot of press coverage besides the ones in which there <u>are</u> a lot of African American players. He sounded hopeful, however, that things are getting better and eventually will be equal.

Education is closely tied to economics. By having to pay more for houses, minorities are often forced to live in lower-income neighborhoods with more populated schools than those for suburban whites. These schools rarely offer the same quality of education, even in the public schools.

Health is another big issue. Urban hospitals are very busy, and many people cannot afford private hospitals. Another major issue is the area surrounding the neighborhoods. Many lower-income neighborhoods are built next to industrial areas or on former landfills and toxic waste sites. This affects the health of the inhabitants who really don't have the resources to fight the environmental inequity.

In an op-ed essay in the New York Times on 9-26-04, Henry Louis Gates Jr. gave some unsurprising but staggering statistics:

- 30-40% of African American children live in poverty.
- If the U.S. had racial equality in education and employment, African Americans would have 2 million more high school degrees, 2 million more college or university degrees, 2 million more professional and managerial jobs, and $200 billion more in earned income.

These statistics are only for African Americans, so what would they look like for all minorities?

ADDING FIELD RESEARCH AND CONTENT
NOTES TO A PAPER

When Nick Broz took a business course on nonprofit organizational effectiveness, he analyzed the mission of the Batavia Volunteer Fire Department and the organization's strengths, weaknesses, opportunities, and threats. The following selection from the introduction of his paper explores the department's mission, using his instructor's checklist to organize information about the fire department he studied. It also alludes to Nick's field research sources, including personal knowledge, interviews, and documents from the fire department.

To supply necessary qualification and context for his field work, Nick also included several content notes, grouped in the paper on a notes page at the end. Major documentation styles such as MLA, APA, and *Chicago* recognize the use of content notes, whether or not they use notes to credit sources. Generally such notes provide information that might interrupt the text discussion, interest only a few readers, or supply more detail than the rest of the discussion. Besides the three notes included in the following selection from Nick's paper, he used two additional notes to comment on the department's fundraising needs and options. If you need to add notes to qualify, expand, or otherwise supplement a research discussion, write them carefully so that they are clear, concise, direct, and relevant.

SELECTION FROM A PAPER REPORTING FIELD RESEARCH
AND USING CONTENT NOTES

The Batavia Volunteer Fire Department

Nick Broz

The Batavia Volunteer Fire Department does not have a mission statement, nor, I think, would its members be interested in creating one. However, if you asked any one of them why they give their time and put themselves in harm's way, they would all allude to the same things. So although it will probably not be put into practice in the foreseeable future, the first thing to do is to combine what I have learned from talking to people and from attending class to create a mission statement. In order to do this, I will follow the questions in Dr. Boyd's "Mission Statement Checklist." Additionally, discussing each question will introduce some of the aspects of the organization that I will be discussing throughout this project.

1. Why do we exist? The Batavia Fire Department exists for the same reason as all fire departments: to protect people from injury not directly caused by another person. Historically this has been fire, but increasingly and especially in rural areas, fire departments are called upon to assist in car accidents and protect civilians in the event of chemical spills or other disasters. What are we trying to achieve? The fire department is trying first to protect the lives and health of victims and second to protect their property.

2. What "business" or "service" are we in? The fire department, strictly speaking, is in the security sector of the service industry. More broadly, it is mostly in the business of fire prevention. How do we achieve it? The department achieves this by providing

education to area schools and by providing physical fire and disaster protection through the use of fire trucks.

3. What is our most important product/service? Currently their most important service by far is physical fire protection, although there are trends that suggest this could be expanded in the future. Focus, boundaries? Technically, the boundaries of the Batavia Fire Department are the townships or parts of townships whose elected board of trustees contract for fire protection. In practice, the fire department responds to calls that it can reach more quickly than other rural fire departments, including some areas that are not taxpayer supported. Our policy direction? The Batavia Fire Department's policies are directed toward providing the best protection possible within the constraints of budget and manpower. Policies are also directed to protect and insure the safety of firefighters.

4. Who are our clients? The clients of the Batavia Fire Department are the residents and businesses in the geographic area that the fire department serves as well as persons traveling through that area by automobile, rail, or air.[1] Volunteers? The volunteers of the fire department are residents of Batavia or the surrounding area who wish to volunteer their time and resources to become members. Donors? At the present time, most donations are received from local foundations and individuals. Other donations that have been unsuccessfully solicited or are no longer in place include grants from various government agencies and fundraising activities. Since there are no shareholders, who is to be served (local, regional, national, international)? The Batavia Volunteer Fire Department's energies and resources are, barring extenuating circumstance, directed exclusively to the local community.

5. Why do they come to us? The township boards are required by state law to provide fire protection to their residents, but they

have a choice of where to go for that protection. For the most part, the clients of the fire department use the service because it is the closest of the available fire protection services. What differentiates us from others? Quality? While it may differentiate itself in some ways from other rural fire departments in the area, the fact that geography and distance play such an important part in fulfilling clients' needs allows the Batavia Fire Department to remain competitive without substantial differentiation. What is our niche (motivation, rallying cry)? The fire department's motivation is that they are helping others. More specifically, since they are serving such a small community, in many cases people needing assistance are friends or family of some of the firefighters. So additional motivation comes from knowing that the people the firefighters help are often connected to them on a personal level.

6. How have we changed in the past five years? The most significant change the Batavia Fire Department has faced is their need to produce a budget each year. In the past, the treasurer always kept track of the monies and kept an excellent, albeit informal, record of costs and projected expenses. Beginning last year the fire department was required to present a budget to the township boards each year in order to have their contract renewed. In other ways, things have changed very little. Apart from a few members retiring from the force or passing away and a few new members joining, the organization has not undergone much change structurally. Some new equipment has been purchased and some members have participated in additional training, but overall the fire department's vision and strategies have not changed.

7. What are our organization's unique strengths and major weaknesses? One of the main strengths of the organization is the high level of commitment most of the members have to the cause. This is important because the nature of the service necessitates

that the members of the fire department be called to volunteer at any time of the day or night. Another strength is that nearly all of the organization's members have lived in the area for most of their lives so they are very familiar with the roads and locations of their prospective clients, which allows the Batavia Fire Department to reduce its response times. In addition, the Batavia Fire Department is incorporated. One of the major weaknesses is the aging of the volunteer force. There are two aspects to this weakness, one in the short term and one in the long term.

There is a level of physical activity that is inherent to fighting fires including lifting hoses, running, and engaging in other strenuous physical labor. Especially when a risk is involved and people are depending on each other for safety, the physical ability of the other members is important. While none of the members of the Batavia Fire Department is infirm, and while some of the older names I recognized on the roster were described as members in "name only," the fact is inescapable that most of the members are my parents' age, in their forties and early fifties. While I have no reason to think that anyone is at risk of not being able to perform the job, my convictions on that could be different five years from now.

The long-term result, if the current trend continues, is that the fire department will begin losing members faster than it can recruit them. There is a limit to the number of members that the fire department can equip, this number currently being twenty people. The limiting factor is the number of fire suits the department has available. This limit is significant because it creates sort of a "one out, one in" membership, which makes it more difficult for the fire department to get new members when it needs them. So in the long-term, the aging of the force could hypothetically jeopardize the survival of the organization.

A second trait that could be considered a weakness is that there are new rules and more formal regulations from many of the organizations and agencies that the Batavia Fire Department deals with. The creation of a budget is an example of a response to that point. There are pressures on the fire department to change the way it does business. While I am confident the fire department will be able to do this, it will be a difficult adjustment to move further away from a more relationship-based way of doing business.

8. What philosophical issues are most important to us? What are our core values? This is a difficult question for me to explore because I would have to be in a very comfortable relationship with any of the members to ask them about their philosophical issues. Anthropologically speaking, I think that a question like that would be enough to seriously damage my insider status.[2] To guess on this, very generally I think that their values are to protect people and help them. I think that the people who belong to the Batavia Fire Department are the kind of people who would go help a neighbor whose house or barn was on fire even if they weren't volunteering as firefighters; they are the kind of people who would stop to help at an accident. I would guess that these people have a strong sense of duty and a sense of obligation to help others.

9. What would be lost if we did not exist? What would be lost is timely response to the community's fire needs. The reason the Batavia Fire Department serves the area it does is because it has the shortest response time to that area. In addition to peace of mind, homeowners' insurance rates are calculated with regard to the distance and rating of the nearest fire prevention facility. I will go into this in more depth later, but the annual cost for my family's home insurance would increase by over $100 if we received our fire protection from the next closest provider.

10. How will we know whether we are performing effectively?
How will we be evaluated? There is no formal process for this
either, that I am aware of. The most likely way is for informal
comments, problems, or praise to be made to individual members of
the organization by members of the community in their social
circle or at their place of work and for these to be relayed to the
rest of the organization during monthly meetings.[3] As you will see,
the fire department's budget has little leeway, so there aren't a lot
of changes they could make even if suggestions were made. At the
extreme end of this, if the fire department were performing
extremely poorly or were not providing enough value for the tax
revenues collected, the township board could refuse to renew their
contract with the township.

From the exploration of these questions I can put together a
possible mission statement. I feel that this mission statement,
while not perfect, does include the purpose, values and vision of
the Batavia Volunteer Fire Department and will make a public
statement about who they are.

Mission Statement

The mission of the Batavia Volunteer Fire Department is to
provide competent, timely fire protection to the residents in our
service area and their property. We will remain an efficient,
effective organization through continuing education of our
members and continuing recruitment and maintenance of our
equipment while remaining fiscally responsible. The Batavia Fire
Department will take care of the community's needs in the present
while preparing ourselves to meet its needs in the future.

[The paper continues with a discussion of environmental data using a Strength-Weakness-Opportunities-Threats (SWOT) matrix, a strategic plan, an action plan with tables showing conservative and optimistic financial projections, an evaluation, and a conclusion.]

Notes

1. At the time I interviewed the Batavia Fire Chief and two other leaders of the department during the Thanksgiving holidays, the two most recent fire calls the department had answered were related to traffic accidents on U.S. Highway 34, which passes directly through town. Both accidents were outside the city limits, and both involved containing potentially hazardous and definitely flammable diesel fuel spilling from overturned vehicles, one a commercial semi-trailer truck and one a farm machine. The largest disaster the department has responded to in the last two decades was an Amtrak passenger train derailment that did occur within the city limits on the main line of the Burlington Northern Railway, which passes directly through Batavia.

2. To make my "insider" status relative to this project perfectly clear, I have lived in or near Batavia, Iowa, all of my life. My mother and her parents and grandparents have lived in Batavia since 1920. My uncle, Dennis McKeever, is the fire chief.

3. During my interviews I was told that local residents who actually have fire calls to their property often express their gratitude by donating money to the "firemen's fund" after such incidents take place. The money donated to the firefighter's fund, which remains outside the formal budget, is used for incidental and less formal purposes such as purchasing refreshments for meetings and buying flowers for the funerals of retired firefighters.

WRITING CHECKLIST

Editing Your Research Paper
Grammar and Sentences

☐ Have you made sure that every sentence has a subject and a complete verb?

☐ Have you corrected any sentence errors such as sentence fragments (incorrectly missing a subject, missing a verb, or not expressing a complete thought), comma splices (two sentences incorrectly connected with only a comma), or fused sentences (two sentences incorrectly connected without any punctuation)?

☐ Have you used the correct form for all verbs, especially those in the past tense (such as *have swum,* not *have swimmed*)?

☐ Have you followed the verb-tense convention appropriate for your field and paper? In a humanities paper, have you used the present tense to describe the work of an author or the events in a literary work (As Hawthorne *recounts* the tale of Goodman Brown, he *describes* the human problem of retaining faith)? In a social science or science paper, have you used the past tense to describe a completed study (Bloom's taxonomy, *published* in 1956, *identified* six levels of literal and analytical reading skills)?

☐ Do all verbs agree with their subjects—singular with singular and plural with plural—even in complicated sentences with other words tucked between the two?

☐ Does each pronoun agree with its antecedent—the word to which it refers—matching singular with singular (*platoon, it*); plural with plural (*soldiers, they*); masculine (*he*), feminine (*she*), or neuter (*it*) with the same; and first person (*I, we*), second (*you*), or third (*he, she, it, they*) with the same?

☐ Have you correctly used adjectives (to modify nouns and pronouns, as in *the child looked happy*) and adverbs (to modify verbs, adjectives, or adverbs, as in *the child jumped happily*)?

☐ Is each modifier—especially a word such as *only, just* or *not*—placed close to the sentence element it describes to avoid creating ambiguity?

☐ Have you used parallel structure—the same grammatical form for related terms—for lists, series, and similar cases (*policies, procedures, and directives; exploring, navigating, and mapping*)?

Punctuation, Mechanics, and Format

- ☐ Have you used commas correctly, adding them before words like *and* when they join two complete sentences, after introductory expressions, between items in a list, and around expressions set off from the rest of the sentence?

- ☐ Have you used apostrophes correctly to show possession (*Roper's theory, Dickens's novel, Chase and Herd's latest survey, the whale that lost its way*)?

- ☐ Have you punctuated quotations correctly, enclosing the exact words from a source inside the marks?

- ☐ Have you used an ellipsis mark (. . .)—three spaced dots—to show where you have left out any words from the middle of a direct quotation? Have you added a fourth dot (the sentence period) before an ellipsis that also ends a sentence?

- ☐ Have you used brackets—[ ]—to enclose, and thus identify as your own, any words that you needed to add to a direct quotation from a source, either to clarify its meaning or to improve its grammatical fit?

- ☐ Have you used the conventional punctuation or other features expected in your citation style when you identify a source in your text or fashion an entry for your list of sources?

- ☐ Have you used capital letters correctly, especially following any special conventions required for entries in your list of works cited, your list of references, or your bibliography?

- ☐ Have you both run your spell-checker and read your draft carefully to be sure that you have spelled everything correctly and used the words you intended?

- ☐ Have you used the correct manuscript form required for your citation style or by your instructor?

Acknowledgments (continued from page iv)

Page 27: Screenshot of Linda Reed, "The Brown decision: Its long anticipation and lasting influence" from the *Journal of Southern History* 70, no. 2 (May 2004): 337. Copyright © 2004 by the Southern Historical Association. Reprinted with the permission of the Managing Editor.

Page 29: David Callahan, *The Cheating Culture: Why More Americans Are Doing Wrong to Get Ahead.* Copyright © 2004 by David Callahan. Reprinted with the permission of Harcourt, Inc.

Page 31: Screenshot from American Medical Association web site and excerpt from "AMA calls on NCAA to ban booze ads" (April 27, 2005), www.amaassn.org/ama/pub/category/15001.html. Copyright © 2005 by The American Medical Association. Reprinted with permission.

Page 40: Screenshot of Tuskegee University Libraries home page, http://www.tuskeggee.edu/Global/category.asp?C=34627nav=CcXC. Reprinted with the permission of Tuskegee University Libraries.

Pages 45–46: Screenshots of Howard University Libraries Sterling keyword search results records. Reprinted with the permission of Howard University Libraries.

Page 50: Entries from the *Readers' Guide to Periodical Literature.* Copyright © by the H. W. Wilson Company. Reprinted with the permission of the H. W. Wilson Company.

Page 51: Screenshot of Boston Public Library Infotrac search results. Copyright © by the Gale Group. Reprinted with the permission of the Gale Group.

Pages 65–67: Screenshots of Google keyword Search results and Advanced Search results. Reprinted with permission of Google, Inc.

Page 81: Screenshots of ASPCA home page and Advocacy Center Action Alert, "New York: Pet Dealer Licensing Law in Jeopardy, Your Help is Needed." Reprinted with the permission of the American Society for the Prevention of Cruelty to Animals (ASPCA).

Page 137: Frank A. Salamone, excerpt from "Jazz and Its Impact on European Classical Music," and editorial listing from the *Journal of Popular Culture* 38, No. 4 (2005). Copyright © 2005 by Blackwell Publishing. Reprinted by permission.

Page 139: Screenshot of Infotrac database displaying excerpt from Frank Louis Rusciano, "James Baldwin: America's Native Son" from *Academic Exchange Quarterly* 7, no. 4 (Winter 2003): 311. Copyright © 2003 by Academic Exchange Quarterly. Reprinted with permission.

Page 141: Title page and copyright page for Isabel Allende, *My Invented Country: A Nostalgic Journey Through Chile,* translated by Margaret Sayers Peden. Copyright © 2003 by Isabel Allende. English translation copyright © 2003 by HarperCollins Publishers, Inc. Reprinted with the permission of HarperCollins Publishers, Inc.

Page 143: Screenshots from PBS web site http://www.pbs.org including excerpt from Davis Larkin, "Tolstoy's War with Love" and PBS Online copyright information. Copyright © WGBH Educational Foundation. Reprinted with permission.

CHECKLISTS, TABLES, AND FIGURES

RESEARCH CHECKLISTS

WRITING CHECKLISTS

TABLES AND FIGURES ON TARGETING SOURCES

TABLES AND FIGURES ON BUILDING A WORKING BIBLIOGRAPHY

SOURCE NAVIGATORS AND STUDENT WRITING

Index

339